A GREAT SACRIFICE

D1596148

THE NORTH'S CIVIL WAR
Andrew L. Slap, series editor

A Great Sacrifice

*Northern Black Soldiers,
Their Families, and the
Experience of Civil War*

James G. Mendez

FORDHAM UNIVERSITY PRESS
NEW YORK   2019

Fordham University Press has no responsibility for the persistence or accuracy of URLs for external or third-party Internet websites referred to in this publication and does not guarantee that any content on such websites is, or will remain, accurate or appropriate.

Fordham University Press also publishes its books in a variety of electronic formats. Some content that appears in print may not be available in electronic books.

Visit us online at www.fordhampress.com.

Library of Congress Cataloging-in-Publication Data

Names: Mendez, James (James G.), author.
Title: A great sacrifice : Northern Black soldiers, their families, and the
    experience of Civil War / James G. Mendez.
Description: First edition. | New York : Fordham University Press, 2019. |
    Series: The North's Civil War | Includes bibliographical references and
    index.
Identifiers: LCCN 2018028220| ISBN 9780823282500 (cloth : alk. paper) | ISBN
    9780823282494 (pbk. : alk. paper)
Subjects: LCSH: African American soldiers—History—19th century. | African
    American soldiers—Family relationships—History—19th century. | African
    American women—Correspondence. | African American families—History—19th
    century. | United States—History—Civil War, 1861–1865—African
    Americans. | United States—History—Civil War, 1861–1865—Social aspects.
    | Northeastern States—Social conditions—19th century.
Classification: LCC E540.N3 M46 2019 | DDC 973.7/415—dc23
LC record available at https://lccn.loc.gov/2018028220

Printed in the United States of America

21 20 19   5 4 3 2 1

First edition

For my loving parents, Larisla and James A. Mendez, Sr.

Contents

Figures

Abbreviations

AD	African Descent
AMA	American Missionary Association
Co.	Company
Col.	Colonel
CRA	Contraband Relief Association
LSASTC	Ladies' Sanitary Association of St. Thomas's African Episcopal Church
LUA	Ladies' Union Association
PAS	Pennsylvania Abolition Society
POW	Prisoner of War
Regt.	Regiment
RG	Record Group
Sgt.	Sergeant
USCC	United States Christian Commission
USCHA	United States Colored Heavy Artillery
USCI	United States Colored Infantry
USCLA	United States Colored Light Artillery
USCT	United States Colored Troops
USSC	United States Sanitary Commission
WAA	*Weekly Anglo-African*
WCRA	Women's Central Relief Association

A Great Sacrifice

Introduction

Mr Abraham lincoln sir I with mutch plasur set down to address you with a few lines to let you know that my husband is in the army and left me hear with a helpless famely and he has not recived any pay and I get no reliefe I would like to know if you please what will be done. . . . pleas rite and let me know." In her letter to Lincoln, Matilld Burr made an impassioned plea for financial help as she struggled to provide for herself and family while her husband was away fighting to preserve the Union, but with no pay, or very little pay, to send home. Burr's letter was a response to the arduous conditions under which northern African-American families had to live and how they were affected by the Civil War. Mattild wrote the letter addressed to Abraham Lincoln on January 18, 1864. Her husband, Charles, was twenty-five years old and a boat-man when he joined the regiment as a substitute on July 18, 1863.[1]

Northern blacks supported the military and the Union in spite of the hard-ships the soldiers and their families experienced. And as the war persisted and the role of black soldiers expanded, families found it even harder to survive under increasingly difficult conditions. Moreover, the patriotism of these fami-lies, though greatly affected, was not broken by the unequal pay issue, which was still unresolved and resulted in continued hardship for them. Soldiers and their families were also not deterred by the racism soldiers faced on the front lines, in the form of excess fatigue duty and mistreatment at the hands of their officers and white Union troops. Black troops faced these obstacles serving in the very seg-regated Union army. Nor were they dissuaded by the racism their families faced at home, in the form of the threat of violence and race riots or limited access to relief resources and aid to help the families survive financially while their main bread-winners were away serving in the army. In spite of these uncertainties and concerns, as well as the threat of execution or enslavement if Confederate forces caught them, black men continued to enlist and serve their country.

When northern black men joined the armed forces of the Union and went off to fight in the Civil War, they were the vanguard of a black community that faithfully supported the Union effort in large numbers and steadfastly sent their men to fight. They did this even though they had to know the sacrifices would be great, not just for themselves on the battlefield but for their families at home. Northern blacks would have to face obstacles and challenges very different from those white Union soldiers and families encountered. From their reasons for supporting the war to their expectations after a Union victory, the participation and experiences of northern black families were at times very divergent from those of the Union's white soldiers, and even their black brothers from the South who also served in the Union army.

This study analyzes the effects of the Civil War on northern black families as they sacrificed for a Union victory, and asks the question, how were black Union soldiers from the North and their families affected by their involvement in the Civil War? In sending their men off to fight the war, black families lost the income these men provided and their presence as fathers and leaders within the family. These losses caused temporary or long-term family disruptions, depending on whether a family member returned home from the war unharmed or injured, or whether he did not return at all because he died while serving. Regardless, the families had to find a way to survive with their men gone, and they did. At the same time, northern black troops had to perform their duties as soldiers while confronting discrimination from Union authorities and white troops, as well as the Confederacy. This they did while acutely concerned about the well being of their wives, mothers, sisters, fathers, brothers, and children.

In addition, this study attempts to gain an understanding of what the family unit expected to gain or lose by the soldier's involvement in the war. Did these African-American families expect financial rewards, greater social acceptance, or political gains in return for their support of the Union? Did they fully realize what was ultimately being sacrificed and that many of their men would not return home, or would return permanently disabled? This study will attempt to discern how the family compensated for the lost income and the loss of male family members. By sending letters to federal government officials, the family members worked actively to get their problems and many inquiries addressed.

I explore these questions by telling the story of northern black soldiers right before the start of the Civil War to early 1866 after the last northern black regiment returned home.[2] The Civil War history of black soldiers is examined from the events leading up to the formation of the first black regiments and their initial participation in minor skirmishes and then major battles, to their role in a Union victory, occupation duty, and eventual return home. However, woven into this history is the story of the families, mainly women and children, who remained at home. Presented in this manner, it becomes easier to grasp, from the beginning to the end of the northern black participation in the war, the interrelation of the battlefront and the Union home front. Each front affected the other front as soldiers and their families went about on a daily basis trying to bear the rigors and challenges of being at war.

By focusing on these questions and how the war affected northern African Americans, this work will highlight the sacrifices made by northern black families, as well as black soldiers, to obtain Union victory. Though northern white families also suffered from the loss of income and the male presence while their men served in the military, the loss was greater for black families as a group because, in proportion to whites and southern blacks, more men in the northern black communities enlisted. Therefore, there were proportionally more black northern families without males around. Additionally, the black families in the North were smaller, consisting of two parents and their children. Also, black families were less likely than white families in similar economic conditions to include older parents, siblings, and cousins living together under one roof. Hence, they were less capable of compensating for losses through the support of older or younger males who remained at home. And black families were less capable of meeting the standard of living obtained prior to the war. Lost wages were not a factor for black Union soldiers from the South because they had not been paid as slaves. In addition, slavery had made the presence of males less of a factor in many slave families, whether or not they resided with their families, but especially if they did not.[3]

While northern black families struggled at home, their men experienced their own difficulties at the front. They had to fight the Union policy to pay black soldiers less than white soldiers. They had to confront hostility from white Union soldiers, many of whom initially did not support the idea of black soldiers, especially not in combat. In addition, the Confederate government threatened to put them into slavery if they were caught, or even to hang them and their white officers as rebels attempting to incite slave insurrections. A greater concern for black troops was the threat of being caught by Confederates and not given any quarter or the chance to surrender. This Confederate practice sometimes led to the murder of black soldiers, such as the massacre that occurred on the banks of the Mississippi River at Fort Pillow, Tennessee, in April 1864. Black Union soldiers from the South experienced these same hostilities at the front, while white Union soldiers did not, unless they were officers in black regiments.

Black families at home also confronted hostility from northern whites who opposed the war, especially after the end of slavery in the South became an official Union goal. An extreme example of this hostility is the New York Draft

Riots, where many innocent blacks were killed and their property destroyed by mobs who opposed the new federal initiative to recruit blacks. The white mobs displayed their anger by lashing out at blacks, any blacks. The families of white northern soldiers did not have to face such hazards. The families of black soldiers from the South were in constant fear of retaliation from Confederates supporters due to the actions of the families' soldiers serving in the Union army.[4]

Because they made a significant sacrifice, these families deserve to have their stories told about their contribution to the Union war effort and how their lives were directly affected by their participation in the Civil War. This book tells their story, not in a secondary manner or as an afterthought to the heroics of the soldiers, but rather, simultaneously and in tandem because the role of northern blacks, both the soldiers and their families, evolved and became more significant from the beginning of their involvement in the war. Until now, the full story of these African-American families has not been truly told because the focus has been on the men who went to war. But the soldiers' story is just one part of the overall sacrifice these families made. The families functioned as a unit before and after the war. Therefore, in many ways they must be examined as a functioning unit during the war, especially because, together, they had to overcome many impediments directly associated with their participation in the war. By examining what was occurring on the home front, and not just on the front line, it becomes clear for readers that though Union families, North and South, deserve to have recognized their efforts to make possible a Union victory, the unique sacrifice of black northern families deserves particular recognition.

Northern black women—mothers, wives, sisters, and female family friends—wrote most of the letters examined in this project. If they did not write the letters themselves, someone wrote the letters on their behalf, which they then signed or put their mark on by writing an "X" next to their names. There is a sprinkling of letters from male family members—fathers, brothers, and family friends—but most northern black men of military age were in a Union uniform at the time, leaving women behind to care for children and the elderly. Or in the case of soldiers without wives and children, their mothers, many of them dependent on their sons, wrote letters to the army inquiring about their sons. Most of the letters from male family members are from fathers.

The letters are addressed to a number of Union military officials. In the majority of cases, it was the Adjutant General of the Union Army, Brigadier General Lorenzo Thomas, who was the recipient. It is not clear how people knew to write to him and request his assistance in resolving their issues, but it could be that, through word-of-mouth, people learned the Adjutant General was the official with the authority to approve their requests. Letter writers quite often wrote to the commanding officer of a soldier's corps or regiment for information. It appears that the intended recipient of the letter depended a lot on how much information the family member had about the soldier's company, regiment, and commanding officers, and how much assistance they received from people more sophisticated and experienced in dealing with the military hierarchy and bureaucracy. Interestingly, a number of the letter writers felt the need to go directly to the top of the Union leadership and addressed their letters to Abraham Lincoln or the Secretary of War, Edwin Stanton.

Family members wrote to Union officials to obtain information, to get problems fixed, and, at times, to influence government officials in their decision making. Usually, these letters were not the first written about a family's problem. Instead, these letters served as follow-up letters to ongoing problems and reflect the feelings of frustration families experienced after weeks or months of trying to get information and questions answered about their soldiers. Thus, the letters served as another attempt at, or means of, dealing with particular difficulties, such as the lack of the soldier's pay. In most cases, the soldier tried to deal with such problems himself through the normal chain of command; however, family members often felt the need to follow up on a soldier's appeal or add information that might help lead to a positive outcome for the soldier. In other cases, a family member made his or her request after not hearing from their soldier for weeks, months, and sometimes years. What is a constant are the feelings of despair, fear, and concern the families felt and attempted to express to Union authorities. The letters used in this analysis were not the only letters sent by family members. Families most often wrote to their soldiers but very few of those letters exist today. However, the letters used in this work are available today because they were originally sent to an army and a government that was very bureaucratic and efficient in its handling of correspondences received. Unlike letters family members first sent to soldiers, which over time were either lost or discarded by their owners, these letters exist because they remained with the government and were eventually deposited in the National Archives in Washington, D.C.

The letters discussed in this book are important for a number of reasons. Collectively, they give a voice to the black family members left on the northern home front, which has not been heard loudly before. The explanations and requests provide for readers a greater understanding of the difficulties the African-American family faced during the war, their conditions as the war progressed, and in rare instances, the expectations of northern black families for fully supporting the war effort. The letters from the black women are the most valuable of the sources used in this study. Though most of the letters are no more than one page, they are significant because they represent the few written primary sources and records left behind by African-American women during the Civil War era. These are their words, sometimes written by them or written for them, in which they are saying what is on their minds and what their needs, concerns, and desires are. Because many blacks were not literate at the time, there exists no other nineteenth-century collection as rich and as numerous by black women.

The war created a situation where there was a need to correspond with the government, and black women, whether literate or not, found ways to get their thoughts and requests on paper and into the right government hands. And in taking these actions and asserting what they felt were their rights, black families achieved something they hadn't before: nearly full participation as citizens, the only limitation being the lack of a universal right to vote throughout the Union. Yet even without the vote, their letters were treated like any other citizen's letter. The letters were usually read, responded to, and acted upon in an official manner. Though the letters don't represent any type of organized or grassroots movement by these families, the act of writing itself verifies that with the right to fight as Union troops in the war came expectations of equality, both with the soldiers and their families, as a recompense for their sacrifices in the war. And in sending these letters, families used an access to the federal government that never existed before because the war represented the first time in U.S. history that black troops were formally a part of the military.[5]

In addition, the letters describe the economic difficulties northern black families endured while their men were away. Usually the person in the military was the main economic provider for the family, but most black families in the North already lived a precarious existence even when the men were home. Most black men worked menial jobs; due to racism and competition with other ethnic groups, that was all that was available to them. Many black women found it necessary to further supplement their families' income by working as domestics. With their main source of income gone, it became even more difficult for families to provide for themselves. The letters discuss what was going on during the participation of black troops during the war, and simultaneously give greater details as to how northern black families struggled.

In rare instances, individual letters give great insight into the minds and thoughts of these family members. These most valuable of writings reveal why northern blacks supported the war and what they expected in return. They discuss loyalty, citizenship, and the pride of a people. These letters are usually, but not always, written by the more literate and articulate of northern blacks and are usually addressed to Lincoln or Stanton. The authors of these particular letters went straight to the top of the Union leadership to make their requests. They also reminded the leadership of why black families sacrificed and how they expected to be treated for their strong support. Northern black families wanted equal treatment under the law. They also wanted the right to vote because it distinctly marked them as participants in the American political process who could use the system to improve the lives of people in their community. And they felt sacrificing for a Union victory and the spilling of the blood of their men on battlefields entitled them to these rights.

These letters also display what historian Gregory P. Downs refers to as a transformed relationship between Americans and their government. People (black or white, North or South) no longer limited their requests to the government for political desires, but now requested more private and personal needs. Only one of the letters used in this project asked for a government appointment, though such letters exist in the National Archives. Instead, what poured out of the correspondences used in *A Great Sacrifice* were stories about the daily struggles of families, concern about their individual soldiers, and requests for resources to provide basic needs (food and shelter). And with these requests, explained Downs, came expectations from families that government could and would act on their behalf.[6]

Southern back families also wrote letters to the federal government. Because literacy for slaves was a crime in the South, such letters were not produced until Union armies took control of formerly Confederate territory, such as southern Louisiana and the South Carolina coastal islands. The letters from southern black families were written for similar reasons as those from northern blacks: information about the whereabouts of their soldiers, the health and well being of their soldiers, and soldiers' pay. However, the newly freed slaves also wrote to address mistreatment by their former masters and white Union soldiers. Still, these letters are far fewer in comparison to those from northern families because the literacy rate (or access to people who could write) was much lower in the South.[7]

The letters consulted in this study were chosen because they provide a better understanding of the plight of northern black families during the war. Often written in the words of the family members themselves, the letters chosen here best articulate the condition of the families in the absence of the soldiers, and the issues affecting them during the war. Depending on the context, all or portions of the letter's content was used.

The letters are original and the text has not been altered. Though many of the letters possess numerous spelling, grammatical, spacing, and punctuation errors, they are reproduced exactly as in their original handwritten form in order to enable family members to speak in their own words. The letters show the level of literacy of many blacks, revealing a higher level of education and refinement of some black northerners. However, the letters also show that the majority of the letter writers were illiterate or nearly illiterate, and their authors struggled to articulate their desires, needs, and emotions on paper. Thus, in their original form, the letters are able to retain their historical value as the real words left behind by the people who lived through the war and endured its many challenges.

The letters show the determination and resourcefulness of many blacks during the war. In spite of the inability to read and write, blacks found other ways of getting their messages out to Union military and government officials. Refusing to be deterred from getting the information they needed, illiterate blacks found other family members, friends, employers, or other associates who could write the letters for them or who could write on their behalf.

During the Civil War, all letters mailed to government agencies regarding soldiers, black or white, were systematically recorded as received. If any action was taken on the letters, such as a government response to the letter's author, these actions were also recorded, usually with specific markings on the letter received by the government, as well as in separate books in which the response letters were copied by hand. Government agencies often responded to family letters in two to three weeks time, and sometimes just a week after receiving the initial letter. It is because of the efficiency of this system and the adeptness of an army of clerks that these letters exist in abundance today.

I made an effort to choose letters that said a lot about the condition of the families in the absence of the soldiers and that best describe, either individually or collectively, the condition of the families and the northern black community during the war. More specifically, the letters chosen for this project fall into three main categories. The first category consists of general inquiries. Families were always sensitive to the whereabouts of their soldiers, and when they did not hear from them for long periods of time, they made inquiries to Union officials. These became the most common requests submitted by northern black families throughout the war and, as the war progressed, these letters became more specific as families asked if a soldier was dead or alive. The second category referred to financial distress. Families sent letters about the lack of funds coming from their soldiers and the state of deprivation, even destitution, that resulted for the family. They wanted to know where their soldier's pay was, and they wanted Union officials to know the family was impoverished because their soldiers were not receiving their pay and thus had nothing to send home. In the third category are requests for discharges. Family members asked Union officials for their soldiers to be discharged. Family members made these requests for a number of reasons: so the male member could come home and work to support the family, because the soldier was in poor health, because the soldier was under-age or had been duped when he enlisted, or because the family felt that their soldier had already performed his duties once the fighting was over.

As much as possible, the letters are presented in chronological order within the chapters. The first letter I used, in Chapter 3, was sent to Union officials in 1863, the first year northern black regiments participated in the war. The latest letter appearing in this study (see Chapter 10) was sent in January 1866. Presenting the letters in a chronological order enables readers to see the trends in the number of letters sent and the evolution of topics. For example, black families wrote very few letters in 1863 because northern black regiments had just begun to be formed and the problems families would face had not yet become acute. However, the number of letters increased dramatically as black troops continued to serve and their numbers increased. In addition, letters requesting confirmation about a soldier's death became more common as the war progressed and black troops consistently proved themselves to be brave and competent soldiers, though letters requesting information about the status and whereabouts of soldiers remained the most common topic of letters from 1863 until northern black troops returned home at the end of 1865. As a result of their proven competency, the number of black men who participated in combat increased, which led to more casualties within their ranks and more letters from their families.

For the sake of clarity, it is important to explain this study's definition of "northern blacks." The term "northern blacks" refers to African Americans who resided in the Union free states, where slavery had not existed for decades.[8] The only exceptions in the use of this term are Delaware and Washington, D.C. Delaware was still a slave state, but slavery there was a diluted and dying version compared to that which existed in the other slave states. There were very few slaves residing in Delaware and the number was decreasing quickly due to natural causes. In addition, Delaware had more free blacks than slaves.[9] And slavery in Washington, D.C. was banned in April 1862, less than six months before the preliminary announcement of the Emancipation Proclamation. The focus of this study is on blacks who were free—either by law or after running away from their masters prior to the start of the Civil War—and their decisions to fight for and support the Union effort. These blacks had been free for years, often decades, and had created lives and communities that were distinctly northern in culture and liberties, though severely limited liberties. Even the former slaves, many of whom had escaped from their southern masters, had assimilated to northern life, specifically the freedoms allowed. Northern blacks went to war for reasons that in many ways were very different from their brethren in the South, who needed to defeat slavery to obtain their freedom permanently or that of their family members who were still in bondage. The distinction is important for appreciating the intricacies and sacrifices made by northern blacks when they chose to support the Union. Consistent with the theme and focus on northern blacks, the bulk of the letters used in this study are from family members who resided in the free states, and not from blacks from the border states (Missouri, Kentucky, or Maryland).

Scholars have written very little on the Civil War experiences of northern black families and how the war affected their lives. Instead, scholars have focused their attention on other aspects of the northern and southern home fronts. The studies completed on the northern home front focused on white families, the economy, and the political atmosphere during the war. The issues that scholars examined in the South are more numerous and include relationships between Confederate soldiers and their families at home as well as relationships between the Confederate government and its citizens and between slaves and masters. These projects also examine the South's economy during the war. The focus on the northern black experience in the Civil War remains centered on military history and not the social aspects of the Union war effort.

This study is different because it examines the effects of the war specifically on northern black families. Most other studies on African Americans during the Civil War focus almost exclusively on the soldiers. While some scholars have highlighted the lives of northern black families, this study, with the use of their letters to Union officials, puts families at the center of the narrative. At the same time, this study tells the story of northern black soldiers during the war and examines how the events and problems at the home front affected the soldiers at the front line, and how many of the problems and obstacles endured by northern black troops directly affected their families at home. Thus, this study's focus on northern black women links them and their survival directly to the everyday lives of northern black troops.

1

Life in the North

Before the War

When war broke out on April 12, 1861, about two hundred thousand African Americans were scratching out a life for themselves in a northern society that was hostile to their very existence. Despite this hostility, a few northern blacks were able to accumulate property and live in a manner similar to white citizens. However, the majority of African Americans struggled to survive at the bottom of the political, economic, and social structure of northern society. Though their lives were better than those of their brothers and sisters in the South who lived under the institution of slavery, northern blacks were marginalized and discriminated against. Whites were successful at creating an environment in cities and towns throughout the North where blacks were legally, economically, and socially designated as a separate, dependent, and unequal group within the community.[1]

In the decades leading to the Civil War, African Americans had to also endure the constant fear of violence and race riots that usually ended with the loss of black property and black lives. Yet blacks found a way to survive in a hostile environment, despite these many obstacles, by building strong social institutions and by organizing and resisting oppressive laws and practices. And in the background were the constant and determined efforts to end slavery.

In spite of the many difficulties African Americans experienced, northern black families in large numbers supported the Union efforts to win the war. Nearly 200,000 black soldiers served in the Civil War—178,975 in the army and the remainder in the navy. Out of the total number in the army, 32,723 were from the North. That number meant 70 percent of all black men of military age in the North—between the ages of eighteen and forty-five—served. For readers to understand what motivated northern African-American families to support the Civil War, despite their hardships, it is vital to examine northern black society during the antebellum era. A review and analysis of the important challenges in this community before the start of the war—such as efforts to gain voting rights, to end discrimination, and to abolish slavery—provide an understanding of how these matters influenced African Americans to both support the Union and participate in the war. Understanding both their struggles and accomplishments sheds light on their motivations for fighting, why they accepted discrimination on the home front and battlefront, and what they expected from America in return for fighting for and helping to save the Union.[2]

By 1860, approximately 225,000 African Americans lived in the northern states. They mostly lived in heavily populated cities in the east, but they also inhabited smaller cities and towns from the Atlantic coast to beyond the Mississippi River. They settled in states as far north as Maine and Minnesota, as well as those states that bordered and had strong cultural and economic connections with the slave states, especially the southernmost parts of Pennsylvania, Ohio, Indiana, and Illinois. Many northern blacks were born free in the North because they descended from families who were free for generations. Others were born free or were manumitted in the South, but emigrated north in search of economic opportunities and increased freedom. Still, many others had escaped from the South as individuals, or as part of a family.[3]

Many African Americans in the antebellum period worked to better their status and obtain from whites the state and federal rights they felt they were deserving of as productive and law-abiding inhabitants of the United States. Whether in Philadelphia, Boston, New York, Chicago, or rural areas, they hoped equal rights would enable them to improve their conditions and open up opportunities for them to succeed in all aspects of American society. However, obtaining these rights was a constant struggle, one with few victories before the war. Yet the struggle itself reveals an active northern black community with established and organized institutions and talented and capable leadership that, in a difficult environment where they were greatly outnumbered, used whatever resources they could to improve their lot. Northern black communities had different access to resources, heavily dependent on their community and the generosity and cooperation of white allies, but they strove for the same political, economic, and social opportunities.[4]

Northern African Americans used their limited resources to organize and try to bring about positive change to end or reduce the effects of discrimination, just as they would as soldiers in the Union army. Black leaders organized within their states to influence and pressure general assemblies, county commissioners, city and village councils, school boards, and other legislative bodies to grant rights to blacks or remove racial restrictions from laws and practices. Blacks possessed limited power, especially due to the lack of access to suffrage. By 1860, only five states (Maine, Rhode Island, New Hampshire, Vermont, and Massachusetts) gave blacks equal voting rights. Alternatively, blacks used both oral and written forms of communication to exert some level of power and influence in the racist environment in which they struggled to maneuver. They gave speeches and resolutions at meetings and conventions. They wrote letters to powerful and influential local authorities and government officials. They wrote letters to black and white newspapers and journals. And they petitioned local and state governments and political organizations to support legislation. In these verbal forms of communication, blacks appealed to logic and to the conscience of whites. When they felt it was necessary, they used Biblical or patriotic themes articulated in the Constitution, asking whites to do what was just and morally right. They also used verbal tactics to garner support from sympathetic and idealistic whites who could be convinced to help them. When they could, blacks used the court system, and when more direct and aggressive action was needed and blacks were willing to take the risks, they boycotted, picketed, and forced their way into offices and courtrooms to take possession of what they felt was rightfully theirs.[5]

Thus, once the Civil War began, northern black men and women were coming from an activist environment in which they were used to confronting the white establishment and actively working to secure their rights. That is why, during the war, they wrote, or had written on their behalf, a large number of letters to get information and redress what they felt were wrongs, especially the delay in families getting pay from their soldiers. Also, because they were accustomed to addressing problems themselves, they seemed to have no reservations about writing to the highest governmental officials, specifically the Adjutant General of the Army, Brigadier General Lorenzo Thomas, Secretary of War Edwin M. Stanton, and occasionally President Lincoln. And along with writing letters, black troops organized and boycotted around such issues as unequal pay. Some troops refused their pay for months; others were more extreme, directly disobeying the orders of their superiors by stacking their weapons and refusing to move. And just as in the antebellum period, blacks during the war always looked to their white allies—influential politicians and public figures with strong abolitionist beliefs—for support. Thus, blacks used every resource they had available to improve their conditions.[6]

The black family was the foremost support group for northern black families. It was the basic and central unit within the community. The family unit's need and ability to share limited resources was paramount in an environment where resources and opportunities were especially limited for African Americans due to racism and discrimination. The average black household in the antebellum North contained four people, usually a married couple and two children. However, many families grew as family members came together in the same household to conserve resources. These family units consisted of older parents, in-laws, aunts, uncles, and cousins. Often, households also included boarders who were not related, but who needed lodging and whose income helped with the family's expenses and precarious financial position. In 1860, about forty per-cent of households included boarders. Black households also lived in close prox-imity to other black families, often in multiple-family dwellings. That is why, dur-ing the Civil War when one person wrote a letter to army officials regarding his or her family member, he or she sometimes included in the same letter multiple requests for other people in the same building who also had a family member in the army and wanted information about him as well.[7]

Black women played significant roles within and outside of the households. Their daily duties at home consisted of shopping for food, cleaning house, wash-ing clothes, cooking, and raising children. Outside of the home, they often held one or two extra jobs because of the underemployment, or lack of steady employ-ment, for black men. The paid work included laundering, cooking, or working as maids for white households, and it added crucial income to the household.[8]

When the family or household needed help and support in meeting the needs of its members, the black community provided the next layer of support by pro-viding its own support services. Long before slavery ended in the North, families and households within the free black community came together to form insti-tutions that combined resources in order to provide necessary services to the community. Usually, municipalities were not willing, due to racism, or able, due to the inpouring of poor immigrants, to provide sufficient aid to blacks. In re-sponse, blacks pooled together their resources and supplied their own welfare, social, educational, cultural, and financial assistance.[9]

These institutions were vital to the survival of many destitute families, though the organizations were limited in overall resources. The African Society was one such organization. Founded in Boston in 1796, it worked toward the abolition of slavery while also supporting people with social-welfare needs, such as widows, orphans, and the infirm. The organization helped the needy by providing finan-cial relief and helping them find employment. In addition, the society adminis-tered wills and provided for burials. Simultaneously, black fraternal organizations also served the black community. The African Masonic Lodge #459, founded by Prince Hall, a Methodist minister, in Boston in 1787, was still a very influential organization in the mid–nineteenth century. The African Masonic Lodge, along with the Odd Fellows, organized in 1843 in New York, worked to abolish slavery and racial discrimination while also providing other vital services to black com-munities. They handed out firewood to needy families, sponsored food drives for the poor, provided financial support to those who were sick and unable to work, and made loans to members and their families.[10]

Northern black women also formed their own organizations, which provided services to the community. The Daughters of Africa Society, formed in Philadelphia in 1821, was an organization made up of approximately two hundred poor and working-class women who banded together to help one another in time of need. In 1832, the black women of Boston formed the Colored Female Charitable Society to help destitute widows and orphans. Daughters of Wesley was a black women's benevolent society formed in New York City in 1827. Also in 1827, black women in New York City formed the African Dorcas Association to supply clothing to children in the African Free Schools. The Afric-American Female Intelligence Society, formed in Boston in 1832, was both a literary and a mutual-aid organization, providing intellectual and educational opportunities to its members, as well as relief services. Many of these organizations also stressed living a moral life, such as the Minerva Literary Association, which was organized in 1834, and the Colored Ladies Literary Society of New York, which was organized by the elite women of the black community, also in 1834.[11]

Even though benevolent societies and other such organizations were available to meet the needs of blacks in northern antebellum society, the church was still the most important institution for African Americans after the family unit. The church, as well as a spiritual sanctuary, was the social and physical place of refuge for all blacks, no matter what their rank or status in society. Black churches were socially active, serving as mutual-aid societies by providing social, cultural, and educational services to the community. In this manner, northern black churches were the center of activity for the entire black community, for northern natives as well as those blacks who migrated from the South as free people or runaways. The aid provided to migrants by the churches was very important because quite often migrants made up a significant portion of a city's population and, without that aid their survival would have been even more difficult, if not impossible.[12]

In addition, the churches served as the center of a myriad of other activities. Black churches were very committed to helping the poor, which they did by providing aid to needy families, holding fundraising events, and pooling church funds together. And because many northern cities had a very transient black population, black churches played a significant role helping these migrants adjust to their surroundings—many of the migrants relocated from the South as free men and women, and others were runaway slaves. The churches provided economic aid and contacts—usually church members—who could help with housing and employment opportunities.[13]

The northern black community had established a long tradition of activism and social protest by the time the Civil War began. The decades leading up to the war produced generations of leaders and activists, including women as well as men. The activists came from the middle-class and working class, the professional and skilled, as well as the semi-skilled workers and unskilled. Their participation in a variety of organizations helped them to develop and hone their leadership skills and prepared them to do battle with whites for greater political, economic, and social rights for African Americans in the North and to end slavery in the South.[14]

African Americans hoped to improve their economic and social status in the North through political access, and protect themselves and their property from the effects of racial violence. For northern blacks, the key to ending slavery and obtaining racial equality depended heavily on securing the right to vote. Blacks were not allowed to fully participate in the political process in most of the North because laws restricted them. New England (excluding Connecticut) was the exception—blacks there actually voted and had equal voting rights in elections. The most common determinant for voting rights, other than gender and age, was property qualifications. After the American Revolution, the laws only became more stringent, making it even more difficult for blacks to vote. In 1807, New Jersey enacted legislation to restrict the voting rights of African Americans, regardless of property. Connecticut and Rhode Island followed with similar measures. In New York, any male could vote who met residency, property, and age requirements. But in 1821, the property requirement was removed for whites, while it was increased from $100 to $250 in landed property for blacks. This action effectively disfranchised the overwhelming majority of free blacks in the state. In 1838, Pennsylvania added the word "white" to the qualifications for voting, thus depriving all blacks of the vote. The practice was even the same in new states, which began entering the Union with their new constitutions specifically banning blacks from voting. Ironically, it was during the period of "Jacksonian Democracy," also known as "the era of the common man," when the franchise was being expanded in the United States to allow white males who were propertyless to participate in the political process, that laws were enacted to exclude African Americans. Black men, regardless of wealth, status, or education level, were excluded from the political process.[15]

In spite of political and economic hardship and second-class treatment, for African Americans, slavery was the preeminent example of racial injustice and, for most, the main target of their national protests. Blacks wanted it abolished once and for all. Frederick Douglass explained this best when he stated, "The distinction between the slave and the free is not great, and their destiny seems one and the same. The back man is linked to his brother by indissoluble ties. The one cannot be truly free while the other is a slave." Northern blacks, though free, knew that just the existence of slavery compromised their own position in the United States and their sense of security. Most believed slavery as an institution was the main cause of racial discrimination against them and their identity and treatment as a people were directly attributed to the view by whites that blacks were only worthy of being slaves. Douglass added, "The free colored man is remembered by the ten thousand petty annoyances with which he meets of his identity with an enslaved people, and that with them he is destined to fall or flourish." Therefore, northern blacks could not help but take a stand on the slavery issue. Struggling to survive at the bottom of the political, economic, and social ladder in northern society, blacks wanted to improve their lives and opportunities for advancement, but the existence of slavery made this task even more difficult. It also did not help that the slave system allowed Southerners, in search of fugitive slaves, to threaten the status of any blacks, free or not, and send them into slavery.[16]

Blacks in the North wanted to abolish slavery not only to free their brethren, but also as a means for racial equality. That is why they were involved in the abolitionist movement, for the end to slavery and an end to the discrimination and injustice all blacks had to endure. That is why northern blacks supported the Union war effort in such large numbers. Though life in the North was tenuous for African Americans, it was better than life in the South. Still, northern blacks gave up the safety and comforts of the North to travel hundreds of miles to put their lives on the line for the Union cause. Some joined to end slavery because they had family and friends who were still enslaved. Others, many of whom came from families free for generations, felt they must earn the rights they desired for themselves and their families. One way to prove your value and worth to your countrymen was to serve, sacrifice and, in some cases, die for your country while it fought for its survival. They also knew the entire race would continue to be perceived as, and treated like, second-class citizens as long as slavery continued to exist. They hoped support for the Union, in the end, would lead to greater political, economic, and legal rights for blacks in the North.[17]

As the 1860 presidential election approached, many blacks, whether or not they were in states where they could vote, were in favor of a Republican victory. Though the party did not campaign for the end of slavery where it already existed, they did support an end to the further expansion of slavery into the territories. And blacks rejoiced when Lincoln won, including Frederick Douglass, who admired Lincoln's non-compromise attitude with the secessionist South. With Lincoln's victory, the South began a movement for secession, starting with South Carolina on December 20, 1861. The other slave states soon followed South Carolina's lead. Blacks welcomed secession and the removal of slavery from the United States. With disunion would come the end to the stranglehold the slave states held on the national government, and the need for the Constitution and the military to be used to protect the institution of slavery. As the slave states continued to secede and government officials debated conciliation plans to stop disunion, African Americans and their white allies opposed any compromises. And blacks were even further enthused once secession resulted in war. They hoped and prayed the war would lead to the destruction of slavery once and for all.[18]

2   A Grand Opportunity

1861 and 1862

On April 12, 1861, hostilities of the American Civil War began with the bombing by Confederate forces of federal troops stationed at Fort Sumter in Charleston Harbor, South Carolina. Abraham Lincoln responded three days later by calling for 75,000 volunteers to serve for ninety days to put down the rebellion. The war's outbreak provided a long-awaited opportunity in the minds of northern African Americans to prove their loyalty to the Union and their worthiness for full citizenship. For the chance to fight and prove their worth, they were prepared to put behind them the legal inequality, economic stagnation, racial violence, and political repression they experienced for decades. For other blacks, this was an opportunity to restore families and reconnect family members long separated by slavery. And for all African Americans, this was a chance to end slavery in America and the mark of inferiority it branded on the black race.

The Rush to Participate

Many people in the North thought the war would be a short and victorious one. In the jubilation of the moment, enlistment offices were flooded with people looking for glory or a chance to prove themselves; blacks were eager to volunteer their services before the chance passed. Prominent citizens offered to raise regiments and donate goods, money, and services for the cause. However, for blacks, it was the opportunity to take an active and heroic role in crushing slavery and the rebellious slaveholders. Blacks responded with outbursts of patriotism by throwing their support to the national government. Many rushed to volunteer to join the military, offering themselves at recruiting offices throughout the North, and deluging the War Department and Lincoln with offers to fight for the Union. Frederick Douglass spurred them on by using his newspaper, the *Douglass Monthly*, to urge free northern black men to be prepared to enter the fight. Douglass explained, "We do most earnestly urge our people everywhere to drink as deeply into the martial spirit of the times as possible; organize themselves into societies and companies, purchase arms for themselves, and learn how to use them." He was convinced blacks would be called upon to serve, explaining, "The present war may, and in all probably will reach a complexion when a few black regiments will be absolutely necessary." And many blacks eagerly followed his lead.[1]

The initial euphoria of these African Americans quickly evaporated when they were told this was not a war in which blacks were welcomed to participate.[2] Interracial unity with blacks in order to defeat the South was not requested nor desired, and outright rejection, both locally and nationally, was the order of the day. Blacks in Cincinnati were insulted by whites and harshly told, "this is a white man's war."[3]

Lincoln had no interest in making the war with the Confederacy a war to end slavery. He knew such a policy was not popular in the North and would have caused the administration to lose the public's support. Hence, his administration minimized the connection between secession and slavery, focusing on putting down a rebellion and restoring the Union under the existing Constitution. At the same time, most of the men who answered the president's call for 75,000 troops marched off to battle convinced in their belief they were fighting to defend the Constitution, preserve the Union, and put a stop to southern aggression—but not to end slavery. Therefore, whites were hardly ready to fight alongside blacks and see them as equals. Even more important at the time, introducing the slavery question was almost certain to tip the balance in the slaveholding border states— Kentucky, Missouri, and Maryland—moving them into the ranks of the Confederates. That is why Lincoln declined the offer when on August 4, 1862 an Indiana delegation offered the government two regiments of black men. He was most aware that losing the border states so early in the war would have been disastrous to the Union's war effort. In addition, no one expected a long war. Many people felt it would be over in ninety days. Indeed, Lincoln believed 75,000 troops were enough to end the rebellion. Thus, there was no need, nor was it worth the controversy, to rely on black troops.[4]

Hurt, outraged, or bewildered, many African Americans began to believe that no service provided to the country would ever free them from racism in America. The African Methodist Episcopal (AME) Church, the North's largest black denomination, advised its members they had no business fighting for a country that openly persecuted them. Frederick Douglass, who was furious over the exclusion of blacks from the fight, questioned the logic of the American government and its people for refusing to exploit the most potent weapon in its arsenal to defeat the South. He could not understand how discrimination and "blind, unreasoning prejudice" could override what he saw as common sense. Other blacks argued, why offer to fight for the country anyway because it intended for slavery to continue. In a letter printed on May 4, 1861 in the black newspaper, *Pine and Palm*, a black man in Chillicothe, Ohio, stated he was disgusted blacks continued to offer their services to a government that, time and time again, rejected their offers and who continued to "oppress them." Another African American, who identified himself as R. H. V., sent a letter to the *Anglo-African*, where he denounced the call to arms, and questioned why blacks were willing to fight and die in a war that would still perpetuate slavery.[5]

We'll Find Other Ways to Serve Until Called Upon

The only bright spot for blacks early in the war was the Union navy's decision to begin enlisting blacks in September 1861, to fill a severe manpower shortage. The Secretary of the Navy, Gideon Welles, issued the order. Severe manpower shortages in the army would contribute to a similar decision only a year later.[6] Until then, however, northern blacks looked for and found other ways to contribute to the Union war effort.

Determined to help the cause while trying to prove they deserved full citizenship, hundreds of these men became cooks and waiters for white officers. Others became laborers, stablemen, and teamsters to drive supply wagons. A group of African-American men from Providence, Rhode Island, who drilled before their offer to fight was rejected, attached themselves instead as servants to a white Rhode Island regiment. Other blacks actually enlisted as soldiers in white regiments. They were so very light in complexion, they were able to pass as white. George W. D. Kirkland was one such soldier. He was the son of Elizabeth Keckley, the dressmaker for Mary Todd Lincoln, Abraham Lincoln's wife. George was very lightly complexioned because his father was Elizabeth's white master. And he used his ability to pass for white to join the army. A member of Company D, 1st Missouri Volunteers, he saw action and died early in the war, on August 10, 1861, in his first battle at Wilson's Creek in southwest Missouri.[7]

George E. Stephens of Philadelphia was also determined to find a way to serve the Union cause. He became a cook and personal servant for Benjamin C. Tilghman at the outbreak of the war. Tilghman was an officer in the Army of the Potomac's 26th Pennsylvania Volunteer Infantry with very strong anti-slavery convictions. He resigned his position as colonel and commander of the 26th to lead the

3rd USCT later in the war when black regiments were organized in the North. The 3rd USCT was organized in August 1863, at Camp William Penn in Chelton Hills, just northwest of Philadelphia, Pennsylvania. Stephens also worked as a war correspondent for the New York *Weekly Anglo-African* while serving Tilghman. Thomas and Robert Hamilton founded the *Weekly Anglo-African* in 1859, and it was one of two newspapers published by African Americans during the Civil War that were read throughout the North. The *Weekly Anglo-African* reported on the everyday life of northern blacks, their efforts to end slavery, and their determination to obtain equal rights in all aspects of their lives in the North. The newspaper also became one of the key vehicles enabling black troops to tell their story about life in the Union army once black soldiers entered the war. Black troops used the newspaper to demand equal rights for themselves, plead for support for their families while away from them, and describe in detail the plight and needs of their newly freed from slavery southern brethren. Stephens was their correspondent in the field. From 1861 to the end of 1862, he provided first-hand reports on the encounters and activities of the Army of the Potomac. In that time span, he also provided readers with a personal view of fugitive slaves, the slave system, and the cruel treatment and brutalization of southern blacks by both southern whites and white Union troops. In addition, Stephens used his position as Tilghman's cook to help runaway slaves escape to Washington, D.C.[8]

From 1863 until the end of the war, he became the voice of the 54th Massachusetts Regiment. He continued his work as correspondent for the *Weekly Anglo-African* while he served as a noncommissioned officer in the regiment. In this capacity, he was in many ways the Frederick Douglass of the Union army. While Douglass was the preeminent black activist, who reported—through his newspaper *Frederick Douglass's Monthly*—on black life and their struggles and accomplishments, Stephens served as a leader in the 54th and provided a first-hand account of the struggles of black troops in the Union army, their encounters with slavery, and their performance as soldiers on the battlefield.[9]

Northern black women were excluded from participating in work supporting the northern war effort just like black men in 1861 and 1862. And just like black men, that did not stop them from finding other ways to participate. They focused their attention initially on the fugitive slaves because, once the war began, fugitives flocked in large numbers to Union lines, arriving hungry, impoverished, and in poor health. Northern black women used their organizational experience, skills, and talents to come to the rescue of these men, women, and children. These women created their own societies, continuing their long history of benevolent and charitable work that was a part of their church and antislavery activities. The knowledge, experience, and skills they gained participating for decades in benevolent activities, often working through black churches, now proved invaluable. They also obtained important experience through their involvement in anti-slavery, literary, cultural, and vigilance organizations.[10]

Black women founded new organizations or expanded the roles of existing ones. The Contraband Relief Association (CRA) was founded in Washington in 1862 by a group of forty women, including Elizabeth Keckley, who served as the first president of the organization and was known as a very good organizer.[11] Keckley used her skills as a seamstress to purchase her freedom and that of her son, George, in 1855. Remembering her own harsh experiences as a slave, she felt African Americans had a duty and obligation to help refugees. While Keckley appealed predominantly to the black community, her compatriot, Harriet Jacobs, appealed to blacks and whites. Also similar to Keckley, Jacobs was a former slave and a seamstress who learned her craft while enslaved. She escaped from slavery in Edenton, North Carolina, where she was sexually, mentally, and physically abused. After she and her children escaped to New York, a white abolitionist purchased their freedom in 1852. After the war broke out, she worked unflaggingly, within and in collaboration with refugee organizations, to raise funds and provide aid for destitute fugitive families. She became a major voice for them, raising awareness of their plight to anybody who would listen.[12]

Some African-American women served as teachers to the refugees. Charlotte Forten went south and taught black refugees in Port Royal, South Carolina, from 1862 to 1864, for the Philadelphia Port Royal Relief Association (later the Pennsylvania Freedmen's Relief Association). She also served as a nurse in a local military hospital and taught wounded soldiers how to read and write while she nursed them back to health. Charlotte, a member of the free, wealthy, and illustrious African-American family, the Fortens of Philadelphia, was a middle-class black woman who took on nontraditional roles for women. Representing the fourth generation of her family who were born free, she followed in their footsteps as a reformer and activist, dedicated to the demise of slavery and the uplift of her people.[13]

By 1863, African-American women were active for almost two years helping fugitive slave families when the Union began forming black regiments in the North. That activity prepared them well to provide similar support to black soldiers. Northern black women began forming blacks-only soldiers' aid societies. These organizations incorporated the support of black soldiers and their families into the mission of existing organizations. For example, the CRA later changed its name to the Ladies' Freedmen and Soldiers' Relief Association, and began raising funds and providing provisions for soldiers and their families, as well as continuing to help freedmen.[14]

A Change in War Goals

By the summer of 1862, Abraham Lincoln decided to *free* all the slaves in rebel territory. This was a symbolic act because he had no authority to free slaves in territory currently not controlled by Union armies. However, the Union army now also became an army of liberation as they conquered more Confederate territory (see Figures 1 and 2). The potential for Union forces to obtain desperately needed manpower was another important factor for the decision.[15]

On September 22, 1862, Lincoln announced he would issue a Proclamation of Emancipation on January 1, 1863, freeing all slaves in areas still in rebellion against the Federal government. Along with giving the war a higher cause for the Union, the Emancipation Proclamation stated that "such persons of suitable condition [former slaves], will be received into the armed service of the United States to garrison forts, positions, stations, and other places, and to man vessels of all sorts in said service." Henceforth, African Americans could enlist into the armed services of the United States. And just months after the Proclamation took effect, northern black regiments were officially organized and trained and finally blacks could be recognized as active and vital participants in the Union's war effort, no longer perceived by most whites as simply onlookers or spectators.[16]

When January 1, 1863, finally arrived, African Americans throughout the North came together to celebrate and observe the Emancipation Proclamation. From morning to afternoon, throngs of northern blacks packed churches, concert halls, and other venues to pray, sing songs, and hear speeches, including the reading of the Proclamation. This was just a build-up to the late afternoon arrival of the official notice from the nation's capital that the Proclamation had taken effect. Frenzied jubilation followed throughout the North—from Boston to New York City, Philadelphia, Washington, D.C., and Columbus, Ohio. Audiences could not restrain themselves, filled with emotion that was released with cheers and shouts of joy (see Figure 3).[17]

Not only did it represent the opportunity for freedom and an end to slavery, but with the Proclamation came the opportunity for northern blacks to finally

Figure 1. African-American refugees escaped in large numbers toward Union lines as the Union Army conquered more Confederate territory. (Library of Congress)

Figure 2. Refugees escaped individually or as whole families, usually carrying with them what little they owned, and needing food, shelter, and health care. (*The Soldier in Our Civil War: A Pictorial History of the Conflict, 1861–1865*, Vol. II, 300.)

Figure 3. On Dec. 31, 1862, African Americans held "watch meetings" (pictured here in Boston) throughout the North to celebrate the Emancipation taking effect at midnight on January 1, 1863. (Library of Congress)

fight in the war. According to William Wells Brown, "The Emancipation Proc-lamation was only a prelude to calling on the colored men to take up arms, and the one soon followed the other."[18] This was the opportunity northern blacks had longed for since the first shots at Fort Sumter. And though they were cynical, distrusting, and still outraged about the reaction from their initial offer to join the fight, they put all that behind them and eventually, though not all at once, supported the Union in great numbers.[19]

3

The Forming of Black Regiments and Success in Battle

A Call for Sable Arms

On January 1, 1863, the Emancipation Proclamation was issued. And though a handful of black regiments had already been organized by the Union in the parts of the Confederacy under Union control—this was done under the July 17, 1862, Confiscation Act—the Proclamation gave official federal authorization to use black troops as part of the Union's war strategy. Thus, the Proclamation provided northern blacks with the opportunity to fight for the country they lived in, prove their worthiness for citizenship, and along with their southern brothers, help bring an end to the scourge of slavery. However, the Civil War would not be the first time African Americans had fought for America. Blacks fought, both as slaves and free men, in every American war, including the Revolution, the War of 1812, and the Mexican-American War. They fought bravely and received accolades from prominent American leaders such as Andrew Jackson, who acknowledged after the Battle of New Orleans (December 1814 to January 1815) that black soldiers played a major role in his victory. Yet in previous wars, black soldiers had never been officially part of the military establishment. They tended to be afterthoughts, operating only at a very local level and on the fringes of any military force. That changed with their participation in the Civil War. From that point on, they served with the regular army of the United States as well as state militias, finally serving in integrated units and regiments of the military in 1948.[1]

Many black men throughout the North joined the newly formed Union regiments. They saw a propitious opportunity they could not let pass. African Americans from the northern states could have either answered the call to serve and put the race in position for greater rights, or they could have stood by as observers, guaranteeing they might never be viewed as citizens of the United States and therefore equal. They hoped that for their loyalty and sacrifice they would be awarded greater rights in the North. In addition, they knew the entire race would continue to be looked at and treated like second-class citizens as long as slavery continued to exist. The Civil War presented an opportunity that might not come again in their lifetime, the chance to end slavery. Sgt. Alexander Altwood, of Company E, 11th United States Colored Troops, best explained the sentiments of African Americans when he stated, "If roasting on a bed of coals of fire, would do away with the curse of slavery, I would be willing to be the sacrifice."[2]

Governor John A. Andrew of Massachusetts, an avowed opponent of slavery, was long interested in arming black men and allowing them to prove their worth to the nation by letting them fight in the war. In January 1863, he requested permission to organize a black regiment from the northern states and on January 26, Secretary of War Stanton authorized him to enlist "persons of African descent" as volunteers for three years of service into separate, meaning segregated, regiments. That order brought into existence the 54th Massachusetts Infantry, the first black regiment formed in the North. Andrew was determined to create infantry units composed of African Americans. As he began organizing it in February 1863, Andrew strongly believed the 54th would set the example and be the model for the other northern black regiments that followed. He believed the regiment would be "the most important corps to be organized during the whole war." He also felt the success or failure of the regiment would resonate throughout the nation and affect any future decisions to use black soldiers in the war. Thus, he made sure the 54th was officered by the best and brightest Massachusetts men who shared his interests in seeing African Americans succeed. He searched the membership of antislavery societies to select Robert Gould Shaw as the regiment's colonel and Norwood P. Hallowell as its lieutenant colonel. Shaw was twenty-five years old and a captain in the 2nd Massachusetts Infantry, and Hallowell was twenty-four and a captain in the 20th Massachusetts. Though maybe not yet committed antislavery men themselves, both men were from staunch abolitionist families, as would be many of the regiment's first officers, the Shaws from Boston and the Hallowells from Philadelphia.[3]

State recruiting agents were sent throughout the North to find enough men for the regiment. Andrew appointed well-known abolitionist George L. Stearns to lead the recruiting efforts to fill the ranks of the 54th and then the 55th Massachusetts Infantries. Stearns established recruiting offices in New York City, Rochester, Buffalo, Philadelphia, and as far west as Chicago. Men came from all the free states, as well as Canada, Great Britain, the Hawaiian Islands, and even Africa, to join the regiment. The recruits arrived at Readville, a town outside Boston, where the 54th's training site, Camp Meigs, was located. Assisting Stearns in raising the unit were prominent abolitionists such as Wendell Phillips and William Lloyd Garrison, and black leaders such as William Wells Brown, Frederick Douglass, and a host of other men and women who volunteered their time and energy.[4] Douglass's two sons, Charles and Lewis, joined. Charles was nineteen years old and a painter when he enlisted as a corporal in Company D. He was later promoted to sergeant in Company B. On March 19, 1864, he joined the 5th Massachusetts Calvary, another black regiment. Lewis was twenty-two years old and, like his brother, a painter when he enlisted on March 25, 1863 and was assigned to Company D. He was quickly promoted to sergeant-major in the same Company. Lewis served until February 23, 1864, when he was granted a disability discharge.[5] The Douglass brothers were the first men from New York to join the regiment. Most of the men who joined were free men from Pennsylvania, New York, Ohio, and Massachusetts, with a good number from the western states.[6]

Even Mary Ann Shadd Cary and Martin Delany, both staunch African-American emigrationists and at the time both living in Canada, returned to the United States and assisted Stearns.[7] Both saw the opportunity for blacks to help end slavery, and they could not turn their backs. Shadd Cary became the only woman officially commissioned and paid as a recruiting agent for the Union army, and she did this while her brother, Abraham W. Shadd, and her cousin, Gabriel Jackson Shadd, both served in the 55th Massachusetts Infantry. Abraham was nineteen years old and a teacher when he enlisted on May 31, 1863. A member of Company B, he was later promoted to Sergeant and then Sergeant Major. Gabriel, a member of Company I, was a shoemaker when he enlisted on June 9, 1863. Anxious to serve, he went off to war even though he was already forty-two years old and his wife had just given birth that April to their second son, while already caring for their two-year-old son. In his zealousness to fill the regiment's ranks, Delany even recruited his fifteen-year-old son, Toussaint L'Overture Delany, who left school in Canada to enlist in the 54th. Toussaint was listed, most likely by his father, as being eighteen years old when he enlisted. As a member of Company D, he served until the entire regiment was discharged in 1865, probably having grown up and matured very quickly in order to perform his duty as a soldier.[8]

Not all northerners agreed with Andrew and Douglass that blacks would make effective soldiers. Many whites felt blacks were naturally cowards who also lacked the necessary discipline and intelligence to function as soldiers. However, as the war progressed, most doubters would become believers. The only people who had full faith from the start in the ability of black troops to perform well were African Americans and their staunchest allies.[9]

In spite of criticism and lingering doubts among many whites as to whether black troops would fight, the 54th was organized in the North, initially at a slow rate—one or two soldiers a day—and then quickly as the work of Stearns and the other recruiting agents began to show results. Many blacks were very cautious when the Union reversed its policy; they recalled the initial rejection of African-American volunteers when the war began in 1861. They questioned why they should fight for a nation that openly discriminated against them. In addition, they doubted the sincerity of the North to treat black troops fairly. As a result, some local black leaders in Boston urged them not to join. Other black leaders, however, seeing the opportunity to end slavery and raise the status of all blacks in America, promoted the creation of the units. These optimists also believed Governor Andrew when he said he would find ways to assign black commissioned officers to the regiment, as well as provide equal pay and bounties to the soldiers. Thus, Andrew, Douglass, and other recruiters, who spoke at rallies and black churches, were able to turn the trickle of volunteers into a steady flow as new recruits arrived at Readville, on the average twelve men a day. Northern blacks began to join in larger numbers, fully aware of the opportunity the war presented them, and by the end of March 1863, the regiment was officially mustered into service. Because of the extraordinary efforts of Douglass, Stearns, and the other recruiters, blacks became so eager to join the war effort that a second regiment was formed, the 55th Massachusetts Infantry. The 55th handled the tremendous overflow of volunteers from outside of Massachusetts. Norwood Hallowell was transferred from the 54th to serve as commander of the new regiment.[10]

Thanks to the efforts of Andrew, black leaders, and Brigadier General Lorenzo Thomas, the adjutant general of the Union Army, the recruitment and enlistment of black troops, both in the North and eventually in the South, was exceedingly successful. Successful recruitment occurred at such a fast pace that the army found itself unprepared. To better organize and centralize the process of raising African-American troops and staffing the regiments with qualified white officers, on May 22, 1863 the War Department established a separate bureau in the Adjutant General's Office. With General Orders, No. 143, the War Department created the Bureau for Colored Troops, headed by Major Charles W. Foster and charged it with raising black troops in the North and the South, and with assigning white officers; it also served as a clearinghouse for all information regarding United States Colored Troops. The creation of the Bureau for Colored Troops was important for two reasons. First, this action signified the important role black regiments would hold as a part of the war effort and the administration's overall plan to win the war. Second, the creation of the Bureau brought order for all aspects of creating and organizing black regiments, including their numbering, under federal control. All newly organized African-American units were assigned United States regimental designations. Thus, troops were no longer fighting for particular states, but were fighting for the United States. Even those regiments originally mustered on the state level were assigned new names and numbers. The 3rd Louisiana Native Guards, for example, became the 75th USCT. The only exceptions were the 29th Connecticut Infantry, the 54th and 55th Massachusetts Infantries, and the 5th Massachusetts Calvary, because they were formed in the North before the new policy.[11]

As in the 54th and 55th Massachusetts Infantries, the troops and non-commissioned officers were all black but the commissioned officers of these new black regiments were white. Lincoln and the War Department felt that keeping white men in charge of black regiments in the segregated Union army was necessary to make the policy of using black troops acceptable to the northern white public, to the border states, and to white Union soldiers. However, African-American troops and their white allies were very disenchanted by the decision to deprive them of black officers. They viewed the government's policy as clearly prejudiced. Just as officials were unsure whether blacks were capable of being competent soldiers, black soldiers were just as unsure of the ability of white commissioned officers to train regiments and then lead them into battle. The policy was the cause of persistent concern among black troops who wanted their own kind to be their officers, people who they felt cared for them and whom they could trust. They were also upset because the government's policy barred from advancement well-educated and talented black soldiers. Blacks were allowed to rise up to the rank of noncommissioned officers, such as sergeants and corporals, where they played vital roles as leaders and intermediaries between black troops and their white officers, but they felt that was not enough. The War Department grudgingly agreed to commission some black chaplains and surgeons—thirteen and twelve, respectively, during the course of the war—but did not budge on combat officers, who remained white until the war was almost over, when a few exceptions were made. To further reinforce the department's decision, General Nathaniel P. Banks eventually weeded out of the army the black officers in the black regiments organized in Louisiana, initially on the grounds that they were incompetent. When that strategy did not work to get rid of all of the unit's black officers, they were ridiculed and subjected to constant public embarrassment, which caused them to choose to resign rather than continue to be humiliated. All the black officers were eventually replaced with whites.[12]

Black Troops in Combat

The most significant test for black troops would be how they performed in battle. The reason most of them joined the military, especially northern blacks who as freemen left their families and secure surroundings, was to prove blacks were worthy of citizenship in America. They put up with what they felt were the Union's racist policies and unfair treatment of them as soldiers because they wanted the opportunity to fight. Black soldiers from regiments formed in the South already showed their mettle in combat, even before the Emancipation Proclamation. These regiments participated in minor skirmishes in Missouri (October 1862), Georgia (November 1862), and, soon after the Proclamation took effect, in South Carolina (January 1863), Mississippi (April 1863), Kansas (May 1863), and Arkansas (May 1863). Nevertheless, it was three major engagements—two battles in Mississippi and Louisiana and the historical charge of the 54th at Fort Wagner in South Carolina—that black troops more than proved their value and worth to white America.[13]

First, members of the Louisiana Native Guards distinguished themselves by showing outstanding bravery at Port Hudson, Louisiana. The 1st Regiment Louisiana Native Guards was the first African-American regiment to serve in the Union forces when they were mustered into service on September 27, 1862. The 2nd Regiment Louisiana Native Guards was mustered into service on October 12, and the 3rd on November 24, becoming the second and third black regiments to serve in the Union forces. All three regiments were armed and trained four miles north of New Orleans, at Camp Strong Station. Also, all of their line officers (captains and lieutenants) were blacks, though, as stated earlier, the Union commander of the region, Nathaniel P. Banks, eventually purged the regiments of all their black officers. They were replaced with white officers, many of whom proved incompetent. Under Banks's orders, the Native Guard was initially relegated to fatigue duty because neither Banks nor other whites knew how they would fight. By the end of May 1863, however, the Union would know.[14]

On May 27, 1863, Banks ordered an attack on Port Hudson on the Mississippi, while General Ulysses S. Grant's forces assaulted Vicksburg. Union forces numbering six thousand men advanced toward the strongly entrenched and well-fortified Confederate forces at Port Hudson equaling twelve hundred men. In the battle, one thousand African-American troops made charge after charge over swampy land with fallen trees while fired upon in rapid succession with rifles and artillery. The regiment continued to fight even under a horrendous barrage of firepower and men falling left and right.[15] Joseph T. Wilson, a member of the 2nd Louisiana Native Guards, described the heroics of the black troops: "Never was fighting more heroic than that of the federal army and especially that of the Phalanx regiments. If valor could have triumphed over such odds, the assaulting forces would have carried the works. . . ." Wilson continued, "The negro regiments on the north side of the works vied with the bravest, making three desperate charges on the confederate batteries, losing heavily, but maintaining their position in the advance all the while."[16] The Native Guards hoped to get support from the white regiments involved in the battle, but help failed to appear since the other regiments were pinned down. As a result, the assault was a complete failure tactically.[17] Nevertheless, even Banks praised the efforts of the troops, in spite of his prejudice toward blacks. He stated in his May 30, 1863 report to the Department of the Gulf Headquarters, "It gives me pleasure to report that they answered every expectation. In many respects their conduct was heroic. No troops could be more determined or more daring. . . . The highest commendation is bestowed upon them by all the officers in command on the right [of our line]." As to the ultimate question as to whether they would fight and be capable soldiers, Banks added, "Whatever doubt may have existed heretofore as to the efficiency of organizations of this character, the history of this day proves conclusively to those who were in condition to observe the conduct of these regiments that the Government will find in this class of troops effective supporters and defenders." Word of the heroism of the Native Guards spread through Union ranks as well as the general northern public, and northern newspapers reported on the bravery of the African-American troops at Port Hudson.[18]

Even before news reached the North about the exploits of black troops at Port Hudson, two more black regiments from Louisiana, along with one from Mississippi, performed admirably under even more intense enemy fire, this time at Milliken's Bend, a Union supply depot just northwest of Vicksburg on the Mississippi River. On June 7, 1863 a force of fifteen hundred Confederates attacked the 9th Louisiana Regiment Infantry (African Descent), later designated the 5th USCT; the 11th Louisiana Regiment Infantry (AD), later the 49th USCT; the 1st Mississippi Regiment Infantry (AD), later the 51st USCT; and the 23rd Iowa Regiment, a battle-hardened white regiment. The Union regiments were guarding the depot when they were quickly overwhelmed in a surprise attack. The black regiments, made up predominantly of newly freed former slaves and field hands, were raw and inexperienced. Lorenzo Thomas formed the regiment just a month before. The 9th and the 11th took the brunt of the rebel attack but, undaunted, the untrained and ill-equipped brave black troops regrouped and used hand-to-hand fighting and their bayonets to turn the tide of the fight into a decisive Union victory. Eleven hundred Union troops engaged in the battle and four hundred became casualties. An astonishing 35 percent of the black troops were killed or wounded, with the 9th losing 45 percent of its men. Similar to their actions at Port Hudson, news of their heroics at Milliken's Bend spread through the Union ranks and to northern newspapers and journals. Grant noted the "gallant" efforts of the black troops at Milliken's Bend and thought they would be "good troops." Other prominent officers who initially ridiculed the idea of using black troops in combat were now becoming convinced of their ability as fighting men. But there was still one more battle ahead before most whites recognized the ability of blacks to perform bravely as troops and that recognition was cemented in their minds. The battle took place before the walls of Fort Wagner on Morris Island, South Carolina.[19]

On February 21, 1863, the 54th Massachusetts Infantry began its very important training at Camp Meigs, outside Boston. By May 13, the regiment was fully organized and equipped. It was presented with its regimental colors on May 18 and was ready for its official presentation to the people of Massachusetts. On May 28, 1863, the full regiment left Camp Meigs and at 9:00 in the morning formed at Park Square in preparation to march through the streets of Boston in a grand parade. Huge crowds of people lined the streets to get a glimpse of the new regiment and thousands of supporters, white and black, showered the soldiers with praise, flowers, and handkerchiefs. The soldiers felt a great sense of pride marching past flag-draped buildings and the State House, and marching in front of a delegation of state and city officials, including Governor Andrew, who came to see the regiment off. Abolitionists Wendell Phillips, William Lloyd Garrison, and other allies in attendance at the parade watched from the balcony as the men marched past Phillips's home. Frederick Douglass was also at the event, proudly watching his sons march by. The regiment stopped to drill on Boston Common and then resumed its march through the city. The regiment marched down State street and over the spot where Crispus Attucks was killed during the American Revolution. Many of the 54th's family members and friends rushed forward to kiss the men, distribute flowers, and then say their goodbyes.[20]

The families of most of the soldiers lived too far from Boston to attend the event, yet included in the throng of well-wishers was a woman who traveled all the way from Chicago to see her two sons off to war. She was very emotional as tears streamed down her face and she kissed and hugged them and wished them goodbye. Many other mothers, wives, and sisters reacted the same way. Also present, but in the background, were "enemies" of the 54th looking to cause a ruckus at the festive occasion. They were not at all supportive of black troops. But good planning on the part of Andrew and Shaw prevented any incidents. Also contributing to the day's success was quick thinking on the part of Boston police, who placed themselves in between possible troublemakers and the soldiers as they marched through the city's streets. After the grand parade and family goodbyes, the regiment then boarded steamships destined for South Carolina.[21]

On June 3, 1863, the regiment arrived in the Palmetto State, where the first shots of the war occurred in Charleston harbor just two years earlier. Now in the war zone, the regiment's first skirmish against Confederate forces occurred in South Carolina in the James Island expedition, July 9–16. Their action on July 16 protected the 10th Connecticut from capture or totally decimation by a surprise attack from the rebels. The 54th's casualties were 14 killed, 18 wounded, and 13 missing in action, all enlisted men. The casualty count included black troops who were captured and then bound and shot or bayoneted, and some were murdered—killed by Confederate troops after surrendering. The same thing occurred in the battles at Port Hudson and Milliken's Bend.[22] The Union forces, including the 54th, then made their way to Morris Island where they were ordered to report immediately to General George Strong. Upon the 54th's arrival, Colonel Shaw reported to General Strong, who was from Massachusetts and a West Point graduate. Earlier, Shaw wrote to Strong stating he felt the 54th was being left out of the planned attack on Fort Wagner. When Strong's brigade was given the assignment to lead the assault, Strong requested that the 54th return from James Island back to Morris Island. After their return, Strong extended to the regiment the honor of heading the assault on the fort. Shaw could have re-fused the offer because his men were exhausted and had not eaten. His men had not rested for two nights, not eaten rations for two days, and were on the march most of the day, yet, without hesitation, he accepted Strong's offer. Shaw probably saw what he felt was an opportunity for black troops to lead a major assault; the opportunity might not be presented again soon, if ever.[23]

The assault force was organized and led by Brigadier General Quincy Adams Gillmore. Gilmore's eye was on Charleston and he was determined to capture the city, a key Confederate trading port. Standing in his way was Fort Wagner, a formidable earthwork, consisting of tons of wood, soil, sand, and marshland, which extended across the neck of Morris Island and was virtually impregnable to a frontal assault.[24]

The six hundred men of the 54th Massachusetts Infantry began the assault in the early evening of July 18. Shaw and his men had a good idea of the hazards before them. The men also knew the previous attempt to take the fort had failed, just days before on July 11. But that did not appear to deter them. About sixteen hundred yards—mainly yards and yards of sand—in front of Fort Wagner, Shaw ordered the 54th to move quickly until within one hundred yards of the fort and then to charge. Knowing the importance of the moment and what was at stake, Shaw told his men "now I want you to prove yourselves" and reminded them the eyes of thousands were watching and would witness and record what the regiment did in the attack that day.[25]

The three-hour battle and the 54th Massachusetts Infantry's charge had two different outcomes for the Union. First, the battle was lost, the fort was not taken, and the casualties were considerable: 246 were killed, 890 wounded, and 391 taken prisoner. The casualty list included General Strong. He was evacuated to New York City, where he died of infection on July 30. The 54th's totals were 34 killed, including Colonel Shaw and three other officers, 146 wounded, and 92 missing in action or taken prisoner. Thus, 272, or 45 percent, of the regiment's 600 men who participated in the charge were casualties. Again, Confederates outraged at having to fight against blacks murdered a number of captured and defenseless black troops, similar to the skirmish two days earlier. Conversely, the Confederates suffered much lower casualty rates: 36 killed, 133 wounded, and 5 captured. Second, in spite of the failure to take the fort, the battle was a great success for African Americans and their allies because it proved black men were capable and courageous soldiers. Even in a major military defeat, the 54th's display of bravery was recognized by both friends and foe; word of their heroism spread throughout the North. One of the brave men was Sergeant William H. Carney, whose valor before the walls of Fort Wagner—saving the American flag while badly wounded in both legs, his chest, and right arm—made him the first African-American soldier awarded the Congressional Medal of Honor, the highest honor awarded by the government to a soldier.[26]

As news continued to spread about the bravery of the 54th, so grew the legends of Colonel Shaw and the regiment. Black troops had to show their mettle in order to be taken seriously as soldiers, something Shaw and his troops both knew. And the only way to do that was in battle, where bravery could be shown in the face of death and destruction. Such was the outcome at Fort Wagner (see Figure 4).[27]

Further Recruitment and Organizing

The heroic actions of black soldiers at Port Hudson, Milliken's Bend, and Fort Wagner proved their value to the Union as a fighting force and stimulated a steady increase in the formation of black regiments organized in the North and South. African-Americans were inspired to enlist and whites were willing to officer them knowing black troops could fight. In addition, the northern public began to reconsider its racial stereotype of blacks lacking the bravery, intelligence,

Figure 4. A depiction of the 54th Massachusetts Regiment's charge on Fort Wagner on July 18, 1863. (Library of Congress)

and discipline necessary to be good soldiers. Following the 54th was its sister regiment, the 55th Massachusetts Infantry, which was organized by June 11, 1863 and sent to Newbern, N.C. on July 21, 1863. The 1st USCT was fully organized by June 30, 1863 in Washington, D.C., and reported to Virginia in July, 1863. The 3rd USCT completed its organization on August 10, 1863 in Pennsylvania. Soon afterwards, the regiment was sent to South Carolina. By the end of 1863, the Union formed eight black regiments in the northern states and the District of Columbia (one from the District of Columbia, one from Iowa, two from Massachusetts, three from Pennsylvania, and one from Rhode Island). The Union formed one hundred sixty-two regiments from the North and South by the end of the war.[28]

Although successful, the recruitment of black troops encountered many difficulties along the way. Several problems were common to black troops and their families such as limited or no bounty payments for volunteering. Bounties were sizable amounts of money that served as an extra incentive to entice men to join the military. There were limited amounts of relief services and resources available to needy families of black soldiers. And as of June 4, 1863, the unequal pay issue, which angered many blacks, helped to keep them away from recruiting stations. These disincentives were learned about through African-American newspapers and journals or simply by word-of-mouth from troops who already enlisted. And they caused many blacks to delay, or hesitate, enlisting. Some northern blacks, anxious to do their part to end slavery and prove their worthiness of citizenship, joined anyway. For southern blacks, ending slavery and freeing their still enslaved loved ones was a greater incentive, though the steady income was an added benefit for enlisting.[29]

An efficient recruiting operation aided the Union to enlist blacks. Through the efforts of George L. Stearns, the recruiting agent appointed by Governor Andrew to fill the ranks of the 54th and 55th Massachusetts Infantries, the Union was able to put together a well-organized recruiting system that employed salaried agents in large northern cities and sub-agents. The sub-agents were paid a fee for every man they enlisted. After Stearns completed his work for Massachusetts, he offered his services to the War Department and on June 13, 1863, he was appointed a recruiting commissioner for African-American troops, with the rank of major. He quickly went to work, first in Philadelphia where he raised eight hundred men in four weeks for the 3rd United States Colored Troops. His success continued even after the draft went into effect in July 1863, when blacks began enlisting as paid substitutes for men, usually whites, who were drafted but had the means to pay someone to take their place in the army. Many blacks chose this route rather than enlisting as a volunteer or draftee without receiving a bounty. Stearns also convinced the government to pay authorized recruiters $2 per recruit, further motivating them to do their job and travel throughout the North, and later into the South. Stearns had further success in the South recruiting into the army slaves liberated by the Emancipation Proclamation as well as escaped slaves, many of whom had managed to reach Union military lines.[30]

Unfortunately for some recruits and their families, financial incentives led to unscrupulous activities on the part of some recruiters. Unsuspecting and uneducated men were duped into enlisting by a handful of unscrupulous recruiters. In addition, these crooked agents, referred to as bounty brokers, often lined their pockets with all or a portion of the bounty money intended for the recruits, and also for their families since most of the money would probably have been turned over to the recruit's family to help them get by financially in his absence. Anxious to secure their fee, some recruiters did not care about the health or age of the men they pressured into enlistment. They enlisted people who did not belong in the military because they were not sufficiently able-bodied and therefore incapable of performing their duties. Many stories surfaced of young boys under the age of eighteen enlisting without receiving proper approval from their parents. Also frequent was the recruitment of black men who were in poor health and who spent more time in the hospital or under an army doctor's care than performing their military duties. All new recruits were required to take physicals before enlisting, but sometimes shady and unscrupulous doctors, for a few extra dollars, approved the enlistment of the sick and unhealthy. More often though, physicians signed off on even unhealthy black recruits because the army, especially as the brutal war progressed, was more interested in filling it ranks than making sure the recruits were healthy enough to perform their duties.[31]

Whether too young or sickly, most of these troops were not in the service very long before their families requested discharges. In one such situation, Mary Ann Douglas, of Washington, D.C., had a letter written for her on August 6, 1863, on which she put her mark and had witnessed. She requested that her son, Daniel, be allowed to return home and help her provide for herself and her other children. Daniel was a laborer and, according to army records, was nineteen when he enlisted on May 19, 1863. Mary's letter was addressed to Stanton and in it she asserted, "About three months ago my poorly son Daniel Douglas enlisted in Co. B. 1st District Col. Vols. Without my knowledge or consent. He is a minor [less than eighteen years old] and was my main support, and since his enlistment I have found it difficult to maintain myself. I therefore ask for his discharge so that I can have his assistance in supporting myself and children." The commanding officer of the 1st USCT, Colonel John H. Holman, recommended the army's approval of Mary's request, not because her son was a minor—the army still believed him to be nineteen years old and therefore, of age when he enlisted—but they considered him sickly and always unfit for duty. According to Daniel in an 1891 pension document, in the summer of 1863 "I got kidney disease" and suffered from back pains, and by 1864 he was suffering from rheumatism as well.[32]

Nonetheless, Daniel ended up serving until his regiment was mustered out of service on September 28, 1865 on Roanoke Island, North Carolina. Pension records verify he actually was nineteen (born on January 25, 1844) when he enlisted in May 1863. His mother probably lied in her letter because she needed him back home to provide for the family. Maybe they underestimated how Daniel's serving and the war would affect the family's livelihood. Unfortunately for his own family later in life, he did not have the same interest in them as his mother had in him. He would abandon his wife and son by the end of the century. He then had two more children (a girl and a boy) with another wife, but didn't support any of his children even while collecting a military pension until his death on

August 8, 1911. He died in Hartford, Connecticut, at the age of sixty-seven and only a couple of years after the birth of his youngest child.[33]

In another appeal for an early discharge, a father wrote asking for the release of his son from service because he was handicapped even before he entered the army and should never have been approved for enlistment. On November 27, 1863, Charles B. Smith wrote a letter to Abraham Lincoln on behalf of his son, Richard Smith, who was a nineteen-year-old shoemaker when he enlisted in the army on June 26, 1863. He was a member of Company A, 3rd USCT. Displaying the strong affections many blacks felt for Lincoln and believing him to be genuinely concerned for them, Smith began his letter, "fine Dear Honorable friend to we por african race." He continued, "Dear Sir I have corse to Write to you About a pre afflicted boy 19 years of age. october 11th 1863 He was persaded off by those Recruiting officers of this Place West chester Co PA and taken into US service Without my knowlage." According to Smith, "this Boy have not had the Proper use of his left Hand for 10 years and together With other afflection in his head and his thumb [he had accidently shot his right thumb off in a hunting accident] . . . he also says that he was not examined Before he was taken off to service."[34] Smith wanted his son sent home to him. He then mentioned three times in the remainder of the letter that he already had three additional sons in the army, implying he and his family were sacrificing enough, so he should be able to get his one sickly son discharged and returned home.

Even before Smith received a response to his first letter, he followed with similar letters to Lincoln on November 28 and December 25, 1863. Maybe he was impatient or maybe he felt he just needed to make the president aware of other pertinent information, but in the November 28th letter, he also mentioned his son had not yet drawn on the "Money Bounty" for joining the military or his "Monthly Pay."[35] The army denied Smith's petition. The army may have made its decision based on the fact that Richard was a military musician, a drummer, not a soldier, something not mentioned in the letters to Lincoln. More likely, it was because Richard had deserted on August 11, 1863. He was captured and arrested on September 15, 1863, spending some time in confinement for desertion and "malicious assault with intent to kill." Despite his transgressions, Richard was somehow still able to obtain an honorable discharge when his regiment was mustered out of service on October 31, 1865, in Jacksonville, Florida. Thus, even though his father described him as being very sickly, Richard survived the war. He also suffered from gangrene of his right foot, which he obtained while enlisted, and which affected him for the rest of his life. In spite of his numerous ailments, which were documented by the Bureau of Pensions, Richard outlived two wives, and received a veteran's pension until his death from diabetes on March 24, 1940, at the ripe old age of ninety-five.[36]

In the case of Hester Anne Laws, of Wilmington, Delaware, her son, Daniel, was both too young and too sick to serve. According to army records, Daniel was a twenty-year-old laborer when he enlisted as a substitute and joined Company G, 6th USCT. At five feet eleven inches, Daniel was very tall for the period and his height may have fooled the army as to his exact age. On October 27, 1863, his mother wrote a letter to Lorenzo Thomas asking for Daniel's discharge because of his bad health and because he was only sixteen when he enlisted without the knowledge of his parents. Hester asserted, "I was in formed to write to you Con Surned my Son for he is very Sick and he is Sutch fear health that I don't think that he coud git well wair he is at and the Doctor toul me to write to you to See if cant git him of for he is very young and was forst in the army a Wite Jentelman unbe nones to his Father and Mother he is very young he is only 16th years of age. . . ."[37] Hester likely was desperate to get Daniel back home for another reason as well: Daniel was working to help provide for the family. Also, she already had an older son, Joshua Laws, serving in the Union army as a member of Company K, 43rd USCT. Joshua was twenty years old when he enlisted on May 16, 1864. He was a laborer before the war.[38]

Daniel and Joshua's father, and Hester's husband, Charles, was unable to support his wife and children because he was feeble and disabled, having injured his back while working as an oyster fisherman. With her two older boys in the army, Hester was left to struggle hard to provide for her crippled husband and three younger boys (ages eleven, nine, and one). In spite of the family circumstances, the army denied Hester's request and Daniel, who wrote home regularly to his mother, served until just before the war ended, when he died of pneumonia on March 15, 1865 in Wilmington, North Carolina. Fortunately for the Laws family, Joshua survived the war and was mustered out of service with his regiment on October 20, 1865 in Brownsville, Texas. However, cases like this produced feelings of distrust as blacks lost confidence in northerners and the government when soldiers were not discharged when requested by relatives. The feelings were especially strong if a recruiter, representing the Union army, had also swindled the soldier and his struggling family.[39]

In spite of racist attitudes, reduced pay, excessive fatigue duty, and other forms of discrimination, blacks continued to enlist in large numbers. Union officials were extremely surprised with the number of African-American troops who joined.

George L. Stearns and his recruiting machine, as well as the efforts of other recruiters, had a lot to do with this success. But more important was the willingness of black troops to give up their livelihoods and leave their families in order to enlist and help the Union win the war. The enthusiasm to join and serve would repeat itself in many northern states.

Altogether, sixteen northern black regiments completed formation in 1864. This number included three from New York. Another one was formed in Massachusetts (a cavalry regiment), one in Rhode Island, two in Ohio, one in Michigan, one in Connecticut, one in Illinois, and seven more in Pennsylvania. Containing Philadelphia, the city with the largest African-American population in the North, Pennsylvania formed more black regiments than any other northern state. Camp William Penn, located just northwest of Philadelphia, was established on June 26, 1863, specifically as a facility where black infantry regiments were mustered into service and trained. The land on which the camp was established was leased to the federal government by the family of Lucretia Mott, a well-known and staunch Quaker abolitionist and women's rights advocate, whose estate was adjacent to the site. Pennsylvania's black regimental numbers were also increased because of the state's close proximity to heavily Democratic states that did not form black regiments—New York (until 1864), New Jersey, and Delaware. Most blacks in these states, anxious to join, simply went to Pennsylvania and signed up with one of its eleven black regiments.[40]

Northern African Americans showed their loyalty by enlisting in proportionally greater numbers than white volunteers. In the North, approximately 37,723 northern blacks would serve in the Union army. This number amounted to 15 percent of the entire black population—men, women, and children—in the North. Thus, a greater proportion of black men served in the Union army than white men. Indeed, recruiting for black regiments became a relatively easy task in the North.[41] Northern blacks continued to support the war in order to preserve the Union, end slavery, and prove themselves citizens worthy of equal rights and equal treatment.

4   The Unequal Pay Issue

By the end of 1863, over eight thousand black soldiers in northern black regiments were assigned to Union armies fighting in the South. They were away from their homes and their families, many for the first time in their lives, and they engaged in military action including combat, where some were killed, wounded, or missing in action. Families began corresponding more frequently with army and Union officials on behalf of their soldiers as the war progressed, and the most common subject in these letters was about the soldiers' pay, or lack thereof. Money became an ongoing and contentious problem for northern black soldiers and their families soon after the men enlisted. And it continued for the duration of the war and, for many, even after the war ended. There were three aspects to the issue. First, African-American soldiers were not paid the same amount as white soldiers, which contradicted what blacks were told when they first enlisted. Second, the army was consistently slow in paying all of its soldiers, whether they were black or white. Third, early in their participation in the war, blacks rarely received a bounty for volunteering, as did most white soldiers. However, the difficulty getting equal pay frustrated and upset northern black soldiers and their abolitionist allies more than any other Union policy.

African-American troops saw the unequal pay policy as unfair and discriminatory, and they protested the policy at every level of state and federal government, convinced they must challenge the racist attitudes they had joined the army to destroy. Black troops felt they were fighting two wars, one against the slaveowning South and another against their own government's racially discriminatory policies. They began doubting whether the sacrifices they and their families were enduring were worth it and whether the government appreciated, or even acknowledged the efforts of blacks.[1]

The letters from home further fueled the sense of anger amongst black regiments, bringing the unequal pay issue to a climax for them and their families, and no group was more affected by the government's policy than the families of black troops. When family members corresponded with the military about the status of their solders' pay, some of them also used the opportunity to remind Union leadership of why black families sacrificed and how they expected to be treated equally—including their pay—for their strong support. These family members did not hesitate to inform Union officials of why African Americans were fighting and supporting the war so unwaveringly.

The Pay Issue Simmers

At first, the War Department paid black soldiers the standard rate paid all Union soldiers, but then the War Department suddenly reversed its policy and announced on June 4, 1863 that black troops were to be paid a lower rate. The Union decided to pay black soldiers $10 a month, but $3 of it had to go toward clothing—thus, black soldiers received only $7 for their personal use. This amount was lower than the $13 that white soldiers (privates) received each month. The War Department's decision to pay all African-American soldiers the same amount regardless of rank—private, corporal, sergeant, surgeon, or chaplain—further angered black troops. Hence, even the highest-ranking black soldiers received less pay than the lowest-ranking white soldier. The Union's decision was based on its interpretation of the Militia Act of July 17, 1862, which stipulated black soldiers get paid $10 a month and one ration, and $3 of the pay could be in clothing.[2]

African-American troops considered the unequal pay policy to be racially discriminatory, and so they protested. Many of them refused to accept the policy under any circumstances because they believed the policy reinforced the racist attitudes they had joined the army to destroy. Protest was greatest in those regiments originally paid the same rate as white soldiers; the 54th Massachusetts Infantry was one of those regiments. Their rate of pay was $13 a month when the regiment first began training in February 1863. But, on June 30, 1863, the regiment was notified of the government's decision to pay them less. In protest, and to draw public attention to the problem, members of the 54th refused to accept their monthly pay until they were awarded the same amount as white soldiers. The regiment was very upset about the pay issue because they understood when they enlisted they were equal to any Massachusetts soldier and expected to be paid accordingly. In support of the his soldiers' decision, Colonel Shaw argued, "The regt ought . . . to be mustered out of service, as they were enlisted on the understanding that they were to be on the same footing as other Mass. Vols."[3]

Black troops were affected in three ways by the War Department's announcement. First, they felt dishonored and discriminated against; therefore, their protest was more about principle and equal treatment. Though they were wearing the same uniform as white troops and performing the same duties as white troops—including dying for their country—they felt the country was saying they were not worth the same or valued equally as white men. Second, it hurt both morale and discipline because black troops felt they had been deceived. The Union's decision undermined their desire to serve and risk their lives for their country. Third, for many black soldiers, the issue was really about their ability to feed and support their families. All of a sudden, the sacrifice made by their families became greater because $7 a month was much harder to live on than $13 a month. This was especially upsetting because the higher rate was even lower than what the families had to live on before the war when most black men worked menial jobs as teamsters, longshoremen and dock laborers, street pavers, cartmen, and hack drivers. The situation became even more difficult for the families of the 54th and 55th Massachusetts Infantries because they would receive no income from their soldiers for over a year. The soldiers of the 54th and 55th were concerned about their families, but they felt it was more important for them *and* their families they be treated as equals to whites, deserving of the same pay.[4]

For Aaron Peterson and his son, Hiram, the disparity in pay was problematic on two levels, principles *and* economic need. On October 29, 1863, Aaron, from Scio, New York, wrote to Stanton about his son's reduced pay. Hiram was a twenty-two-year-old mechanic when he was drafted into the army in July 1863. Because New York had not yet formed any black regiments, he was assigned to Company G, 2nd USCT, a black regiment organized in Arlington, Virginia. Aaron asked if $7 a month was all that a colored soldier drafted from the state of New York was entitled to receive: "My son supposed & so did I that he would receive the same pay as white soldiers." Aaron felt obligated to write to Stanton after receiving a letter from his son dated October 24, 1863, in which Hiram stated he was happy to serve but was very unhappy about the reduced pay, which made things difficult for him to provide for himself. He also stated he did not even have money for a stamp to mail the letter he sent to his father, which was probably even more frustrating for Hiram given that he had just been promoted to sergeant on September 1, 1863. Yet under the government's current policy, he was not entitled as a *black* sergeant to any more money than a private. Hiram hoped his father could find out more about why the pay was less for colored soldiers.[5]

When Aaron Peterson wrote to Stanton about his son's pay, he reminded Union officials that his son was deserving of the pay because "He is a truly loyal boy and says he will serve his Country faithfully." Peterson ended the letter stating, "Your reply will settle the matter and will be appreciated by a colored man who is willing to sacrifice his son in the cause of Freedom & Humanity." In these few words, Peterson clarified that, not only his son, Hiram, was sacrificing himself, but the whole family was making a sacrifice, too. Hiram represented the entire Peterson family when he did his duty, in a cause they all considered worthy. Both men appeared to have faith in their government and acted as if the government had unknowingly made a mistake. Maybe even Secretary of War Stanton did not know about the reduced pay.[6]

Black troops from the North and South discovered avenues to protest the government's decision, though their options were limited. As mentioned earlier, the 54th and 55th Massachusetts Infantries refused almost to a man, including its officers, to accept the reduced payments, which they felt was "insulting and degrading." Seven times the paymaster mustered the troops to pay them and seven times they refused to accept the pay. Before long, the government owed the men eighteen months of salary. Governor Andrew sympathized with the men and agreed they were recruited under false pretenses and were deceived. To rectify the problem, he offered to pay the men the monetary difference out of the state treasury, but the men refused, feeling acceptance of the offer would only validate the Union's decision to differentiate between them and white troops. Similar to the 54th and 55th, the 1st, 2nd, and 3rd South Carolina Infantries—later designated the 33rd, 34th, and 21st USCTs—also refused to accept the reduced pay. Thus, the South Carolina Sea Islands, where all five regiments were located at the time, became the center for opposition and protests against the unequal pay policy. And in some of the most extreme cases, protests led to open revolt. In late 1863, members of the 3rd South Carolina Infantry openly protested the army's pay policy. They "stacked their arms and refused to perform duty until the army granted equal pay." Sergeant William Walker led the men and was charged by his superiors with mutiny. He was executed in February 1864 as an example to other protesters. This extreme punishment was not only rare but it was also ineffective in ending the occasional acts of individual protest.[7] Still, the troops continued to perform their duties. According to an anonymous 54th Massachusetts Infantry soldier who wrote in December 1863 to the *Boston Journal*, "For four months we've been steadily working, night and day, under fire. And such work! Up to our knees in mud half the time—causing the tearing and wearing out of more than the volunteer's yearly allowance of clothing—denied time to repair and wash (what we might by that means have saved), denied time to drill and perfect ourselves in soldierly quality." He ended saying, "All this we've borne patiently, waiting for justice." The overwhelming majority of black troops continued to perform their duties faithfully, though frustrated, while hoping for justice to be done.[8]

Another way that black soldiers protested their unequal pay was by publicizing their mistreatment in letters to newspapers. Troops sent a stream of letters to newspapers and journals. The papers they wrote to were predominantly black-owned and –operated, such as the New York *Weekly Anglo-African* and the Philadelphia *Christian Recorder*, as well as white abolitionist newspapers such as the New York *National Anti-Slavery Standard* and William Lloyd Garrison's Boston *Liberator*. These papers were willing to publish letters from the soldiers. Northern black soldiers were especially proficient at this strategy because they were literate unlike most soldiers from the South who were former slaves.[9] One of the letter-writers from the North was Sergeant George E. Stephens. Once the 54th Massachusetts Infantry was formed, Stephens ended his service as a cook and personal servant for a Union officer in the Army of the Potomac's 26th Pennsylvania Volunteer Infantry. He continued to work as a reporter for the *Weekly Anglo-African*, now a member of Company B of the 54th. On September 20, 1863, he wrote from Morris Island, South Carolina, questioning the need for a special law from Congress to pay black troops what they rightly deserved once they enlisted. He explained, "There seems to have been no provision made to pay colored soldiers. . . . Does not the deed of muster secure the services and even life of the man mustered into the service to the government? And does not this same deed of muster give a man title to all pay and bounties awarded to soldiers bearing arms? I believe that, 'by law, we are entitled to the same pay as other soldiers.'"[10] The army simply needed to do what was right and pay black troops what they righty deserved. No new laws were needed.

A member of the 55th Massachusetts Infantry, referred to as "Wolverine," reminded readers equality was the goal of black troops and what they deserved. Wolverine wrote from Folly Island, South Carolina, to the *Christian Recorder* in December 1863, and explained why accepting Governor Andrew's supplemental pay offer would endorse and legitimize the unequal status of black soldiers. He proclaimed proudly, "Let our faces be black, but our hearts be true, you will find us true and loyal and obedient, and all qualities pertaining to a soldier. A true and rather singular idea for a colored man to wish to be placed on equal footing with a white man! Why not? Can't we fight just as well?" Wolverine continued, "We showed our qualities at Port Gibson and Wagner. . . . All the compensation that we ask is to give us our rights, and don't be dodging around every corner as if you owe us something, and your conscience is getting the upper hand of you. . . . Our motto: 'Liberty and Equality.'" No other extra acts were necessary, neither from the federal nor the state governments. Black troops had done their part, now the army needed to do what they promised to do, pay them as equal partners in the struggle for victory.[11]

African-American soldiers also wrote letters and sent petitions directly to government officials about equal pay in an attempt to get a change in policy. Corporal James Henry Gooding, of Company C, 54th Massachusetts Infantry, wrote one such letter directly to President Lincoln: "Now your Excellency, we have done a Soldier's Duty. Why Can't we have a Soldier's pay? You caution the Rebel Chieftain, that the United States knows no distinction in her Soldiers. She insists on having all her Soldiers of whatever creed or Color, to be treated according to the usages of War." He continued, "Now if the United States exacts uniformity of treatment of her Soldiers from the Insurgents, would it not be well and consistent to set the example herself by paying all her Soldiers alike?"[12] Gooding was a twenty-six-year-old seaman from New Bedford, Massachusetts when he enlisted in the army on February 14, 1863, one of the first recruits for the 54th. A highly literate soldier, he frequently wrote letters to the *New-Bedford Mercury*, a white-owned abolitionist newspaper that regularly published them. He reminded the president that black soldiers fought and died just like white soldiers and were therefore deserving of the same pay. He also explained how black families suffered just as much as white families when their soldiers died while serving. "Today the Anglo Saxon Mother, Wife, or Sister are not alone in tears for departed Sons, Husbands and Brothers." In a rare instance of discord amongst blacks, Gooding pointed out to the president how northern black troops were very different from southern blacks who were enlisted as contraband or "slaves freed by military necessity." Instead, they were free by birth and deserved to be paid as men who were thinking and acting for themselves when they enlisted and chose to serve their nation. Statements making the distinction were uncommon. Nevertheless, the overwhelming majority of African-American troops, whether from the North or South, free or slave, together protested the unequal pay policy and worked for all black troops to be paid equal to whites.[13]

Adding to the frustrations of black troops was the knowledge that their family at home was struggling to put food on their table as well as a roof over their heads, while the soldiers themselves at least received their rations and had the basic necessities as soldiers. George Stephens's family situation best depicts the stress both soldiers and their families experienced because of the lack of pay. Other than a $50 bounty payment from Massachusetts for enlisting, he had not been paid for six months, since November 1863, when his regiment, the 54th Massachusetts Infantry, arrived in South Carolina. During that time, his family, which consisted of his wife, Susan, her three sons from her previous marriage, and her mother, was on the verge of destitution. Stephens became desperate after learning his family had become dependent on private charitable organizations, probably those organized by blacks and abolitionist friends. Stephens received a month-long furlough in November 1863. He returned home and likely moved his family to cheaper living arrangements. He then returned to his regiment at the end of December. Like Stephens, many members of the 54th and other northern black regiments had similar, if not worse, stories of families in financial distress.[14]

Determined to get the pay issue resolved, soldiers and their families continued writing. Troops wrote to family members and friends who, like Aaron Peterson, proceeded to write to government officials on behalf of the soldiers. Often the family members and friends would write about the effects of the lack of pay on the soldier's family. Public pressure from abolitionists and other allies of black troops highlighted what was becoming an embarrassing situation for the administration. Lincoln and the army did not look favorable in the eyes of the northern public when black troops were receiving less pay while being wounded and killed next to white troops on the battlefield. Eventually a solution would have to be reached. Unfortunately, that solution would not be reached until long after many African-American soldiers had fought and died for their country.[15]

Duty First: The Battle of Olustee

The year 1864 saw black troops engaged in more action, having proven their ability as competent soldiers in the previous year—at Port Hudson, Milliken's Bend, and Fort Wagner. Less than two months into the new year, black troops were part of a major campaign, the Florida Expedition, which was the largest campaign waged in the state of Florida during the Civil War. Black troops participated in the campaign's key battle, the Battle of Olustee (or Ocean Pond).[16] And they performed bravely, even as the unequal pay issue was moving from simmering to a boiling point.

The campaign was led by Major General Quincy A. Gillmore, who had organized the assault on Fort Wagner and was now commanding the Department of the South. Union forces largely ignored Florida during the war, but seeing an opportunity, Gillmore was determined to put Florida under Union control. In January 1864, Gillmore went about assembling an expeditionary force totaling 7,000 to 7,200 troops. Eight regiments participated in the expedition, including three black regiments, the 8th USCT, 1st North Carolina Colored Infantry (which would later be designated the 35th USCT), and the 54th Massachusetts Infantry, which was commanded by Colonel Edward N. Hallowell. Gillmore chose thirty-nine-year-old Vermont native Brigadier General Truman Seymour to lead the Florida expeditionary force in the field. With his appointment of Seymour, Gillmore ensured the Florida campaign was led by the same two generals who designed the ill-fated July 18, 1863 assault on Fort Wagner.[17]

On February 17, 1864, Seymour ignored the advice of his staff and repeated warnings that a Confederate force equal in size to his awaited him. He had grand visions, instead, of victory and moving deep enough into Florida to take the state capital at Tallahassee. Unknown to Union forces, by the end of the day on February 18, Confederate forces equaled about 5,200 men, up from less than 1,200 before reinforcements began arriving. Ironically, some of them were veterans who repulsed the charge on Fort Wagner back in July 1863.[18]

The battle was a bitter defeat for Union forces. Confederate casualties were estimated at 950 while the Union suffered 1,861 total casualties out of the 5,500 men Seymour took into combat that day, worse Union casualties than at Fort Wagner. The 8th USCT bore the brunt of the rebel onslaught. More than 310 of the 8th's 575 officers and enlisted men present that day were killed, wounded, or missing. The regiment, composed primarily of free blacks from Philadelphia, had landed in Jacksonville just two months after training at Camp William Penn and saw its first action the day of the battle. The men performed bravely, wavering at first under heavy musket and canon fire, but then holding their ground for some time and not running. But their inexperience—they had not even completed their shooting training—doomed the regiment.[19]

General Seymour soon realized his planned assault was a disaster and the Confederate force was a lot larger than he initially expected. He then focused on stopping his army from being annihilated. He used the other two black regiments—the 1st North Carolina and 54th Massachusetts, along with mounted cavalry and the 7th Connecticut—to provide a shield while the rest of the expeditionary force retreated. This strategy resulted in the 1st North Carolina suffering heavy losses with 230 of its 600 men killed, wounded, or missing. The 54th ran double-quick time for over a mile to get into the battle. The 54th lost 86 of the 495 men who went into battle that day, but they stopped the Union defeat from being a total rout; they were the last regiment to leave the field. Corporal James Henry Gooding was one of the 54th's losses. He was captured and wound up in the Civil War's most infamous prisoner-of-war camps, Camp Sumter, located in Andersonville, Georgia. He suffered for five months before dying there on July 19, 1864. Gooding was the member of the 54th who the previous year wrote

the eloquent letter to Abraham Lincoln protesting unequal pay for black soldiers. African-American troops, like Gooding, were initially lucky to have been
taken prisoner and moved to Andersonville because many wounded and captured blacks from the 8th USCT, 1st USCT, and 54th Massachusetts Infantry were
executed by Confederate troops after the battle. Also a casualty was sixteen-year-
old Toussaint L'Overture Delany, who was just ten days from his seventeenth
birthday. He was wounded in the right breast "by a flying missile of some kind."
He survived the wound.[20]

The four-hour battle was over by 6:30 PM. Supporters of the 54th in Boston
blamed Seymour for the defeat. Nonetheless, black troops took pride in their
bravery under fire but put the blame for the defeat directly on the generals in
charge. According to George Stephens, in a March 6, 1864 letter to the *Weekly
Anglo-African*, the battle was a "stupendous ambuscade." "Our men fought well,"
explained Stephens, "but could not withstand, in their disorganized condition,
the shock of battle."[21]

Even at Olustee, in the midst of battle, black troops never forgot how un-
equally the Union was treating them, yet they continued to perform their duties
admirably and bravely. For example, as the 54th threw down coats and knapsacks
to lighten their load as they rushed to get into the battle, they cried "three cheers
for the 54th and seven dollars a month!" Thus, as they went off directly into the
killing zone, many of them not to return, they reminded others they were still
receiving unequal pay as they risked their lives for the Union.[22] Edward D. Washington, a member of Company B of the 54th, and a veteran of Fort Wagner, where
he was wounded, commented on the irony of African Americans performing the
same duties as white troops at Olustee, yet for less pay. He explained how he felt
in a letter from Jacksonville, Florida, dated March 13, 1864 and addressed to the
Christian Recorder. He stated, "Now it seems strange to me that we do not receive
the same pay and rations as the white soldiers. Do we not fill the same ranks? Do
we not cover the same space of ground? Do we not take up the same length of
ground in a grave-yard that others do?" He continued, "The ball does not miss
the black man and strike the white, nor the white and strike the black. But, sir,
at the time there is no distinction made; they strike one as much as another. The
black men have to go through the same hurling of musketry, and the same belch-
ing of cannonading as white soldiers do."[23] Like Washington, their performance
at Olustee caused African-American soldiers to further question how the Union
could pay them any less than white soldiers. And when idle time and the mo-
notony of camp life returned for these troops, their questions would change into
greater anger and, eventually, mutiny for some.[24]

The Unequal Pay Issue Boils Over

January 1, 1864, was the first anniversary of the Emancipation Proclamation, which the 54th Massachusetts Infantry and other black regiments in the Department of the South celebrated with speeches and the beating of drums. The gathering of African-American troops and three thousand freed slaves at Camp Shaw on Morris Island to hear speeches by the noncommissioned officers helped to improve morale, at least temporarily. But as the year began, the 54th and 55th were eight months into their bold demonstration against the Union's decision to pay them less than white soldiers. And they continued to refuse to accept reduced pay, which they felt was an affront to their manhood and their race, until the Union policy was reversed and their pay was made equal to white soldiers. Sergeant William H. C. Gray was one of the organizers and speakers at the celebration on January 1. He reminded listeners why they were there as soldiers and why they refused to accept reduced pay. Gray stated, "What are we here for? For money? No! But to strive by deeds of valor to add still more to the accumulated testimony of negro patriotism and courage, and to contend even against overwhelming odds for our just and rightful dues." He continued, "We should not have it said that knowing our rights we did not stand up for them. Let us vindicate our manhood by our conduct."[25] The solemn day eventually came to a close. But, every new day of the new year increased the soldiers' anguish and reduced their morale because they knew their families were struggling at home. As morale sank among the black troops, especially after the Union defeat at Olustee in late February, dissension in the ranks increased throughout the Department of the South. In addition, rather than reducing discontent, Confederate executions of the captured soldiers from the 54th and other black regiments only increased their anger and frustration and pushed them closer to mutiny.[26]

The breakdown in the relationship between black troops and their officers only compounded the problem in the 54th. Many of the regiment's officers were killed or severely injured after the charge at Fort Wagner. They were replaced with men who were not dedicated to the abolitionist cause, as were many of their predecessors. Instead, many of them were outright racists, having joined the 54th because of the promotion opportunity. And the troops were very aware many of their new officers joined black regiments looking for advancement, having little or no concern for the troops they were commissioned to lead. As a result, trust between the 54th and its officers disintegrated. And the pay issue further undermined the trust because the troops did not think the men leading them cared about the principle of their pay boycott or the financial plight their families were in. This in turn highlighted what black troops thought was another racist policy on the part of their government, the refusal to appoint black commissioned officers. Black troops fervently believed black officers would not only treat them better but would fight harder for their demand to be paid and treated as equal soldiers to whites.[27]

Talk of mutiny among the troops became more intense and threats became more real as tensions swelled throughout the ranks. In anonymous letters to Colonel Edward N. Hallowell, the regiment's commanding officer, the men of the 54th threatened they would refuse to fight unless they were immediately awarded equal pay. Others talked openly of refusing to follow orders unless they received their full pay. Discontent increased as word spread throughout the army that other black regiments had stacked their weapons in response to the pay crisis and were shot for their actions. It was around this time the regiment learned about the fate of Sgt. William Walker, just nine days after black troops fought so heroically in the disaster at Olustee, Florida. On February 29, 1864, in Jacksonville, Florida, Walker was "shot to death with musketry at 9:00 AM," executed for leading a mutiny. The revolt occurred on November 19, 1863, when members of the 3rd South Carolina Colored Infantry (later designated the 21st USCT) protested the army's pay policy by stacking their arms and refusing to follow orders and perform their duties until they were paid equally. Walker, a member of Company E, was twenty-two years old when he enlisted on April 24, 1863 at Hilton Head, South Carolina. He was later promoted to Sergeant and appointed to Company A. Now he was charged for leading his men in a mutiny.[28]

Walker wrote a letter on February 7, 1864 in a last desperate gasp to reverse the army's decision. He begged to be released from confinement and allowed to return to duty. He explained his plight in the letter: "I Have been now Some Three Months A prisoner in the Provost Guard House I am now awaiting Sentence of Court-Martial Charged With Crime I am Entirely Guilty of I have always done my duty as a soldier and a man and I Hope to do so in future my former good character Has never been doubted."[29] Walker then described his and his family's suffering. It is this suffering that probably reached a climax for him and caused him to adamantly disobey direct orders from his superiors. According to Walker, "I am Suffering very much in consequence of my Close confinement absence from my family who are Suffering from want and destitution my family receives no assistance Whatever from Government and I Have received no pay for the Last Six months Causing them and myself to suffer much."[30] Walker stated he simply wanted to be released from confinement and return to duty, for which he would "never give you [the Provost Marshall] cause to regret your Kindness."

Walker ended his letter by stating his good character could also be vouched for by his former captain, "Captain Worden of the Monitor Montauk," who he served for valiantly as a boat pilot in the Union Navy before enlisting in the army.[31] Walker was executed in spite of his final plea.

The army hoped that these actions would serve as an example to other protest-ers. Though executions were rare, they was used by military authority as a warn-ing so disgruntled soldiers, like George Stephens, would see what their fate would be if they continued to protest against unequal pay. Stephens was still working as a war correspondent for the New York *Weekly Anglo-African*, while serving as a sergeant in the 54th. He stated, "I suppose it [the situation] required a victim to show the colored soldiers in the department what they must expect if they don't take the money [the] government offers them, however paltry."[32] The strategy proved to be an ineffective means to ending the protest, intensifying it instead, and it did not slow down the likes of Stephens, who continued to use his letters to inform readers of the crisis and the unequal treatment of black soldiers. As he explained in a February or March 1864 dispatch to the *Weekly Anglo-African*, "In the army every pledge made on our enlistment has been broken—every prom-ise remains unfulfilled." And referring to Union officials, he stated, "Those to whom we looked for the fulfillment of these promises, the maintenance of those pledges, and for that protection secured by every nation for its defenders, have proved to be, in the hour of trial, foes to our every interest."[33]

Tensions continued to increase, especially when the regiment was not in com-bat but instead idle, and the soldiers of the 54th continued to write anonymous notes to their commanders, declaring their intention to refuse to fight. But they also contemplated more aggressive action. On April 17, 1864, as the regiment was being moved from Florida, several soldiers planned to seize the transport and steam it to New York. But they could not convince enough of their comrades to follow through with their plan. Once the transport finally reached its intended destination, Folly Island, it required the grabbing and shoving of a soldier down the gangplank to get the troops to leave the vessel. Another incident on Folly Island led to the death of a disgruntled soldier. On May 1, 1864, Private Wallace Baker took his time falling into an assembled line, and without his weapon and equipment. He adamantly refused when ordered to get them, blatantly insubor-dinate to the officer in front of all the men. And when a lieutenant grabbed him and shoved him toward his tent, he fought back, eventually striking the officer twice in the face. Baker then snatched the lieutenant's drawn sword from him and struck him violently with it multiple times. The other black troops ignored the lieutenant's request for help, first the sergeant and then the enlisted men.

Baker was screaming and hollering when he was finally subdued by the lieutenant with the help of another officer, and then locked away in the guardhouse.[34]

Baker's trial was held on June 16. The presiding officers at the trial knew the
reason for Baker's disobedience was the unequal pay issue. They tried to find
mitigating circumstances to prevent the inevitable but the reality of the situation was that Baker committed mutiny and struck an officer. The military code
required he be put to death. On June 18, the order was carried out and Baker was
executed in front of the entire regiment. In attendance at the execution, Stephens
explained, "[He] died like a soldier. . . . He bade the boys a hearty 'good-bye.'"
Stephens applauded Baker's conduct before his execution: "No man ever met his
death with less trepidation. . . . During all the ceremonials of the execution . . .
he remained firm, and when he spoke no tremor could be detected in his voice."
Stephens's detailed description of the Baker incident, including the execution,
was published in the *Weekly Anglo-African* on July 9, 1864.[35]

The allies of black troops—influential politicians, public figures, and especially white officers of black regiments—intensified their efforts to get the Union
army leadership to resolve the unequal pay issue following Baker's execution. The
unequal pay issue hurt black soldiers and their families both physically as well
as psychologically and no one was more aware of this than their white officers.
Many of these same officers became the best spokesmen for black troops, especially the abolitionists. Both Hallowell and the commander of the 55th, Colonel Alfred S. Hartwell, denounced the execution of Baker. Lieutenant Colonel
Charles B. Fox, of the 55th, blamed the federal government for Baker's death
because of its unfair pay policy. In addition, both Hallowell and Hartwell continued to press Governor Andrew to compel the War Department to pay the men
equally. Hallowell informed the governor the unequal pay issue drove men to
such desperation the officers would be forced to shoot the regiment's soldiers to
prevent anarchy, an action he thought would be deplorable. In a letter addressed
to the assistant adjutant general of the army, Captain Samuel Breck, Captain Hallowell recommended that if the issue was not resolved, all black troops who were
promised equal pay "should be mustered out of the service" on the grounds of a
breach of contact on the part of the Federal government. He included in his letter to Beck a letter he had received from the mother of one of the black troops
under his command in the 54th who struggled to provide for her family. Some
of the 54th's white officers were so disgusted with the entire affair they resigned
their commissions.[36]

These acts of disobedience and the threat of total mutiny continued. And
they coincided with news of the massacre of black troops at Fort Pillow, Ten-

nessee, by Confederates. On April 12, 1864, a Confederate cavalry force equaling 1,500 troops and led by former slave trader and future leader of the Ku Klux Klan, General Nathan Bedford Forrest, attacked Fort Pillow and its Union force of 557 soldiers, half of whom were black. The fort sat on the banks of the Mississippi River, and the Federal forces serving there consisted of the 6th United States Colored Heavy Artillery (USCHA), the 2nd United States Colored Light Artillery (USCLA), and Major William F. Bradford's Tennessee Calvary Battalion of white Unionists. Both black regiments were organized in the South, primarily with former slaves. The Union forces surrendered but what followed was the murdering—by means of shooting, beating, stabbing, hacking, burning, or drowning—of Union troops, specifically the black troops, even as they begged for mercy. The Union casualties equaled 231 killed, 100 wounded, and 226 taken prisoner in the battle and subsequent massacre. The Confederates lost only 14 men, with 86 wounded. Also, some of the killed and wounded were black women and children. They were the relatives of the black regiments who manned the fort, who often followed their soldiers as refugees. African-American troops were outraged when they heard reports about the massacre. They considered it a heinous act. Black troops rallied around the cry of "Remember Fort Pillow" throughout the remainder of the war, promising to exact revenge on the Confederates. As the news of Fort Pillow continued to spread, there was a general call by the allies of black soldiers to resolve the pay issue quickly since black troops were facing more dangers, and thus having to display more bravery, than was required by white troops.[37]

The white press sometimes supported black troops as well. The *Chicago Tribune*, a Republican newspaper, took an interest in the effort by black troops to get equal pay. In an editorial on January 28, 1864, the newspaper argued that "*no additional legislation [was] necessary*" to equalize pay. Instead, prejudice against blacks was the culprit and the newspaper blamed the War Department for choosing to make a distinction between black troops and white troops. On May 1, the *Tribune* further stated the black soldier was as good as any soldier. He was oppressed with duties that lightened the burdens of white troops and he faced more dangers than whites, especially if captured by the enemy. The *Tribune* continued, "He [the black soldier] deserves equal pay with the best, and has been promised it." The newspaper then showed in print the stark difference between the rate of pay for white and black troops in all ranks. While white soldiers were permitted to purchase clothing themselves from the $13 they received, blacks soldiers had $3 taken out automatically from their $10 monthly pay, thus reducing what black troops actually received to $7 a month.[38]

	White	Colored
Sergeant Major	$21	$7
Quartermaster Sergeant	21	7
First Sergeant	20	7
Sergeant	17	7
Hospital Steward	30	7
Corporal	13	7
Private	13	7
Chaplain	100	7

The unequal pay policy put a tremendous strain on black families who had very few, if any, alternate avenues to obtain support or relief. What in 1863 was a trickle of letters from family members complaining about the lack of funds became a roaring river in 1864, as the euphoria of finally being able to fight and prove their worth as citizens turned into despair and anguish for African-American soldiers and their families throughout the North. A demoralized soldier in the 6th USCT explained these feelings in a letter to the *Christian Recorder* on February 8, 1864: "Really I thought I was a soldier, and it made me feel somewhat proud to think that I had a right to fight for Uncle Sam. When I was at Chelton Hill I felt very patriotic; but my wife's letters have brought my patriotism down to the freezing point, and I don't think it will ever rise again; and it is the case all through the regiment." Feeling black troops were used like slaves, the soldier signed the letter "Bought and Sold."[39]

Family members wrote to their soldiers explaining the conditions they were living under without financial means. Also, the letters from home told stories of destitute, homeless, and starving families—women and children, the old, and the infirm. "Bought and Sold" revealed, "When I was at home I could make a living for [his wife] and my little ones; but now that I am a soldier they must do the best they can or starve. It almost tempts me to desert and run a chance at being shot, when I read her letters, hoping that I would come to her relief. But what am I to do?"[40] George Rodgers of New York wrote in a letter to Abraham Lincoln, "I have a wife and 3 children neither of them able to take care of themselves and my wife is sick. And she has sent to me for money and I have no way of getting any money to send to her because I can't get my pay. And it goes very hard with me to think my family should be home suffering."[41] A soldier in the 8th USCT described his own and his family's agony in a March 1864 letter to the *Christian Recorder*: "My wife and three little children at home are, in a manner, freezing and starving to death. She writes to me for aid, but I have nothing to send her; and, if I wish to answer her letter, I must go to some of our offices to get paper and envelopes." He continued, "With all this, they want us to be patriotic and good soldiers; but how can we when we see, in our minds, the agonies of our families? When we lie down to sleep, the pictures of our families are before us, asking for relief from their sufferings. How can men do their duty, with such agony in their minds."[42] It upset Rodgers and the soldiers from the 8th to know their families were struggling and as their main providers they could do little about it. Many of these soldiers began to question their own manhood, believing they failed as husbands, fathers, and sons, by not providing for their struggling families.

The letters from home made the men feel despondent and desperate to act. At every mail call some soldier received a letter about the suffering of his family. They showed and discussed the letters with each other. According to a captain in the 54th Massachusetts Infantry: "By every mail they received letters setting forth the sufferings of their families." Then the soldiers made sympathetic officers aware of the desperate situations their families were encountering. They expressed their anger and frustration and they blamed the Union for forcing them to have to stand up for equal pay and treatment. As "Bought and Sold" revealed, some contemplated desertion to go and help their families. Others chose mutinous acts, such as Walker and Baker. All the while, black troops continued to write letters to federal and state officials demanding they be given the pay they were promised. They wrote directly to Governor Andrew who, when the regiment was formed, promised they would be treated as equal to white soldiers. They signed their names on the letters to him, stating they would no longer fight for a government that treated them as unequal citizens.[43]

The families were the people most affected by the pay issue, and they were not willing to just sit and wait for the issue to resolve itself. Rather, family members not only wrote to their soldiers but also joined their troops in writing to Union officials—influential politicians, the War Department, and even the president. Union officials became their final resort for many northern black families to gain some type of relief, and so they went straight to the top, to Lincoln.[44]

Nancy M. Weir, of Rochester, Massachusetts, also wrote to Abraham Lincoln, not once, but twice, in two of the most articulate letters from a northern black family. Nancy wrote to Lincoln on February 8, 1864, informing him why blacks were fighting—to save the Union. She also explained how she fully supported the president and the war effort. Moreover, she and her family "consented" to her son joining the army, knowing at the same time they would be greatly affected by the loss in income. Her son, James S. Weir, was an eighteen-year-old farmer when he volunteered and enlisted in the army on November 26, 1863. He was a member of Company D, 54th Massachusetts Infantry. She related in her letter, "Sir it is with a deep sense of my duty that I attempt to forward a few lines to inform you sir of the circumstances connected with my sons enlisting in the 54th Mass Regiment." She continued, "he is as good a young man I will venture to assert as can be found though belonging to the 'So Called unfortunate' Colored race feeling for the government Hearing her Crisis of distress in the great struggle for national life." Hence, they answered the call to save the Union, in spite of the "unfortunate" treatment the race experiences in their country. Nancy explained, "I consented for him to go to the rescue not heeding the consequences my self & 7 seven children was depending on him My husband an aged minister of the gospel." So even though James was the main financial provided for the family, the family let him serve. However, she continued, "But after enlisting the United States pay Master refused to give him one cent [of bounty] so he went to the battle field with sorrow of heart because of the helpless ones dependent on him we see drunkards because of their hue receive that wich is due to all equally." Believing Lincoln to be a fair man, Nancy stated, "I truly believe sir that you are not in favor of injustice in this matter I humbly ask if it is in the order of your administration that he might be restored to us again if his services is not worth as much as other mens." She ended with, "For the people of color are praying day & night to your hands to be supported untill this great struggle proves victorious on the side of the Union."[45]

It upset Nancy Weir to know the government treated "drunkards" better just because they were white, while her son who "is as good a young man" as any was discriminated against. She reminded Lincoln that in spite of her son's "sorrow of heart" worrying about the fate of his family, he still went to the battlefield and continued to perform his duties. And this she said just twelve days before the 54th again performed bravely at the Battle of Olustee on February 20, 1864. On March 3, soon after the battle, Edward N. Hallowell, the colonel of her son's regiment, forwarded her letter to the Assistant Adjutant General, Captain Samuel Breck. Hallowell included Nancy's letter probably because it was so poignant and very representative of the plight of black families struggling to survive. Hallowell recommended in his letter that all black troops be mustered out of the service on the grounds of a breach of contact on the part of the Federal government regarding equal pay and because "many of their families have suffered severely" because "the government has failed to fulfill its contract with them [the soldiers]" to pay them the bounty, wages, and rations that were promised them.[46]

Nancy refused to be deterred by the army's response to her first letter. She sent another letter to Lincoln on January 9, 1865. She informed him in the second letter of her family's financial crisis since her son had not received the $402 bounty promised him when he enlisted as a Union soldier. She focused on trying to obtain his bounty rather than his regular pay, probably because the regiment's boycott had ended and the men had received their back pay in the fall of 1864. According to Nancy, "He left a good business with no other motive than to serve his country & as a good Christian supposed his bounty would keep his dependent mother with 9 in family from distress but his disappointment has caused him much grief on account of our adverse circumstances."[47] Nancy made an important point by stating not just what the family was going through but also what her son was going through worrying about the well being of his mother and siblings. Most of James's fellow black soldiers were just as affected and were on the verge of mutiny due to worrying. To understand the state of mind and the struggles of black Union soldiers from the North, it is important to understand what their families were experiencing because of their absence from home. As Nancy explained best in her letter, "Grocers with whom in times past we have dealt hundreds of dollars with supposed was our friends but since the election would have sold me out in 6 days." "But the Constable of our ward," she continued, "is a union man & would not we had to mortgage my sewing machine and household goods for 60 days for the sum of $7200 costs making is $8000 the sixty days will expire on the 13th day of February next 1865 I humbly beg sir if I can obtain an part of it that I may receive such information."[48] Nancy's letter showed how desperate families had become to pay for their basic necessities. Having probably used up all of the credit available to her at the grocer, Nancy mortgaged what was a prized possession for any family, a sewing machine. It was probably also the primary means for the family's income at the time. She also mortgaged the family's other household goods, just to feed the family, and now the loan was due or she would lose the possessions.

Coincidently, the local grocers wrote many of the letters from northern African-American families because many blacks were illiterate and it was the grocer to whom they were indebted for payments for food. The grocers probably saw it in their best interest to write the letters for the families to get what was owed to them by the families. Similarly, landlords and landladies, as well as physicians, looking to get paid for goods or services already rendered to struggling families, often wrote letters. The army responded to Nancy on January 30, 1865. They stated her son was not entitled to a bounty because he enlisted prior to

July 28, 1864, when Congress passed legislation making black volunteers eligible for bounty payments. They suggested she contact the "State of Massachusetts" for information to see if her son was due a bounty through the state.[49]

More northern black families, like the Weirs, toiled to overcome severe financial difficulties as 1864 continued. They and their allies continued to write letters to Union officials. John Bland, of Birdsboro, Pennsylvania, wrote a letter to Stanton on behalf of the families of four northern black soldiers on March 28, 1864. Bland explained, "They left behind four families that are destitute, The wife of one of them was just to see me and preped me to write to you and inform you that these men have never yet received one cent of wages due them, So they [the four soldiers] write home, They belong to Company 'E' 8th Regiment Penn Col Volunteers, Their names are, George Tolbert, Israel Bodily, John Hart, David Johnston."[50] George Tolbert was twenty-four years old and a laborer when he enlisted as a draftee on October 5, 1863. Israel Bodily, whose correct name was Bourdney, was a twenty-year-old farmer when he enlisted on November 5, 1863. He was a member of Company I, not E. John D. Hart was a laborer and already thirty-four years old when he enlisted on October 5, 1863. David Johnston, whose correct name was Johnson, was also thirty-four years old and a laborer when he enlisted as a draftee on October 5, 1863, the same day as Tolbert and Hart. The army responded to Bland on April 28 1864, stating steps were being "taken to facilitate the payment of the regiment."[51] The army was referring to the discussion going on at the time in Congress to equalize the pay of black and white soldiers. Simultaneously, African-American troops, many of their officers, and abolitionist leaders and organizations continued to pressure Governor Andrew to demand the federal government change its policy. The pressure caused Andrew and the state's politicians to lobby Attorney General Bates and Secretary of War Stanton to equalize the pay. This occurred even while acts of disobedience and mutiny among black troops were on the increase in 1864. Andrew also obtained the help of Charles Sumner, who in turn argued the point with Stanton and lobbied senators and congressmen who served on committees that oversaw the military.[52]

Finally, on June 15, 1864, the incessant pressure from northern black troops, their families, and their allies caused the government to reverse its previous policy. The continued pay boycott by black troops became an embarrassment to the Lincoln administration, who came to realize it made a serious error in judgment on the unequal pay issue, especially in their delay to resolve it. Now under pressure from several fronts, Congress passed the Army Appropriation Bill of 1864, authorizing equal pay for black troops retroactive to January 1, 1864. Not satisfied with just partial reimbursement, Andrew, Sumner, and others continued to pressure government officials until July 1864, when Bates finally reversed his previous opinion and ruled that the 1862 Militia Act did not apply to black soldiers who had been "free" since the beginning of the war. This new interpretation of the law meant northern black troops, most of whom were free men before the war began, were now paid at the same rate as whites, retroactive from the time of their enlistment in 1863. However, soldiers who were runaway slaves or newly freed were not eligible for the equal pay. For some inexplicable reason, Congress did not go all the way to right the injustice of unequal pay. Therefore, commanding officers of black regiments took it upon themselves to become creative in order to get around this restriction and to avoid a potential morale problem if some men saw other men getting more money for performing the same duties.[53]

Colonel Hallowell of the 54th contrived what became known as the "Quaker Oath," in which a soldier swore that, before April 19, 1861, "no man had the right to demand unrequited labor of you, so help you God." By taking this oath, the men were able to meet Bates's latest requirements for equal pay. The oath upset some of the men who were free all their lives, as were many in the 54th and 55th. They saw it as demeaning. Other men, knowing they actually were runaway slaves, were upset with taking an oath and swearing to God; they felt were lying to God. Other northern black regiments also used the oath. But it did not apply in regiments made up predominantly of men who clearly were still slaves after the war began. Many of them were ex-slaves who escaped to Union lines and then were recruited into the army. And this included just about all the black regiments formed in the South, such as the South Carolina regiments, including the 1st South Carolina Colored Volunteers, which was in service five months before the 54th Massachusetts Infantry. Hence, the South Carolina regiments continued their protest for another nine months until Congress finally decided in March 1865, just one month before the war ended and almost two years after the 54th was formed, to provide equal pay for all Union regiments regardless of their status of freedom, retroactive to when they enlisted in the army. The change in policy was a tremendous victory for all African Americans, regardless of the delay in gaining full equality in pay.[54]

After the Union finally changed its policy and decided to honor its promise to pay at least some black soldiers equal pay, it took time for the funds to get to the soldiers and their families. The troops continued their boycott of unequal payments and they continued to send their letters until the funds were eventually distributed. Seventy-four members of Company D, 55th Massachusetts Infantry signed a letter dated July 16, 1864, addressed to the president. In the letter, they reminded him why they left their homes and families to help the Union cause.

They explained, "That to us money is no object we came to fight For Liberty justices & Equality. These are gifts we Prise more Highly than Gold For these We Left our Homes our Famileys & Relatives most Dear to take as it ware our Lives in our Hands To Do Battle for God & Liberty."[55] They also reminded him that, in spite of unequal pay, they continued doing their duties: "after the elaps of over thirteen months spent cheerfully & willingly Doing our Duty most faithfully in the Trenches Fatiegue Duty in camp and conspicious valor & endurance in Battle as our Past History will Show." Therefore, they felt they had "sufficient" reason to demand their pay or to be discharged because they enlisted expecting the government to honor its pledge to pay them properly. The letter ended with a threat that if they did not receive relief further actions would be taken: "Be it further Resolved that if imediate steps are not takened to Relieve us we will Resort to more stringent mesures."[56]

George Stephens of the 54th also continued to lambast Union officials for what he felt was their cruel and unequal treatment of blacks. He expressed the anger and frustration of his comrades. He explained in an August 18, 1864 letter to the WAA, "In the Revolutionary War, and the War of 1812, colored men fought, and were enrolled, and paid, the same as the whites; and not only this, were drilled and enlisted indiscriminately in the same companies and regiments. Little did out forefathers think they were forging chains for the limbs of their own race."[57] Thus, Stephens argued the Union was only hurting itself by not treating blacks equally as soldiers, as the nation's founders had. By not incorporating them "indiscriminately" within the military forces as equal partners, the Union was hindering its ability to win the war. He also believed that the boycott was going on for so long and resulted in so much pain and suffering that black troops would never get what they deserved. And even if they did, he did not know whether the wrong experienced by blacks could ever be forgotten. Stephens stated, "Nearly eighteen months of service—of labor—of humiliation—of danger, and not one dollar. An estimable wife reduced to beggary . . . what can wipe out the wrong and insult this Lincoln despotism has put upon us? . . . There is not the least sign of pay, and there are hints from those in authority that we will not get paid, and will be held to service by the terror of our own bullets."[58] Just two days later, Stephens continued to press the issue, stating in another letter to the WAA, "Eighteen months in the army and not one dollar of pay! Eighteen months of unrequited service for a country that believes the liberty of colored men a matter of secondary importance. . . . Eighteen months of unrequited service for a country—the one only of the nations of the earth that has proclaimed a deed of universal outlawry against the African race."[59] Stephens was not about to reduce the pressure on the Union government until black troops received what was rightfully theirs—respect and equal pay.

Because it also took some time for the news of the change in policy to reach the families, and even longer before they received any funds, families continued to write letters to Union officials. Rachel Ann Wicker, of Piqua, Ohio, wrote to Governor Andrew on September 12, 1864. She described the suffering black families experienced, including hers, because of the government's unequal pay policy. Rachel's brother, Robert Wicker, was nineteen years old and a farmer when he joined the army on May 13, 1863. He was a member of Company B in the 55th Massachusetts Infantry. Rachel vented her frustration: "Sir I write to you to know the reason why our husbands and sons who enlisted in the 55th Massichusetts regiment have not bin paid off I speak for my self and mother and I know of a great many others as well as ourselves are suffering for the want of mony to live on. . . . I think it a piece of injustice to have those soldiers there 15 months with out a cent of mony for my part." Rachel felt it was especially unfair that people like her brother left their home states to go to Massachusetts to join the 55th. She continued, "These soldiers helped to fill Massachusetts' quota for soldiers yet they were not paid. I cannot see why they have not the same rite to these 16 dollars per month as the whites or even the soldiers that went from Ohio. . . . I wish you if you pleas to answer this letter and tel me why it is that you still insist upon them takeng 7 dollars a month when you give the poorest white regiment that has went out 10 dollars."[60] Rachel's letter was forwarded from Massachusetts to the U.S. Adjutant General's office and on October 10, 1864, the army replied back to Massachusetts stating the recent appropriation bill approved black soldiers pays at the same rate as white soldiers, effective June 15, 1864.[61]

Finally, payment day arrived for the 54th and 55th. Between September 28 and October 5, they received their full pay, sixteen months for the 55th, and eighteen months for the 54th after beginning their unequal pay boycott. In jubilation, African-American troops shot off canons and then sang and danced into the night. They were overjoyed they won both a great victory for equal rights and for their race in America, and they could finally send home greatly needed funds to their struggling families. An overjoyed soldier who called himself "Fort Green" described his joy in a letter to the *Christian Recorder*: "If we should not be again deceived, our distressed wives and children will hail the happy moment to be relieved from suffering and they may with glad hearts offer up prayers and tears for the speedy end of this great rebellion."[62] Sergeant John F. Shorter reported the men were so overjoyed that, on October 10, they organized a celebration, which included a procession, speeches, resolutions, toasts, music, and a banquet, to commemorate the successful drive for equal pay.[63] Sergeant Gabriel P. Iverson, of the 55th, told the *Christian Recorder* on October 14 about the resolutions adopted at the October 10 celebration. The troops resolved to remain committed to a Union victory and "the work of crushing this wicked rebellion and preserving the national unity," to continue to prove their "fitness for liberty and citizenship," and to forgive those who questioned their "motives" and who failed "to give us support and sympathy" in the battle for equal pay, and they thanked "those of our friends at home who stood by us throughout our trials and privations."[64]

Unfortunately, there was one damper on this historic occasion for black troops and their families. Some families never saw the fruits of their eighteen-month sacrifice because of mismanagement of funds by some troops or fraud by others who preyed upon them. Having not been paid for so long, most of the troops who could be paid were suddenly in possession of more money than they ever had, or would ever have, at any one time in their lives. Consequently, soldiers who were not disciplined with their funds lost them gambling or purchasing lavish items such as jewelry or watches. Some purchased useless items like alcohol or sexual gratification from the many prostitutes that followed the army. Others became targets for unsavory white officers who promised to hold funds for soldiers but instead robbed them. According to Luis F. Emilio, a captain in the 54th, the army paymaster needed $170,000 to pay the 54th. Of that amount, $53,000 was sent home via Adams Express, the usual way soldiers' families received funds, and eventually another $47,000 followed. It is not clear if the other $70,000 ever reached the homes of needy families or was wasted through the "lavish and foolish expenditure of money on the part of some."[65]

Still, the unequal pay issue was a major victory for northern blacks. Not only were black soldiers now paid funds that went a long way to help their struggling families, but just as important, they got the Union government to take a major step in accepting them as equal partners in the war. There still remained major inequalities within the army. The prohibition against black commissioned officers and the assignment of excessive fatigue duties still angered black troops, but at least their wages were equal, regardless of the color of the soldier.

Slow Pay and No Bounties

Although one financial difficulty was resolved when black troops won the battle to gain equal pay, there still remained the inability of the army to pay its soldiers, black and white, on time. The Paymaster General's Department had a very difficult task getting pay to regiments often on the move in the theater of war, far away from Union borders. Soldiers' pay lagged weeks, and more often months, behind because of the difficulties. Troops were supposed to be paid no later than every other month but, in reality, regiments were lucky if they were paid every four to six months and often did not see their pay for six or twelve months. And when payday finally arrived, troops often received anywhere from three to twelve months of pay all at once. Generally, northern blacks sent their pay home to family members to pay for the family expenses. The problem for most black families was they lived from paycheck to paycheck, making it very difficult to pay the bills and bridge long gaps between pay periods.[66]

Even the 54th, once paid in September and October of 1864, would not get paid again until June 1865. This time, however, it was not because of the reduced pay issue or any kind of boycott. The pay was simply late. Even when the paymaster finally arrived, Adams Express representatives were needed to facilitate the process of sending the pay home to family members. Like paymasters, they also had difficulties keeping up with advancing armies. And once again, it was the families who suffered when pay did not arrive on time, especially northern black families, who, because of their already precarious existence economically, were more likely to agonize when funds were delayed.

The lack of access to bounties only exacerbated the families' financial problems because few black recruits received a bounty for enlisting, which was quite different from white recruits (see Figure 5). Bounties were sizable amounts of money that served as extra incentives to entice men to join the military. Both the Union and Confederate governments offered bounties, though the Confederates offered substantially smaller amounts. Union bounties were provided by federal, state, or local governments—sometimes all three at once—and could be very substantial, anywhere from $25 to $400. So they proved an effective recruiting tool. They were sometimes paid in full when a soldier enlisted but more often in two installments, one at the point of enlistment and the rest when a soldier mustered out of the army. The purpose of withholding payments was to make sure a soldier did not desert. Initially, African-American soldiers were not eligible to receive the federal bounty for volunteering to enlist in the army. White soldiers had received bounties since the third month of the war, but blacks did not gain access to this financial incentive until the middle of 1864. If a bounty was offered, its amount was reduced. Union authorities often felt that granting recruits their freedom and allowing them to join the Union army was enough for blacks; therefore, they were not deserving of bounties. The Emancipation Proclamation freed blacks from former Confederate territory, but it had no affect on northern blacks. Northern blacks were already free and were frustrated by the Union's policy not

Figure 5. At a recruitment office in New York City, white recruits had access to several types of bounties while black recruits did not, which further angered black troops and their families. (*The Soldier in Our Civil War: A Pictorial History of the Conflict, 1861–1865*, Vol. II, 108)

to offer them bounties. Nonetheless, black troops, whether from the North or newly freed, lost out on funds that could have contributed considerably to their families, especially given that their regular army pay was not only reduced, but rarely paid on time as well.[67]

Soldiers' Family Relief and Aid

Making matters worse, black families faced discrimination from many of the soldiers' relief organizations and societies, which emerged in the North to provide food, shelter, and money to families struggling to survive while their men were away fighting the war. It also did not help that black families had to deal with the rising costs of basic necessities while having limited access, often due to discriminatory policies and practices, to jobs and emergency resources from state agencies as well as from the private aid societies.[68]

For northern African-American families, the first option for relief from their financial straits was self-help in the form of employment. Many female family members were forced to find work to help provide for the family, but usually the only work available was domestic or washerwomen jobs that paid wages at a fraction of those earned by men. The industrial demands of the war—an enormous army had to be armed and supplied—and the government's granting of numerous contracts for wartime production meant that a great number of manufacturing jobs opened up in the North for women. Unfortunately for black women, racial discrimination meant that these more lucrative jobs were not available, leaving black women with few prospects for gaining economic stability of any kind while their male family members were away serving their country. A more significant problem was that many African-American women worked jobs that paid less, even before their men went off to war. Because racism kept many black men from having access to better paying jobs or being properly compensated within the jobs they already had, black women worked outside the home as a necessity. Now with the men—husbands, sons, fathers, and brothers, all of whom played crucial roles in the family's income—sending back inadequate and late financial support, an already difficult existence became perilous. Women and children were forced to live in crowded and unhealthy conditions, while the women worked long hours washing clothes, scrubbing floors, or other domestic jobs paying meager wages. Women with children found it even more difficult because of the issue of childcare when they were away working; often, the children were left unattended. And even when women moved in with other kin—such as parents, in-laws, and siblings—which was a common practice during the war in order to avoid being destitute, they still suffered hardships. Though they could share expenses, such as rent and food, the newly configured families could not replace the funds brought in by the breadwinners before the men went off to fight.[69]

Families also dealt with steadily increasing inflation, which reduced the value of the little funds they had access to and caused further hardship. Inflation caused prices to rise 100 percent throughout the period of the war. The price for staples such as beef, coffee, sugar, eggs, and bread, and important commodities such as coal, wood and clothing, went up to rates higher than when families were intact and men were adding regularly to the family income. Wartime taxation also drove prices up as the government looked for ways to finance the war.[70] Rachel Ann Wicker made Governor Andrew aware of this problem in her letter when she wrote to him on September 12, 1864, complaining about the suffering black families were experiencing because of the government's unequal pay policy. Wicker revealed, "when provision and clothing wer Cheap we might have got along but every thing now is thribble and over what it was some three year back it matter not if every thing was at the old price." Families were forced to forgo replacing clothing, purchasing medicine, and visiting the doctor because the cost of simply eating and providing shelter was so high.[71]

Limited access to adequate employment coupled with pay that was inadequate or withheld proved especially frustrating for northern black families whose soldiers served in regiments formed in states other than their home states. Often, the family was denied relief from the state where the regiment was formed because neither the soldier nor his family were considered citizens of that state. Yet, the family could not get relief from their home state either because state officials did not classify the soldier there as an enlisted man. This caused soldiers and their families to lose out on aid provided by local communities as well as state governments. Wisconsin, like many northern states, authorized bounty payments to volunteers and then paid those funds directly to the wives and children of soldiers' while the soldiers were away. At the same time, local communities in Wisconsin also made monthly payments to a soldier's wife, $5, and children, $2 each. Beginning in April 1861, Philadelphia provided $125 (which amounted to $1.25 per week) to the families of volunteers.[72]

Many northern black families, like George Stephens's family, were not eligible for such funds from their home state because, anxious to serve and prove their worth as soldiers, they rushed to join the 54th and 55th Massachusetts Colored Regiments. Stephens was one of three hundred blacks from Philadelphia who joined the 54th, and one of the regiment's companies was made up entirely of Philadelphians. Like Stephens, they and their families became ineligible for financial relief from their home state. In Massachusetts, the friends of the black regiments did what they could to help aid families who were struggling financially. This usually meant contributing money and clothing to them. But providing similar help to the families of troops from other states, such as Stephens and numerous others, was beyond the means even of these friends. The ordeal and suffering of his family served to frustrate and anger Stephens and caused him to question the Union's view of black troops. Hundreds of other northern black troops and their families reacted the same way. So frustrated was Rachel Wicker that she complained in September 12, 1864 to the army that her husband (or brother), Robert, would have done better by never joining the 55th. Wicker stated, "I think if Massichusetts had left off coming to other states for soldiers the soldiers would have bin better off and Massichusetts saved her credit." Probably in agreement with her was George L. Stearns, the recruiting agent appointed by Andrew to fill the ranks of the 54th and then the 55th Massachusetts Infantries. Almost singlehandedly, he was responsible for Massachusetts' success in filling its ranks with blacks from other northern states. Then, he saw those same troops denied the equal pay they were promised, with devastating impact on their families. As a protest, he resigned his position in March 1864.[73]

The home-state issue was also a problem for families living in northern states that chose not to form black regiments. Their states—Delaware, Minnesota, and New Jersey—went through the entire war without forming an African-American regiment. Norwood P. Hallowell, colonel of the 55th and brother of Edward M. Hallowell, compiled statistics on the 55th, which he felt was a typical northern regiment. Hallowell disclosed, "Of the 961 enlisted men in the regiment, the largest number (222) were born in Ohio, followed by Pennsylvania (139), Virginia (106), Indiana (97), Kentucky (68), Missouri (66), and Illinois (56). The remaining 207 men were born in eighteen states (including eleven slave states), the District of Columbia, Nova Scotia, Canada, Africa, and places 'unknown.'"[74] This diversity meant a large number of families whose soldiers served in the 55th had difficulty receiving aid both from Massachusetts and from their home state.[75]

Among the northern states, New Jersey was unusual because of the large number of blacks from the state who served in the Union army and because of the hostility of its political leadership to the idea of African Americans as soldiers. Historical records show approximately 2,782 black Jerseymen served in the Union army, although the federal government only credited the enlistments of 1,185 black soldiers to the state. The discrepancy occurred because many of them served for regiments created outside of New Jersey because the state chose not to form any black regiments. The Emancipation Proclamation was not viewed very favorably in New Jersey, a state bordered by a slave state, Delaware, and in close proximity to another, Maryland. New Jersey had very close social and economic ties to the South, as did its neighbor to the north, New York. In addition, the state's governor, Joel Parker, opposed the Proclamation and stated his opposition to its measures, including the enlistment of African Americans. If John A. Andrew of Massachusetts was the northern governor who was the quintessential supporter of African-American troops, Parker was his exact opposite, holding very racist views of African Americans and their qualifications to be soldiers. Parker was a Democrat at odds with the Lincoln administration. Yet he and other New Jersey Democrats knew they could not undo what was happening; more and more black men took the initiative and joined the Union war effort. So instead, they chose not to cooperate fully and refused to form black regiments. Not to be deterred, black men from the state simply went to other northern states and signed on with the 54th and 55th Massachusetts Infantries, or with New York regiments. But most simply crossed the Delaware River and joined one of the many Pennsylvania black regiments.[76]

The families of the black soldiers were hurt the most by New Jersey's policy. Rosanna Henson, of Mt. Holly, New Jersey, wrote about her family's financial difficulties in a July 11, 1864 letter addressed to Lincoln. According to Rosanna, "Sir, my husband who is in Co. K. 22nd Regt U.S. Cold Troops (and now in the Macon Hospital at Portsmouth with a wound in his arm) has not received any pay since last May and then only thirteen dollars." Again showing the faith blacks had in Lincoln, she continued, "I write to you because I have been told you would see to it. I have four children to support and I find this a great struggle. A hard life this! I being a col'd woman do not get any state pay. Yet my husband is fighting for the country." She reminded Lincoln that even though her family received no support from their home state, New Jersey, her husband sacrificed for their country.[77]

Rosanna felt racism had more to do with her not having access to soldiers' family relief from New Jersey than any procedural problems. This increased her frustration because she knew that her husband, Benjamin, was fighting—and being wounded—for a country that discriminated against African-American soldiers. Benjamin was a farmer and was already forty-two years old when he enlisted on January 4, 1864. On June 14, 1864, he received a shell wound in action at Petersburg, Virginia. The injury left him hospitalized. A fragment from the shell crushed Benjamin's right elbow joint, leaving him disabled, and led to an early discharge from the army on April 1, 1865. Rosanna's brother, James M. Johnson, who enlisted the day after Benjamin, served in the same regiment as her husband, but in Company I. On July 18, 1864, her letter was referred to the Paymaster General of the U.S. Army but it is not clear whether she ever received a response.[78]

Julia Piner encountered similar difficulties trying to get relief from her state, Pennsylvania, even though she had two sons in Pennsylvania regiments. The first son, David T. Jones, was a seaman and already forty years old when he enlisted in the army on December 22, 1863. He was assigned to Company D, 22nd USCT. The second was Joseph Piner, who was twenty-one years old and a laborer when he enlisted in the army on August 29, 1863 and was assigned to Company H, 6th USCT. One son was mistakenly enlisted under New Jersey rather than Pennsylvania. On August 12, 1864, Julia wrote to Stanton for help in resolving her problem. She contended, "My son David T. Jones left me a certificate which I send you it was made out for New Jersey when he should have had it made for Philadelphia as he was mustered in here at [camp Wm Penn and] marched from here I cannot get any relief on his bounty in consequence." Explaining her financial condition and that of her sons, Henson continued, "They [the corrected forms] may be of use to a widow and hope that you will get me the certificates necessary to get the bounty relief I have been married twice and my two sons are step sons.... P.S. Neither of my sons have had any pay since their enlistment and I am very bad off."[79] Julia included in her letter to Stanton a letter from James Simon, who was a Lieutenant Colonel in a USCT, to the U.S. Sanitary Commission and the Philadelphia Ladies Relief Association in support of Julia's request and corroborating her account of her destitute condition and poor health. The Sanitary Commission, in turn, wrote a letter to the Ladies Relief Association on Julia's behalf. A month or so later, the army received all four letters and, on August 23, denied her request to have David's enlistment credited to Pennsylvania and not New Jersey. The letter from the Adjutant General's Office simply stated "that the rules of the dept will not permit a change to be made." Julia remained ineligible for state relief.[80]

Northern black families had some success getting aid from the white soldiers' relief societies and agencies as well as the black relief organizations, but such aid was limited, especially because the focus of these organizations was the sending of provisions to troops at the front lines and in hospitals. However, at times black families were denied aid from the white-run organizations simply because of prejudice. During the war, approximately 7,000 soldiers' relief societies existed in towns and cities throughout the North, which together made up a wide network that was operated on a large-scale by northern women dedicated to providing necessary supplies to soldiers. Some of these societies had formal ties to national relief associations such as the United States Sanitary Commission (USSC), which had official government sanction and the blessing of the Lincoln administration; the Woman's Central Relief Association (WCRA), which late came under the authority of the USSC; and the United States Christian Commission.[81]

The focus of the soldiers' relief organizations was easing the suffering of the soldiers. The organizations provided medicine, clothing, hospital supplies, bedding, foodstuffs, and other supplies soldiers needed, especially when they were convalescing. They also sewed, rolled bandages, and collected money for soldiers. They raised most of their money by organizing and sponsoring fairs, both large and small, and bazaars in major cities throughout the North. Cities, states, and regions tried to out do one another's fairs in what became a competition to prove who was the most patriotic and committed to the nation. These events were so successful that, by the end of the war, thirty Sanitary Fairs had earned about $4.4 million through the sale of general admission tickets and the sale of patriotic goods, clothing, housewares, artwork, handcrafts, farm produce and products, services, entertainment, and a variety of other items, most of it donated, including cash. And thanks to their efforts, these societies helped to save the lives of many sick and wounded soldiers. Later in the war and immediately after the war ended, many of these organizations began to help families apply for the back pay and for pensions of deceased soldiers.[82]

African-American soldiers and their families received some relief from whites. However, it was usually from the white friends and allies of colored troops, who sent supplies to men serving in the black regiments of Massachusetts and who supported their families by providing aid to them in the absence of their men. In addition, the Chicago branch of the WCRA helped black families by bringing food and fuel for women, seeking medical care for them and their children, raising money to pay back rent, and helping to pay for burials when they or one of their children succumbed to the harsh conditions they had to live under. Some soldiers' aid societies also wrote letters for illiterate and injured black soldiers, as well as for the soldiers' suffering families. Many of the letters inquired about pay issues, governmental aid for soldiers' families, and the well being or whereabouts of troops. However, members of the relief societies and organizations were made up predominantly of middle-class white women, who concentrated on helping white troops. They did not necessarily go out of their way to exclude blacks, but they did not reach out to them either, or to black women to join their organizations.[83]

Undaunted, northern African-American women did what African Americans have always done when denied access to opportunities and resources due to discriminatory laws and practices. They created their own institutions and provided for themselves. By organizing their own societies, black women were continuing their long history of benevolent and charitable work that was a part of their religious and antislavery activities. By 1863, when black regiments were being formed in the North, some black women, who were predominantly middle-class and from urban areas, organized exclusively black soldiers'-aid societies and associations. Similar to northern black men rushing to join northern black regiments in order to prove their worth as soldiers and worthy citizens, black women quickly took on the task of supporting African-American troops, thereby proving their worth and value as patriotic women.[84]

Naturally, many of the women who joined these organizations had male relatives serving in the Union army. Lucy Stanton Day, the first black woman to complete four years of college course work, was a member of the Colored Ladies Auxiliary of the Soldiers' Aid Society of Northern Ohio and her stepbrothers served in the 54th Massachusetts Infantry. And Mary Ann Shadd Cary, the only woman officially commissioned and paid as a recruiting agent for the Union army, also worked as a paid fundraising agent for a Chicago relief agency, while her brother, Abraham Shadd, served in the 55th Massachusetts. Sojourner

Truth was employed by the National Freedmen's Relief Association in Washington, D.C., helping destitute black refugees from the South.[85] She did this while her grandson, James Caldwell, enlisted in the Union army. Leaving his family's home in Battle Creek, Michigan, he went to Massachusetts and on April 17, 1863, he enlisted in the 54th Massachusetts Infantry. He was only nineteen years old at the time. These women were not acting out of benevolent disinterest by helping provide for the war-time needs of their male family members: husbands, fathers, brothers, sons, and friends. More importantly, they were doing their part to help win the war and defeat slavery. Together, black men and women knew what was at stake for the entire race as men served in the Union cause on the battlefield and women served collectively at home, dedicated in their efforts to make sure black troops had the support they needed to sustain the war-effort.[86]

African-American soldiers' relief societies existed throughout the North. In Philadelphia, the city that sent the most northern black troops to war and where fourteen USCT regiments were recruited, there existed several organizations whose members came from the leading black families of Philadelphia. The Ladies' Union Association (LUA) was established on July 20, 1863. Miss Amelia Mills was the organization's president, Miss A. Morgan its vice-president, Miss M. V. Brown the recording secretary, Mrs. Elijah Davis the treasurer, and Miss Caroline (Carrie) R. Le Count the corresponding secretary. After the war, Le Count, a public speaker, activist, and elementary school principle, played a major role in finally ending discrimination on public transportation in Philadelphia. In 1867, when a Philadelphia streetcar conductor barred her from entering the vehicle due to her race, she filed a lawsuit against the streetcar company and won. She was also the fiancée of abolitionist, civil rights activist, and army recruiter, Octavius V. Catto. The LUA hosted a fair at Concert Hall on April 17, 1864, to raise funds for black soldiers. In August 1864, the organization provided desperately needed provisions (watermelons, peaches, citrons, apples, sundry pies, cakes, and tobacco) and nursing to sick and wounded black soldiers at Summit Hospital in Philadelphia.[87]

African-American women in other large and small cities throughout the North organized to do their part to help black soldiers. The Ladies Sanitary Association of St. Thomas's African Episcopal Church (LSASTC), which was formed as an auxiliary of the USSC, was committed to do its part in ending slavery and defeating the Confederacy. The Colored Soldiers' Aid Society of Chicago was formed in April 1863. In Ohio there existed the Colored Ladies Auxiliary of the Soldiers' Aid Society of Northern Ohio, organized in June 1863 in Cleveland, which focused its relief efforts on the sick and wounded soldiers of the 5th USCT, an Ohio black regiment. In Norwich, Connecticut, the Ladies' Aid Society arose to provide support and aid to the soldiers of the newly organized 29th Connecticut Colored Infantry. Black soldiers' societies were even formed in northern states that did not form black regiments, such as Delaware. The Colored Soldiers' Aid Society of Wilmington provided relief to black regiments formed in other states, indirectly supporting black men from Delaware, who had left the state to join black regiments formed in Boston, Philadelphia, and elsewhere. So prolific were black relief societies they were also formed in border states and cities in the South, specifically in areas under Union control such as Norfolk and Portsmouth in Virginia, Washington and Newbern in North Carolina, and Louisville in Kentucky, to name a few. These organizations predominantly supported black regiments formed in border states and the Confederacy.[88]

Like their white counterparts, black relief organizations staged fairs to raise money and collect goods to help soldiers and their families. In the May 20, 1864 edition of the *Liberator*, The Colored Ladies of Massachusetts made "An Appeal to the Public" for donations for an upcoming fair: "It being well known that the men composing the 54th and 55th Regiments Mass. Vols. have, since they have been in their country's service, received no pay, and also that hundreds of them have fallen in defense of the American flag, leaving here in our midst their poor, suffering and destitute wives and children." The appeal continued, "The Colored Ladies of the Massachusetts, *knowing* the urgent necessity there is, just at this time of doing for these suffering ones, are preparing to hold a Fair in this city. . . . Donations, either of goods or money, will be thankfully received."[89] Obtaining donations in this manner, relief organizations relied heavily on the generosity of the general public, as well as the public's ability to give. However, with already limited resources and funds, both black and white relief organizations saw their assets and energy further reduced because of their efforts to help the rapidly increasing number of black refugees in the South and those who made their way to the North, such as to Washington, D.C. That is why some organizations, like the Freedmen and Soldiers' Relief Association of Washington, referred to both "freedmen" and "soldiers" in their official names. On February 26, 1865, the LUA reorganized itself to focus on freedmen, though the organization still supported black troops.[90]

Relief organizations raised and distributed funds in order to provide relief for freedmen and women. The organizations were very aware of the crisis emerging when former slaves crossed into Union lines. The refugees generated an outpouring of charity and assistance in the form of desperately needed food, clothing, and medical supplies. The efforts by white women to help black refugees were usually led by those associated with antislavery work. However, providing relief to two groups was especially difficult for the African-American organizations because, while most white women focused exclusively on soldiers' relief, black women embraced two causes, soldiers' relief and support and relief for the former slaves. Black women's organizations considered the two causes to be inextricably combined. They provided aid to soldiers by raising funds and providing clothing, money, and food to sick and wounded soldiers and relief to the needy families of soldiers. In addition, the organizations paid for transportation for troops to return home to their families. Simultaneously, they also organized to help provide supplies and aid to refugees fleeing slavery.[91]

Continued Financial Difficulties

Financial difficulties did not disappear for northern African-American families when the war moved into 1865. Most of them continued to struggle financially and some were at the point of destitution. Yes, black troops won a major moral victory in 1864 when Congress approved legislation for black troops to receive pay equal to white troops. But that decision applied only to black troops who were considered free before January 1, 1863. Most of the troops who met the requirement were from the North, belonging to regiments formed in the northern states, such as the 54th and 55th Massachusetts Infantry. Furthermore, although black soldiers were now receiving the same pay as whites, the army still struggled to pay all of its soldiers, black and white, on time. Consequently, families continued to suffer, especially black families, who were already enduring economic hardship before the war, and could least adjust to the loss of funds from their breadwinners. And northern black families continued to have limited access to most state and local soldiers' family relief resources, or organizations affiliated with national relief associations such as the USSC and the WCRA. They also continued to have a hard time if their soldiers did not serve in regiments formed in their home states.[92]

Desperate for help, black families persisted in their petitions and inquiries to Union officials about the pay of their soldiers. For example, Ruby Cumback, of Mamakating, New York, wrote a very articulate letter to Stanton asking about the pay owed her husband, Oliver. Oliver was a twenty-six-year-old farmer when he enlisted on December 9, 1863. Desperate for money and suspicious that something was happening to keep funds from her family, Ruby wanted to verify what his rate of pay was and then to know why she had not seen any of it: "Mr Edwin Stanton sir I adres these lines to you though I am a colored Woman I hope you will not think me impertinent my husband enlisted in the 20th U S Cold Troops now stationed in Camp Parapet near new orleans he has been in the service 15 months and all the wages I have received is 25 dollars which makes it very distresing to me with 4 small children." She continued, "he is unable to write or read writing and I sometimes think that he is swindled by persons writing his letters if you can only let me know if they are paid in full and if they get 16 dollars per month please let me know as I am anxious to know and confer a great favor on a suffering woman I am willing to bear any just thing but to work hard and him be robbed is trying."[93] On March 8, 1865, Ruby's letter was referred to the Paymaster General of the army but it is unclear if she received a response.[94]

Ruby had good reason to fear that someone was taking advantage of her husband's illiteracy and swindling him. Some black soldiers were taken advantage of by unscrupulous recruiters and white officers who embezzled their funds. But her husband's difficulties arose from his own shortcomings. He had been found guilty of being absent without permission, engaging in improper conduct, and being drunk while on guard duty. The punishment for such infractions was lost pay, sometimes a month's pay. When Ruby made her inquiry, she did not know he was reprimanded for breaking several military rules. And it does not appear Oliver told his wife what accounted for the loss of at least some of his pay.[95]

Samuel Peterson's situation was similar to William Chandler's in 1864. When a struggling family's soldier came home, their financial difficulties were sometimes exacerbated if he was wounded and could not readily work to provide for the family. Samuel Peterson was home recovering from wounds he suffered at the Battle of Olustee on February 20, 1864. After the battle he was captured and served time as a prisoner of war in the infamous Confederate prison at Andersonville, Georgia. His brother, Peter Peterson of New York City, wrote a letter to Stanton asking to be reimbursed for money he spent helping his wounded brother. He found it difficult to provide for his brother and probably felt it was the army's responsibility anyway, especially given that Samuel was wounded in the line of duty. According to Peter, "Stating that my brother Samuel Peterson, coloured, has been drafted and Served in Comp. H Eight U.S. Regt. Infantry Since 1863. He was wounded and taken prisoner at the Battle of McAllister Florida, and was Send from there to Andersonville as a prisoner, where he was kept from that time until the fourth of March last." Peterson continued, "He reached the Union lines on the 15th of March as a paroled prisoner and reached his home at Perth Amboy N. Jersey on the 18th last." Though Peter was steadily employed, it was difficult for him to pay his bother's health-related bills. Peterson explained, "All his expenses did fall upon me, being a Servant myself. . . . I was obliged to hire a nurse for 58 days at the rate of $1.50 and board. The doctor's bill will be very heavy on me. So I do not know what to do to help myself." The situation was especially difficult because his brother had not received any of his regular pay from the army, a detail that Peter stressed: "In the last place I suggest that my brother . . . has never received more than two months pay since he entered the Service of the United States."[96]

On May 30, 1865, the army responded to Peter stating, "You should look to your brother for compensation, as there is no appropriation from which you can be remunerated." According to Samuel's service records, the army owed him three months of back pay for the time he spent as a prisoner of war, but the army did not address this in its reply to Peter. Instead, the army's reply claimed his brother was entitled to rations while a prisoner of war, implying he was not due any back rations from the Union during that period. The army also presumed his brother *had* received his rations from the Confederacy. What is not clear is why Samuel was not receiving his regular pay. He had not yet been mustered out of the army. Because that did not occur until June 10, 1865, he was still on the army payroll and, therefore, entitled to his monthly pay. Samuel Peterson's situation showed that, even if a family was lucky enough to have their soldier return home, often the soldier, became a burden to his family if he was wounded and unable to work. And as Peter Peterson discovered, there was very little help coming from the federal authorities.[97]

Even in the spring of 1865, as the war drew to an end, families whose soldiers served in regiments formed in states other than their own continued to have problems getting aid from their local relief agencies. This was especially a problem for African-American families from the District of Columbia. The Union's capital sent 3,265 black soldiers to fight in the war, more than enough men for three regiments. However, only a third of that number served in the 1st USCT, which was organized in D.C., while the remaining men served in other northern black regiments. Many of them enlisted in the 54th and 55th Massachusetts Infantry. Because the majority of black soldiers from D.C. served in a regiment raised outside the District, families had difficulties proving to D.C. relief agencies their soldiers were serving in the military. And the families could not get relief until they provided necessary documentation or certificates of proof.[98]

On March 8, 1865, Assistant Inspector General William H. Sinclair wrote a letter to the Inspector General, Colonel James A. Hardie, on behalf of the struggling black families in the city. According to Sinclair, "There is a charitable organization in the city for the relief of the families of soldiers who are credited to this District, which has extended its benefits to the families of colored soldiers, when, they have been furnished with the proper certificates showing the company and regiment to which the soldier belonged." But he was perplexed that, "Recently Col. Foster has declined to give the regiment certificates of service on the ground that it would be furnishing information contrary to orders, and that the certificates might be used for other purposes or sold by those who received them."[99] It was the responsibility of the army's inspector general's office, to which Sinclair was assigned, to investigate and examine the actions of army officials to ensure they were complying with established policies of the army. The inspector general was also responsible for making sure army resources were not wasted or misused. Thus Sinclair argued, "These families are in a suffering condition, and need the aid of the society." He acknowledged he did "not think there is much danger of the certificates being improperly used" and so he "would recommend that Col. Foster be directed to give certificates to such families as may be entitled to them." Sinclair's superiors took his petition into consideration but decided to deny it, stating that the military certificates *could* be misused. Instead, the army suggested, the relief agency should not be so strict with its requirements for proof of military service before granting relief to needy families of soldiers.[100] Of course, this disagreement between government agencies did nothing at the time to resolve a desperate situation for families most in need of resources.

Compounding the claimants' difficulties, even aid provided by soldiers' relief organizations became more limited to northern black families. As the war drew to a close, these organizations continued to raise money and provide some support to soldiers and their families, but they were shifting their focus away from the soldiers to the thousands of newly freed men, women, and children, who were in even greater need of food, shelter, and health care. Many of the former slaves were refugees following behind Union armies that could not provide for them. Others, looking for food and shelter, flocked to southern cities that recently fell to Union armies, such as Charleston and Atlanta. Others huddled in one of the many severely overpopulated refugee camps that sprang up throughout the South and were riddled with disease. In response, relief organizations that already had agents and teachers in the South helping refugees adapt to freedom redirected their limited resources to help the rapidly growing number of freedmen. This was especially the case for relief organizations formed and run by blacks, who were committed to helping their southern brethren. Even the LUA, which had been formed on July 20, 1863 to support black soldiers, reorganized on February 26, 1865 to expand its mission to include the support of freedpeople. Though they provided vitally needed resources to the newly freed, there was now less available for northern families still struggling to survive while their men were away serving.[101]

African-American boy and girl.
(Library of Congress)

African-American woman and child.
(Library of Congress)

African-American soldier and woman.
(Library of Congress)

African-American woman and two children.
(Library of Congress)

African-American woman and child.
(Library of Congress)

Sojourner Truth holding a picture of her grandson James Caldwell, who served in the 54th Massachusetts Infantry. (Library of Congress)

Violence on Two Fronts

On July 31, 1863, Hannah Johnson wrote a much more universal letter. She attempted to speak for all black people about their participation in the war effort and their offer of support for the Union. Johnson wrote from Buffalo, New York, to Abraham Lincoln insisting black soldiers, like her son, deserved equal protection if taken prisoner by Confederate forces. Johnson, whose son was a member of the 54th Massachusetts Infantry, wrote in response to the threat by Jefferson Davis, the Confederate President, to send black soldiers into slavery or have them executed if captured by Confederate forces. Davis made the threat in December 1862 because the idea of arming blacks both angered and terrified southerners, who lived in fear of slave insurrections, especially in states where the black population was greater than or equal to the white population. On May 1, 1863, as the 54th was still being organized, trained, and equipped, the Confederate Congress gave substance to their president's threat by passing a joint resolution authorizing him to classify as an insurrectionist any captured officers of black regiments and requiring they be put to death. African-American soldiers, on the other hand, were to be delivered to the Confederate states where they were caught. Free blacks would be seen as insurrectionists and put to death, while slaves who had run away with the Union army would be returned to slavery.[1]

On July 30, 1863, just one day before Hannah Johnson wrote her letter, Lincoln countered the Confederates with a proclamation asserting that the Union would "give the same protection to all its soldiers [black and white]" and would severely punish any offenses by Confederate troops against any Union soldiers. Offenses included the enslavement, torture, or murder of soldiers. Despite the Confederate insistence on the death penalty, there were many instances where Confederate forces actually treated captured officers of African-American regiments and free black troops as prisoners of war, though their treatment may have been worse than other Union POWs. Moreover, it is unclear how often former slaves were returned to their masters. The Union, on the other hand, never followed through with Lincoln's threats, even when there was proof some black troops were murdered after surrendering during battles in the upcoming months and years. The president's words were one thing, but the Union found it too difficult to determine whether a crime was committed and which Confederate soldiers were guilty and should be punished. Thus, in reality, Lincoln's threat was somewhat of an empty one.[2]

Hannah Johnson supported the Union war effort and felt African Americans owed it to their country to stand up and fight for it when called upon. Johnson stated, "My Son went in the 54th regiment, I am a colored woman and my Son was Strong and able as any to fight for his country and the colored people have as much to fight for as any." She also felt black soldiers were obligated to take on the same risks as white soldiers. According to Johnson, "Now I know it is right that a colored man should go and fight for his country, and so ought to a whiteman." However, their risks should not be any greater: "I know that a Colored Man ought to run no greater risques than a white, his pay is no greater his obligation to fight is the same." However, she felt strongly black soldiers deserved the same protection as white soldiers if they were taken prisoner. Therefore, she urged Lincoln to demand this of Confederate forces, stating that she let her son enlist in the army knowing Lincoln would protect him and other black soldiers. Johnson insisted, "So why should not our enemies be compelled to treat him the same, Made to do it." Johnson also reminded Lincoln what was stolen from African Americans because of their enslavement—their labor—and demanded they be given their due, equal protection. Near the end of her letter, she exclaimed passionately, "Robbing the Colored people of their labor is but a small part of the robbery their souls are almost taken, they are made bruits of often. You know all about this Will you see that the colored men fighting now, are fairly treated." Not bashful, Hannah made clear her expectations of President Lincoln and the Union to keep its commitment to its citizens and protect them. And she had no qualms about going straight to the top, the president, to make her demands. Her letter shows she fully understood why blacks supported the war, what the effects of slavery were, why slavery needed to end, and what African Americans expected from the Union as equal participants in defeating the South.[3]

Black troops and their families suffered from several kinds of violence inflicted on them alone. Johnson's letter discussed the risks blacks took merely by enlisting and wearing the Union uniform. But there was also an epidemic of violence inflicted by rebels on black troops after black troops had surrendered or been captured. As early as 1863, evidence existed at Port Hudson, Milliken's Bend, Fort Wagner, and other battles that black troops were murdered after being captured or while surrendering and laying down their arms. Often these soldiers were killed while tied up or roped together. "No quarter" was a yell often heard by black troops under attack by Confederate forces. The phrase meant rebels would kill all black troops, even if they were disarmed or captured. Black troops continued to join the army and support the Union cause in spite of this risk; they and their families remained undeterred from their goals. The fear of being murdered or enslaved if captured actually caused black troops to fight even harder and more ferociously. But it gave their families even more to worry about as their men went into battle.[4]

In addition to worrying about the massacre of unarmed soldiers, African-American family members in the North faced violence themselves at home. But, in their case, their assailants were not Confederates, but white northerners. In the antebellum North, blacks were often victims of individual acts of racial violence as well as periodic race riots resulting in the death of numerous blacks and the destruction of their property. The fear of violence was experienced communally because having men in uniform did not diminish the likelihood of becoming victims but actually made black families an easier target because the men, who would have acted to protect them, were away serving in the army.[5]

Danger at Home: Race Riots

The most extreme cases of violence during the war occurred in Detroit and New York City. On March 6, 1863, Detroit experienced its first race riot, which took place as the 54th Massachusetts Infantry was being organized and several black men from Michigan had already joined the regiment. The impetus for the riot was an alleged sexual crime committed by a black man on February 26, 1863 and the legal proceedings that ensued. But tensions in the city had been building for months because the North was faring badly in the war and needed more men to fill the army's ranks. White Detroiters believed the war had evolved into an abolitionist crusade to free slaves, so they jumped to the conclusion that African Americans, whom they disliked anyway, were the cause of the war.[6] It also did not help that Michigan began drafting men in February 1863, several months before federal conscription began, in order to meet the Union demand for more manpower. The perception that the war aims had changed and that the war was now being conducted to end slavery infuriated whites, as did the actions taken by the state to get more soldiers. For whites who did not agree with the war, the city's black population became the visible target for their anger. Using all of these issues to criticize the management of the war was the Detroit *Free Press*, the pro-Democratic, anti-war, and anti-Negro newspaper, which employed malicious and inflammatory reporting to whip the white population into a frenzy over the alleged crime committed on a white girl by a black man. The *Free Press* incited white anger further by asserting once freed, blacks would head to the North to take away the jobs of those whites who were drafted and fought to free them. Anti-war Democrats added to the hostility against blacks by claiming freed blacks would also live in their neighborhoods, lowering the reputations of those communities and areas of the city. And even worse, black men would cavort with their daughters.[7]

The riot began on the last day of the trial. The mob was upset the government was protecting a black person they felt deserved to hang. The mob focused their anger on the black community located near the courthouse, beating any black person in their sight and destroying black property.[8] The mob moved quickly to the black neighborhoods physically attacking blacks, throwing rocks and bottles at their homes and businesses, and destroying their property. Many blacks ran for their lives, such as Marcus Dale, his wife, and three children. When the home they were sharing with two other black families came under attack by a hail of stones and bricks hurled by rioters, the families had to escape to avoid being killed. Mrs. Dale was able to flee the house "with one child in her arms and two children hanging to her." The house was set on fire by the rioters and the last to leave it was Marcus, who was badly burned on his face and was also bleeding after a stone hit his face. The Dales barely got away before their home was burned to the ground, along with all their possessions. They and the other families in the house escaped. Unfortunately, Marcus also lost his job because the cooper shop, where he was employed, the largest black-owned cooper shop in the city, was adjacent to his home, and this was also burned to the ground by the mob.[9]

Desperate to end the violence and the wanton destruction of property, federal troops were called out from nearby forts. At 8:00 in the evening, a detachment of the 19th United States Infantry arrived from Fort Wayne and minutes later five rifle companies of the 27th Michigan Infantry arrived from Ypsilanti. And by 11:00 PM the riot was over. Nevertheless, the city was still aglow as the fires set by the mob continued burning through the night. In the end, two innocent people were dead. Many African Americans were badly beaten and injured but, amazingly, only one was killed. Many buildings were looted and damaged, while thirty-five were burned to the ground, leaving two hundred blacks homeless. The loss of life and devastation was not as extensive as what other northern cities previously experienced during race riots, such as in Cincinnati in 1829 when a mob drove half the black population out of the city. However, it was Detroit's first, and life in the city was never the same for its black community, which was severely shaken and terrified.[10]

The worst acts of mob violence against African Americans in the North occurred in New York City July 13–16, 1863. The cause of the riot was the implementation of the military draft, known as the Enrollment Act, passed by Congress on March 3, 1863, to meet the Union army's serious manpower need. Similar to Detroit, whites believed the war had become an abolitionist crusade to end slavery, especially after the Emancipation Proclamation took effect on January 1, 1863. With the passage of the Enrollment Act, many working-class whites also believed the draft would force them to fight for the rights of blacks, who would then head north to take their jobs. Working-class whites were also upset by the clause of the Enrollment Act that allowed a person to pay $300 for exemption from the draft. Because only the wealthy could afford to pay such an amount, poor and working-class whites felt the war was becoming a fight for the poor to fight and die while the rich stood by and watched. The Democratic politicians hammered at these points, especially the Peace Democrats, or "Copperhead" faction, of the party, and Democratic-leaning newspapers, such as the staunchly Democratic *New York Herald*. Thus, they helped to intensify the anti-Republican and anti-black feelings that led to the riots.[11] Or, as the *New York Times* asserted, "The assiduous fanning of every malignant passion by a portion of our public Press, and by platform demagogues, has at last resulted in an open outbreak." Another factor was the intense competition between low-income whites and blacks as they fought over limited resources and menial jobs. As important as these factors were for creating conditions that were ripe for the riots, the primary cause was intense racism against blacks, which sustained the riot as it spread throughout the city and increased in violence.[12]

The riot began on Monday morning, July 13, as officers administering the new draft law began drawing the names. Groups of angry men, many of them of Irish decent, similar to Detroit, expressed their opposition to the draft by attacking the draft officers, and so began the riot. The offices where the draft was held also went up in smoke. The mob, which had swelled in numbers, initially focused on military officials, government buildings, and anyone who got in their way. However, by that afternoon, the rioters turned their attention to black people, and just that quickly the draft riot became a race riot. According to the *New-York Tribune*, "An attack was made upon colored men and boys in every part of the city during the day, crowds of from 100 to 500 persons hunting them like bloodhounds." In the next three days, rioters went almost unchecked in the streets, and any black person or black-owned property the mob could get their hands on was attacked. Some of the victims were even the family members of black men who were already serving in the Union army. Also targeted by rioters were the homes of prominent Republicans and abolitionists, the offices of the *New York Times* and the radical Republican *New-York Tribune*, and any businesses that employed blacks.[13]

But African Americans and their property bore the brunt of the attacks. And the mob's chants of "Down with the bloody nigger!" and "Kill all niggers!" could be heard in the streets. Blacks were pulled off streetcars and beaten. In the streets, they were chased like animals and brutalized. On the second day of the riots, Charles Jackson, a waiter, was leaving work in the evening when he was spotted by dock workers who instantly chased after him. He tried to escape them but was overtaken within a block. His attackers did not appear to know him personally, but disliked him simply because he was a black man, and just as bad, because they encountered him near the docks they may have thought he was also a dock laborer, an occupation in which they felt blacks were their competitors. Once they cornered him, they beat him up badly and attempted to kill him by cutting his throat. They then threw what they thought was his dead body into the water. However, Jackson was still alive and the shock of the water brought him to his senses. He swam to safety, but he had lost a lot of blood and was in too much pain to move any farther so he held on to the dock and waited for daylight. The next day, he was discovered half dead in the water by two people who pulled him out, attended to his needs, and had him sent to the hospital, where he recovered from his wounds.[14]

Jackson was actually one of the lucky ones because many victims in the New York City riots lost their lives.[15] Even more disturbing, women and children were also targeted by the mobs, often resulting in the death of the victims.[16] Susan Reed, a widow, and her two children, a baby and her seven-year-old crippled son, Joseph, lived with her mother, Mrs. Simmons. On the morning of Wednesday, July 15, Mrs. Reed, a laundress, went on an errand to return clothes to their owner, concerned that they might be destroyed in the riot if her home were attacked. While she was away, the building they resided in, which was fully occupied by blacks, did actually come under attack by the mob. Mrs. Simmons tried to find a place of safety for herself and the two children, but in the confusion, she became separated from the seven year old, Joseph, who was confronted by the mob and "savagely" beaten. Perhaps because of his disability, he could not keep up with his grandmother as they tried desperately to get away from their assailants. However, before the mob could finish off the job by hanging him, a very brave Irish fireman named John F. McGovern swooped him up, fought off rioters, and took him off to safety. In spite of the heroics of McGovern, Joseph died from his injuries the next day. Mrs. Simmons and the baby did survive the attack, but the family's home and property were destroyed.[17]

White rioters, who at their peak reached 4,000 to 5,000 strong, also smashed and looted black-owned homes and property, and even burned their dwellings to the ground. As in Detroit, many black families were left homeless and destitute. On Thursday morning, the mob's destruction was visible for all to see.[18] According to the Committee of Merchant's *Report*, "The scene presented was desolate beyond description. Not a vestige of glass remained in the windows, the sashes were gone, the doors presented the appearance of lattice-work with the apertures very large, and great heaps of bricks and stones were piled upon the stoops and dispersed about the floors of the rooms."[19] Already struggling to survive day-by-day, many blacks lost everything they owned, as well as a roof over their heads.

The police fought the mob bravely and courageously on July 13 and 14, with help from a few hundred troops. But, they had only partial success because they were greatly outnumbered and unprepared for the reaction to the drawing of the names for the draft. It required several regiments of the Union army, rushed by the War Department from Pennsylvania, where they had just participated in the victory at Gettysburg, to bring order to the city. On July 15 and 16, the battle-hardened soldiers arrived, about 4,000 men altogether, and went through the city and poured numerous volleys into the ranks of the rioters, killing and wounding many and bringing the riot to an end. By July 17, additional federal troops arrived and a semblance of peace returned to the city.[20]

In the end one hundred people were left dead. Those killed included men, women, and children. They were black and white, and they ranged in age from three days old to sixty-three years old. Many more people were left injured, homeless, destitute, and wondering, *why them*? Thousands of African Americans went into hiding wherever they could in the city, including police stations. Others became refugees, fleeing the city altogether, and went to the upper part of Manhattan, Brooklyn, Long Island, New Jersey, or any place they could find safety and shelter. Some hid in swamps or camped out in the woods along the Harlem River, while others headed to Canada, never to set foot in the city again.[21]

Unfortunately, very few of the rioters were ever brought to justice, and those that were arraigned received light sentences because it proved too difficult to convict them of the more serious crime of murder. Not surprisingly, the city's black population was greatly reduced after the riot, down 20 percent from 12,581, who lived there in 1860, to only 9,943 in 1865.[22] And for those who did return to New York, it was very hard to find employment, making recovery from the riots even more difficult. Employers refused to hire them, fearing that doing so would trigger more riots by whites with their businesses becoming targets for destruction.[23]

George Stephens and the men from the 54th Massachusetts Infantry felt devastated and disillusioned when they heard the news of the riots. Violence in the South from rebel troops and civilians was anticipated but black troops were disheartened to hear about the violence at home in the North. They thought wearing the Union army uniform and fighting and dying alongside white troops would have made a difference in the minds and hearts of northern whites. Instead, they found out their families faced hatred and violence in the North at the same time black troops faced hatred and violence in the South. The Simmons family's situation best exemplified the menace northern black families faced at home and at the front. Sergeant Robert J. Simmons, the son of Mrs. Margaret Simmons and the uncle of Joseph Reed, was a member of Company B, 54th Massachusetts Infantry. He was born in Bermuda but resided in New York City when, as a twenty-six-year-old clerk, he went to Massachusetts and joined the 54th on March 12, 1863. He was considered a fine soldier, well educated and brave. He was promoted to First Sergeant after only five days in the service. Three days after his family was terrorized in the race riot, and unaware the mob had burned his home and killed his nephew, Robert participated in the 54th's charge at Fort Wagner where his arm was struck by a musket ball. He was captured in the battle, had his arm amputated, and died several weeks later, on August 20, in a Charleston jail where he was held as a prisoner of war. Thus, he and his family made the ultimate sacrifice at home *and* on the battlefield, while supporting the Union.[24]

Similar to the 54th, other black regiments had family members who were victims of mob violence during the riots. William B. Powell, Jr., who was serving as an assistant surgeon, found out that his father, William B. Powell, Sr., a black abolitionist leader, entrepreneur, and physician, had his hotel vandalized. It was one of the few hotels in the city owned by an African American and one of the few establishments where blacks could rent a room. Powell and his family fled over the roofs of nearby buildings to escape the mob. They were able to reach a friend's house where they stayed in the cellar until 11 PM, and then went to the police station. From there, they were escorted to the dock to take a boat to New Bedford, Massachusetts, where they waited out the riot. Even if they had known, it probably would not have mattered to the mob that the older Powell had just received a commission in the navy and his son was already in uniform. They would have destroyed his property anyway.[25]

Unprotected Black Families: Fear of Individual Acts
of Violence Against Them and Kidnapping

Missing from the many letters to federal officials is any mention by northern family members of the physical danger they faced at home. This is surprising in view of the long history of race riots in the antebellum North as well as the riots in Detroit and New York City. Although nothing similar had occurred since the incident in New York in July 1863, and would not for the remainder of the war, African Americans always had to be vigilant of the possibility of another riot. In addition, they had to be just as vigilant about the possibility of individual acts of violence against them; there was always the threat of getting singled out and becoming the victim of violence. With most northern black men away in the Union forces, black families were an easier target for those wanting to do them harm. Letters about such problems do not exist among those sent to military officials, particularly the Adjutant General's office. Maybe families wrote to their soldiers about violent occurrences or the fear of violence, but they do not seem to have written to Union officials about this.

Nevertheless, on April 1, 1865, H. G. Mosee, a black man, wrote to Stanton about the treatment of black families in New Albany, Indiana. According to Mosee, "Sir I H. G. Mosee take my pen in hand to inform you of the hardships and troubled of Colored Soldiers wives here it makes my heart bleed to see how they are treated some are starving some are robbed out of all their poor husbands leave for them." Mosee explained how these blacks were coming from over the border in Kentucky: "those persons are the so called Contraband they have made their way to this place and no Men with them or the greater part of them the most of them have come from Kentucky." The blacks in New Albany tried to help them the best they could but the military needed to provide support: "We, the Colored people of this place do all we can to help these poor people and I thought by applying to you that we would be a great deal better off."[26]

Mosee described how women and children were robbed and, in some cases, even kidnapped, a common occurrence in the North long before and even during the war. From the American Revolutionary through the end of the Civil War, free blacks, some of whom had been free for generations, lived in constant fear of getting kidnapped and sold into slavery, with little to no recourse within the American legal system. With black men away fighting in the war, their family members became easier targets for kidnappers looking to make a quick profit by selling them into slavery in the South. The value of slave labor in the South continued to increase since the African slave trade ended decades earlier. It did not matter to the kidnappers if their victims were free (freeborn, manumitted, or purchasers of their freedom) or fugitives. It also did not matter that kidnapping was illegal in the United States. The nation's racist laws against blacks enabled kidnappers to boldly flourish. The laws were purposely created to aid masters and slave-hunters.[27]

The Fugitive Slave Act of 1793 stated that northern authorities were required to cooperate with authorities in slave states, or their representatives or agents, in the apprehension of fugitive slaves. Also, the slave in question had no say on his or her status and the master, or his agent, simply had to inform a judge or magistrate that the person in question was a fugitive. This legal process not only aided those in pursuit of fugitive slaves, but it also made it very easy to kidnap blacks who were born free. In addition, the aforesaid agents were empowered to transport fugitives back to their masters, and anyone who inhibited or interdicted the agent in the exercise of his duties, or who rescued a fugitive slave, was subject to a fine of up to $500 and imprisonment up to a year. Refusing to obey what they felt was an unjust law, northern blacks of all classes and backgrounds worked together to free fugitives or at least make their detection and recovery as difficult as possible for slave catchers and officers of the court. The African-American community took great pride in its efforts to help fugitive slaves and considered every successful attempt as a victory over the slave system and injustice.[28]

The fugitive slave issue was of paramount importance to all blacks because it greatly affected their status, even if they were free. Blacks lived constantly in the fear of suddenly being thrown into slavery. Some blacks and abolitionists were able to use the courts to their advantage. This was especially so in New York, where blacks were helped by a series of measures passed by the Whig-dominated legislature and signed into law by William Seward. As governor, Seward showed himself to be an ally of blacks. On occasion he blocked the extradition of runaways to the South, resulting in legal battles with southern governors. And with the signing of the new legislation, he gave fugitives in New York State greater rights to protect themselves from being returned to slavery, including the right and guarantee of a jury trial if accused of being a fugitive. This legislation gave fugitives the most protection that they had ever had before and more security than blacks had in any other northern state at the time. Other blacks did not depend on the law but instead used physical force to protect themselves and others in order to secure their freedom. In 1837, a mob surrounded a courthouse in New York City and attempted to use force to free William Dixon, a fugitive slave a magistrate ruled against and ordered his return south into slavery. The mob gave

Dixon a knife and dagger to help him in his escape. Though the police recaptured him, he won his freedom on appeal.[29]

Nevertheless, slave catchers remained a real threat, especially because there was money to be made from returning slaves, or simply enslaving free blacks. Working-class blacks were particularly vulnerable in northern cities with close commercial relations to the South because many of them were employed in service jobs (at hotels, restaurants, and docks), which made them very visible to city visitors from the South. Black seamen also were highly vulnerable. Middle-class blacks, on the other hand, were less exposed because of their close relationships to abolitionist whites who could provide them with hiding places or money to flee to Canada or Europe. However, blacks continued to organize to help each other and to hide fugitives; they did not want to be dependent only on white allies. In New York City, the African Society for Mutual Relief helped hide fugitives, as did David Ruggles's New York Committee of Vigilance, which was formed in 1835. Ruggles was a man of action. His committee used the devices and resources of working-class and middle-class blacks and whites to create a movement within the New York City black community of hiding and freeing fugitive slaves. It existed for seven years, but not before saving approximately 1,373 fugitives and free blacks from slavery.[30]

Free blacks became even more at risk of kidnapping after Congress enacted the Fugitive Slave Act on September 18, 1850. The act strengthened considerably the Fugitive Act of 1793. The new version made available federal officials, in all states and federal territories, to help in the capture and return of fugitive slaves to their masters. Even stricter, the new act required not only federal officials, but also ordinary citizens—even those in free states—to assist in the capture, confinement, and transportation of the alleged fugitive. The new law provided no opportunity for the alleged escaped slave to claim otherwise. The accused could not even speak on their behalf in the required judicial hearing to determine the accused's proper status. This made it easier for a slave-catcher to simply accuse *any* black person, free or not, of being a fugitive and hoisting that person off into slavery. And thanks to federal law, the slave-catcher had at his disposal federal marshals or ordinary citizens to help him. If these authorities did not cooperate, they were liable for a stiff penalty, but they were much more likely to cooperate because they were paid a fee for every fugitive slave they captured. And if a person was found to have aided or provided food or shelter to a fugitive, he or she was subject to six months' imprisonment as well as a stiff financial penalty.[31]

The 1850 law generated many fugitives who decided to leave the United States for Canada. Many of them had lived free in the North for years. The fear and risks of being apprehended became too great for them. Outraged by the law, members of the African-American community refused to be beaten by it, and instead worked even harder to protect those fugitives who remained. The protection of fugitives became the most important concern for northern black communities. Protecting fugitives also had a unifying effect amongst all blacks. Many African Americans saw the fugitive laws as a direct attack on the rights of all blacks, fugitive and free, and the legislation brought into the fold more blacks willing to be militant in order to protect those rights. Blacks saw the need to defend themselves, even if it meant the use of violence. Many even armed themselves in order to prevent their kidnapping or that of their families, and enslavement South.[32]

The use of force was escalated in a few cases when northern blacks participated in calculated acts of violence against the slave system. In 1854, the abolitionist community attempted to free a fugitive slave, Anthony Burns, and prevent his return to slavery in Virginia. A mob made up mainly of armed blacks attempted to secure his freedom from the federal courthouse in Boston, where Burns was held. They smashed the windows of the courthouse and used a battering ram to tear down the door and gain entrance to the building. In the building, Burns was guarded by U.S. marshals armed with sabers and billy clubs. Yet the crowd still fought with them and, in the ensuing battle, a civilian deputized under the provisions of the new Fugitive Slave Act, was stabbed and killed. Others in the crowd and the marshals received minor injuries when several shots were fired from the crowd. The attempt to release Burns failed and two military companies arrived to restore order. Burns was eventually tried and returned to slavery. Still, the incident revealed the intensity of black militancy and showed the degree to which blacks were willing to go to free a fugitive and attack what they construed as the invasion of the North by the slave system. Frederick Douglass also strongly encouraged such action in *Frederick Douglass's Paper*. In a June 2, 1854 column titled "Is It Right and Wise to Kill a Kidnapper?" he commended those blacks who attempted to free Burns, stating they were justified in their use of violence in self-defense against slave catchers.[33]

With most of the black men gone to war, it became even more difficult for black families to protect themselves, especially in states with governments less willing to protect them and in closer proximity to southern borders. That's probably why Mosee called for federal help. He argued the military needed to step in and assign someone to protect these families. In addition, Mosee disclosed, "Such conduct could by any reasons be prevented if one Colored Man had Military Orders to see after such persons this would be stopped such as kidnaping and carrying

soldiers wives and children back into Kentucky and going into their houses steal-
ing what they have." Mosee continued, "and because the Colored Women have
not a White Witness they cant do any thing they can stand and look at their own
proporty but cant get it because they have no White witness or Military Man to
speak in their favor."[34] He went on to describe how the "Contrabands" were putting black men in jail and forcing them to join the military as substitutes in order
to get out of jail. And once the black men had enlisted, the whites would steal
their bounty money. According to Mosee, these whites found ways of swindling
unsuspecting black soldiers out of pay destined for their families. His suggestion
was for Union soldiers to provide a Freedmen's Bureau type agency for blacks
in the North as they had for freedmen in the South. He explained that "if ever
the poor Colored population wanted a Beaureau it is here." In his letter, Mosee
also asked to be commissioned as a recruiter. The army responded to Mosee, approving his commission, but there was no response to his unusual suggestion to
create a northern Freedmen's Bureau or his other proposal for protecting black
families from violence.[35]

There was also a threat to northern blacks of getting kidnapped by Confederate forces. On rare occasions when the Confederate army entered northern
states, they kidnapped African Americans and sold them into slavery. The un-
lucky blacks were sent south under guard. This happened when Robert E. Lee
moved his army out of Virginia, through Maryland and into Pennsylvania in
June 1863, resulting in the seminal three-day battle at Gettysburg on July 1–3.
Blacks in Maryland and Pennsylvania began to hear the stories of Confederate
forces kidnapping African Americans—men, women, and children—when the
troops moved further into Union territory.[36] Rachel Cormany, a white woman
from Chambersburg, Pennsylvania, which was only twenty-five miles from
Gettysburg, described what she witnessed in late June 1863 as Confederate forces
engulfed the region:

[The Confederates] were hunting up the contrabands & driving them off by
droves. O! How it grated on our hearts to have to sit quietly & look at such
brutal deeds—I saw no men among the contrabands—all women & children.
Some of the colored people who were raised here were taken along—I sat on
the front step as they were driven by just like we would drive cattle. Some
laughed & seemed not to care—but nearly all hung their heads. One woman
was pleading wonderfully with her driver for her children—but all the sympathy she received from him was a rough "March along"—at which she would
quicken her pace again. It is a query what they want with those little babies—

whole families were taken. Of course when the mother was taken she would take her children."[37]

Blacks residents quickly fled from the potential path of the Army of Northern Virginia and became refugees to avoid becoming kidnapping victims. This included many African Americans in Gettysburg, which had a "significant" and very active free black community. Many refugees ended up in Philadelphia, Harrisburg, the mountains, or anyplace they could find refuge and safety. It's not known how many blacks were kidnaped by the Confederates during the Gettysburg campaign and sold into slavery, but the numbers are estimated at least in the hundreds.[38]

Danger at the Front: "No Quarter"

At the battlefront, African-American troops continued to fight under the threat of being singled out for hostile treatment by the Confederates. They feared being murdered after being captured and taken prisoner. Black troops who no longer were a threat to the enemy were murdered by Confederate forces at Port Hudson, Milliken's Bend, Fort Wagner, and Jackson (Louisiana) in 1863; Fort Pillow and—only six days later—Poison Spring (Arkansas), the Crater and Saltville (both in Virginia) in 1864; Selma in 1865; and many other battles. In addition, Confederates murdered wounded soldiers and their white officers by hanging, bayoneting, and doing other gruesome things. And the situation only got worse when the Confederacy began falling apart near the war's end; scattered rebel forces took out their anger on black soldiers. African-American troops and their officers also encountered roaming bands of Confederate deserters and guerrillas, usually on horseback, who harassed Union armies. On the occasions they caught a black soldier, the result was usually torture and death. Since the first use of black troops in combat in 1863, the Union threatened to retaliate if captured black troops were enslaved, or if they or their officers were executed. However, Union officials could do little besides stop the exchange of prisoners of war until the Confederacy agreed to recognize black troops officially as soldiers and treat them as such. Instead, the Confederates ignored reports of the atrocities committed on helpless soldiers from black regiments.[39]

Yet Confederate policy or practice toward black troops did not have the desired effect. In the face of the realities of being murdered—and hundreds were—black troops and their officers did not shirk from their duties, as the Confederates hoped they would. New recruits, very aware of the danger, continued to join and veterans continued to perform their duties.

Black troops resolved to fight harder and with more determination, with no thought of surrendering.[40] After the war, Joseph T. Wilson, a member of the 54th Massachusetts Infantry, explained, "The massacre at Fort Pillow had a very different effect upon the black soldiers than it was doubtless expected to have. Instead of weakening their courage it stimulated them to a desire of retaliation; not in the strict sense of that term, but to fight with a determination to subdue and bring to possible punishment, the men guilty of such atrocious conduct."[41] And even in the last days of the war, the memory of Fort Pillow remained strong. Black troops did not forgot and they continued to rally around the cry of "Remember Fort Pillow." Thomas Morris Chester, the only black correspondent for a major white newspaper during the war, the *Philadelphia Press*, recalled a February 14, 1865 encounter between black soldiers and Confederate prisoners. As several hundred of the Confederate prisoners were boarding a truce ship, nearby black soldiers, who were witnessing the boarding, goaded the Confederates. The ship was taking the rebels south to be exchanged for northern troops imprisoned in the South. The black troops told them if they had fallen into the blacks' hands during battle, there would be no need for an exchange. According to Chester, "They [black soldiers] reminded the Johnnies that they had not forgotten Fort Pillow, which was still their battle-shout." Thus, through their continued encounters with Confederates, black soldiers made sure the rebels knew they had not forgotten the atrocity, and they were ready and willing, if given the opportunity, to exact their revenge.[42]

Even with the threat of violence against them in the North as well as the South, by northern whites as well as southern whites, northern blacks continued to enlist and support the Union war effort. This even included blacks from Detroit and New York City. The Detroit *Advertiser and Tribune* reported that weeks after the riots many black men were going to Massachusetts in order to enlist in the 54th. According to Charles Lenox Remond, a prominent black abolitionist in Detroit, over two hundred black men were enlisted in Detroit for the 54th.[43] African-American families surprised people with their continued support, despite experiencing cruel and brutal treatment. A white person who witnessed the Detroit riot expressed puzzled amazement at this behavior on the part of African Americans. He stated, "There is certainly something mysterious about them. On the one hand they are being mobbed, and everything that is sacred to a people to make a country home dear are denied them, in many of the large Northern cities. And on the other hand they are marching off to the call of the Government as if they were sharing all the blessings of the most favored citizens!"[44] And months after the bloody and destructive riots, they continued to join up. On September 25, 1863 in Detroit, Marcus Dale joined the only black regiment formed in Michigan, the 102nd USCT (formerly the 1st Michigan Colored Infantry), which was organized on May 23, 1863. At the time he enlisted he was twenty-nine years old and it was less than seven months after he, his wife, Mary, and their three children lost their possessions and ran for their lives. Marcus was in Company C, where he rose to the rank of sergeant, and served until the regiment mustered out on September 30, 1865, in Charleston, South Carolina.[45]

After the riots in New York City, Charles Jackson, who was badly beaten in the riots, thrown in the river, and left for dead, enlisted as a twenty-three-year-old draftee on September 1, 1863. The New York native became a sergeant in the 8th USCT, which was formed in Philadelphia. Chased by murderous rioters, Alexander Newton ran for his life through the streets of New York City during the riot. Like many blacks, he left New York for good after the riots, settling in New Haven, Connecticut. But, on December 18, 1863, the twenty-six-year-old mason joined the 29th Connecticut Volunteers, where he became a sergeant.[46]

Figure 6. Tremendous adulation was on display at the public gathering for New York's first black regiment—the 20th USCT. (*The Soldier in Our Civil War: A Pictorial History of the Conflict, 1861–1865*, Vol. 2, 228)

On March 5, 1864 the 20th USCT, the first of three black regiments formed in the state, marched down Broadway, just nine months after African Americans, like Jackson and Newton, were hunted like animals through the streets of New York City and where blacks—men, women, and children—had run for their lives, chased by bloodthirsty mobs who destroyed black-owned property and killed and injured hundreds of African Americans. Undaunted by the riots and the fear of another occurring in their absence, black men continued to show their support for the Union by using the opportunity presented by the Union League Club to join the New York regiments. In December 1863, advocates of black troops in New York received authorization directly from the War Department to form the state's first black regiment. To achieve this goal, they were forced to work around Democratic Governor Horatio Seymour, who was strongly opposed to the idea of black soldiers. In fewer than sixty days, 2,300 men enlisted and, on March 5, 1864, troops of the first regiment, the 20th United States Colored Troops, paraded through the streets to great joy and excitement from many in New York City's black community and its white supporters (see Figure 6).[47]

George Stephens pointed out in an August 7, 1863 letter to the *Anglo-African* on the New York City draft riots that "Our relation to the government is and has been that of unflinching, unswerving loyalty." Thus, in spite of the violent and hostile treatment they had received, African Americans would remain loyal to the Union and to the cause. These men still wanted to serve their country.[48]

6   Information Requests

In 1863, northern African-American family members sent fewer letters than they would later, as the war progressed. The formation of the first black regiment from the North, the 54th Massachusetts Infantry, did not start until March and was not completed until May. Other regiments were quick to follow, and as more black men enlisted, more black families attempted to adapt their lives to having their loved-ones and breadwinners away from home. As these black families struggled to adjust to not having their men around and began to react to the problems black troops faced while in uniform, they began sending more letters to Union officials. Though few in number, the 1863 letters reveal a lot about the concerns most important to family members during the war. A marked increase in the formation of black regiments occurred in 1864, resulting in many more letters to Union officials from family members, friends, and allies. And these letters continued to paint a clear picture of the struggles of black families while the war progressed and continued to give it their stalwart support.

The Simplest of Requests: How or Where Is My Soldier?

With a lot more northern black men in the military, the everyday results of the war suddenly affected many more black families. Whatever affected the soldiers would eventually touch their love ones, whether it was reduced pay or the lack of it, battle wounds, capture by the enemy, or death while serving. The letters in 1864, much more so than those in 1863, display these concerns, but with greater intensity and frequency. The first questions for most families was, where is my soldier? Families were always sensitive to the whereabouts of their soldiers, and when they did not hear from their soldiers for long periods of time—usually after making numerous attempts through letters to reach them—they made inquiries to Union officials. Throughout the war, these types of letters were the most common from northern families because not knowing the whereabouts and well being of their soldiers caused much distress to family members. The longer the war lasted and the more black troops enlisted, the more letters were sent to Union officials from family members, or others on their behalf, seeking answers about their soldiers.[1]

O. D. M. Baker, a lawyer and local Democratic politician in Poughkeepsie, New York, wrote one such letter on June 29th, 1864. He wrote to the Adjutant General, Brigadier General Thomas, asking what company of the 20th USCT Private John Pero was assigned to. Pero was a thirty-year-old farmer when he enlisted into the army on January 18, 1864, probably anxious to join one of New York's newly formed black regiments. According to Baker, Pero's family had not heard from him in a "long time." Baker was a claims agent and he wrote a number of letters to Union officials on behalf of black family members searching for information on the whereabouts or well being of their soldiers. In this instance, the army responded on July 9, saying Pero was in Company K, 26th USCT, the second black regiment formed in New York, and as of April 3, was reported "present" for duty in Matagorda Island, Texas, where the regiment was assigned. It is not known if the army's response put Pero's family at ease in any way. What the family did not know was Pero never lived long enough to finish his training at Rikers Island, New York. His service record revealed he died in the regimental hospital on February 17, 1864, less than one month after enlisting. Similar to the confusion about his whereabouts with the regiment in April, there was confusion about how he died. The family would not find out until January 1865 he died of pneumonia, a disease probably attributed to the severe weather new soldiers encountered while quartered at Rikers for their initial military training. John left behind a wife, Elizabeth, and six children, ranging in ages from ten to three, and a seventh with whom Elizabeth was pregnant with when he died. With her husband dead she had to find a way to provide for herself and their children on her own.[2]

In a similar letter, dated November 3, 1864, information was requested about the welfare of Private James Johnson of Company H, 20th USCT. As a twenty-year-old laborer, James enlisted in the army on December 15, 1863, one of the first recruits for the first black regiment formed in New York. Similar to Pero's wife, the Johnsons did not appear to be literate; James put his mark on his enlistment documents and the letter to the Adjutant General was written on behalf of his wife. The letter asserted, "[She] has not heard from him since as May last. Will you please inform me what the latest report concerning him is." It was written and signed by Homer Augustus Nelson, of Poughkeepsie, New York, the Democratic congressman from New York's Twelfth District and a former Union officer. He wrote a number of letters to Union officials on behalf of African-American family members.[3]

In a letter dated December 1, 1864, Lucy Freeman, of Middleton, Massachusetts, described for Union officials the anxiety she and her family felt after losing touch with her brother, Charles Brown, a member of the 54th Massachusetts Infantry. Charles was twenty-four years old and a farmer when he enlisted as a substitute on September 29, 1863. The letter was addressed to Abraham Lincoln, stating, "We wish to obtain information of oure beloved brother who enlisted in the 54th Collard Rigement, this last fall an was stationed on Galloupes Isilan . . . was removed South . . . and since we can obtain no information of the rigement whatever." Lucy stated, "If you would oblige us by Sending us a line . . . you would Greatly oblige your humble friend an an releive many anxious harts if we could asertain whare the rigement was we could write to him and if he is still living could hear from him." It is unlikely Charles's family was aware of the outcome at the Battle of Honey Hill and the 54th's role there because it took several days, and sometimes weeks, for mail to reach its destination. Mail carriers tried their best to keep up with armies on the move, but all families—black and white—felt frustrated when trying to keep track of their soldiers through the mail. Eventually Charles's family had a lot to be concerned about because the 54th suffered many casualties in the battle. Many black families, however, experienced greater frustration due to a longer wait for information, especially because many of them first had to find someone like O. D. M. Baker or Congressman Nelson to write the letter to the army.[4]

The solicitations for information about the status and well being of soldiers were so numerous the Adjutant General's office created a standard form for family members to complete when making inquiries. Along with the general information about the soldier, his regiment and company, and any physical identifiers, the form also asked who the nearest relative was and when the soldier was last heard from. The relative making the request signed the form, or put his or her mark, and had the form witnessed. The document was especially helpful for family members who could not write or articulate their needs in a letter, as well as for the military because it provided all the vital information needed by officials to identify a soldier, and provided it in an easily read and understood manner. African-American family members from the North used this document extensively. On October 7, 1864, Elizabeth Gaines, of Philadelphia, completed the form inquiring about her husband, Noah Gaines, of Company I, 54th Massachusetts Infantry. A thirty-four-year-old laborer, he enlisted in the army on April 26, 1863. Elizabeth stated she had not heard from him since June 12, 1863. The army responded with the bad news that her husband was reported missing in action on July 18, 1863, the day of the famous charge of the 54th at Fort Wagner. He was later classified as killed in action on the day of the charge. Used in this manner, the form served as a useful device for both the families and army officials to share information and for thousands of family inquiries to get responses more efficiently.[5]

Regardless of the availability of a standardized form, letters remained the mode of communication most families chose to make their requests. In a personal letter, rather than the sterile military form, they could stress their need to obtain information and underscore the frustration and anguish family and friends suffered while awaiting some word about the loved one. On November 2, 1864, Mrs. S. J. Bell, of Iberia, Ohio, asked for information from the army about the whereabouts of her son's regiment, the 8th USCT. Something she could not do in a standardized form, she implored, "Will you allow me the pariveledge of thus addressing you I hope you will excuse me if I am to fast but I wish to know where the 8th Col Regt is stationed." A letter, like Bell's, allows for the following impassioned plea: "In the name of suffering humanity I ask this matters of imediate importance. . . . will you oblige a suffering widow by telling me where the regt is at this time." The person who wrote the letter for Mrs. Bell, and also served as a witness to her plea for information, added that Mrs. Bell was "poor" and "afflicted." On November 10, 1864 the army sent her the information she requested about the regiment's whereabouts.[6]

The most common requests for information were sent by families desperate to know whether their soldiers were dead, alive, or badly wounded, especially since the Union army, itself a large bureaucracy, was very slow at getting important information to families. This was especially the case when a soldier was dead or wounded because Union procedure required officers complete specific paperwork to confirm a soldier was a casualty—dead, wounded, or captured—and to stop the soldiers pay. If a soldier's death was confirmed, an inventory was made of his belongings so they could be shipped to his family. Additional paperwork was completed to record whether the soldier was owed any bounties or back pay, and in most cases the soldier was owed months of back pay, now belonging to his family.

Because of the slowness of the army, families often first found out about the death of their loved one through other soldiers who wrote letters directly to the soldier's family or who had returned home. Families also found out about loved ones when newspapers printed letters from soldiers describing battles and casualties, as well as from casualty lists, which were often printed in newspapers.[7] The families in turn contacted the military, often having to make several requests, to get official notification from military officials. They sent their letters and then in turn had to wait, usually anxiously, for a response from the army. The waiting was particularly difficult if a family knew their soldier's regiment recently participated in a major battle with a large number of casualties and if the family had not heard from the soldier in a number of weeks or months.

With very little information about their soldiers, family members had to go about their daily lives not knowing for sure if their loved one was dead, captured, or laid up in a hospital somewhere badly wounded. The wife of Samuel Waters experienced such uneasiness while worrying how he was doing after the Battle at Olustee. Samuel was a twenty-three-year-old laborer when he was drafted into the army. He enlisted on September 23, 1863, and was appointed a sergeant in Company C, 8th USCT. The 8th was one of the regiments that participated in the battle on February 20, 1864, and the black regiment that suffered the most casualties. A letter was written on Mrs. Waters's behalf because she heard Samuel "was supposed to have been wounded & taken prisoner in the Battle of Olustee, Florida." The letter writer described Mrs. Waters's state of mind while she dealt with the possible wounding of her husband or the chance he was taken prisoner by Confederate forces, who she surely feared might execute him or sell him into slavery. The letter professed, "She is suffering mentally and pecuniarily." On July 29, 1864, the army replied and indicated Samuel Waters was captured by the enemy but had been listed erroneously as "killed in action." Of course, the news did not do anything to ease Mrs. Waters's mind about the inhumane treatment, or lack of treatment, he might have been getting at the hands of the Confederacy. Unfortunately for Samuel Waters, many of the Union soldiers captured at Olustee ended up at Fort Sumter in Andersonville, Georgia. His wife eventually found out that Andersonville was, in fact, where Samuel died on June 30, 1864, from the wounds he sustained at Olustee; he had to have a leg amputated and he never recovered from his injuries.[8]

Emotions were heightened for families when they needed information to verify a soldier's death rather than just trying to find out where the soldier or his regiment was stationed. That was the state of mind of Sarah Lewis, of Philadelphia, who put her mark on a letter transcribed for her by John Keefe. The letter was written on November 2, 1864 and Sarah asked for information from Stanton about her husband: "Hon Sir I have heard that my husband was killed in battle as I have not heard from him for several months I seem to think it must be so, he enlisted in the colored troop here Sept his name is Alexander Lewis private in Co G 6th Regiment US Colored Troop Pennsylvania Enlisted Sept 16th 1863 and went from camp Wm Penn, Pa." She continued, "This is to beg you to let me know if he is recorded among the killed in the War Department and you will relieve me of much pain of mind and oblige."[9] Sarah had reason to be concerned because the 6th USCT played a major role in the June 15, 1864, assault on Petersburg, Virginia, when the regiment suffered casualties. Alexander was twenty-five years old and a farmer when he enlisted in the army on September 3, 1863 as a substitute. He survived the assault on Petersburg, but by August 31, 1865, the army listed him as a deserter after he was not heard from since March 16, 1865, when the regiment was on maneuvers.[10]

Harriet Banks, of Allegheny City, Pennsylvania, was experiencing similar distress when she wrote to Union officials on October 26, 1864, asking about her son, James E. Banks. Like Sarah Lewis's husband, James was a member of the 6th USCT. He was a twenty-two-year-old laborer when he was drafted, enlisting in the army on July 14, 1863. Harriet complained she did not receive a response to her previous inquiries and discussed how she felt not knowing the condition of her son. She revealed, "I write a few lines now in hopes of hearing something of my son . . . whether he is dead or living, for I have written again and again without receiving a reply." Harriet continued, "You or any kind friend of Co C that will be so kind as to give me any information of James E. Banks . . . will confer a lasting favor on a widowed and distressed mother for James is my last child left me but one." James was wounded and did spend some time in the hospital. That may have been why he was unable to stay in contact with his mother. Eventually, he recovered and rejoined his regiment; he was discharged with them on September 20, 1865.[11]

James Thomas Davis of Brooklyn, New York, expressed similar sentiments as Harriet Banks when he complained about the problems he encountered trying to obtain information from the army about his brother-in-law, George Harris of Company I, 26th USCT. George was a laborer and already thirty-four years old when he enlisted in the army, on February 8, 1864. On September 19, 1864, Davis wrote to the Adjutant General: "Mr Thomas adjutant general Sir i would bege the information of my brother in law who inlisted in the new york twenty sixth reaiament company I by the name of George Harris we saw the reporte in the news paper of his death in battal and that is all the information that we have learned from him since he left new york." Davis continued, "I have roat five or six letters to him an have not received any answer from them I allso roat to the captian of the company I have not hay any Sir any information of him will be thankful receive by his brother in law he inlisted in the twenty six new york colored troops."[12] Prompting the family's concern might have been news the 26th participated in a battle on John's Island between July 5 and July 7 where the regiment suffered a number of casualties. Davis did not get a reply to his letter. Angered and frustrated at not getting a response, Davis sent another letter on December 5, 1864 to the Adjutant General. This time he felt the need to speak for all African Americans about the difficulties they encountered trying to get timely information about their soldiers. Davis began the second letter similarly to the first but then added the following: "We have wroat several letters to the officers of the regerment but we have not reseaved any answer from eather of them yet Sir if you can give his poor family and friends any informattion of his whearabouts it will thankful reseaved we poor colored people have a ver hard time to get the slightes informattion of our friends and relation in the army."[13] This time Davis received a response, probably stating his brother-in-law was accounted for. George survived the war and was mustered out with his regiment on August 28, 1865.

James T. Davis's letters reveal the problems families encountered when trying to obtain accurate information from and communicating with Union officials, especially for the families who had to go on with their lives not knowing the whereabouts or well being of their soldiers. The family of white soldiers also experienced delays getting accurate and up-to-date information about their soldiers. But many northern black families were illiterate—most of them did not have a family member as articulate as James Thomas Davis—and had almost no access to people of authority who could champion their cause. Hence, the turnaround time on getting a letter out to Union authorities and getting a response was delayed much longer for northern black families.

Of course, not all letters were as expressive and as descriptive as those of Harriet Banks or James Thomas Davis. Many contained just a few lines of information the army needed in order to identify the soldier and his regiment. Jane Harris, of Baltimore, Maryland, wrote such a letter to the Adjutant General, asking about her son. James was a volunteer who enlisted in the army on August 2, 1864. He was twenty-two years old and employed as a clerk. Jane's letter of November 16, 1864, asked, "Dear Sir, As I have heard that my son James T. Baker [of] Co F 28th Regt USC. Troops was killed please favor his distressed mother with a reply." The army answered her letter verifying her son was dead. He was "shot through the head" and killed on September 30, 1864 while on picket duty around Petersburg, Virginia. In the army less than two months, James died before the army ever paid him. His mother would have to file an application to collect his back pay and any bounty money due him.[14]

In addition, non-family members who wrote on behalf of the family tended to write shorter letters. On November 16, 1864, a Mrs. Banks of Hollidaysburg, Pennsylvania wrote a letter to the Adjutant General for the family of John Brown. Brown was a thirty-one-year-old laborer when he enlisted on December 3, 1863.

Mrs. Banks simply stated, "Sir, John Brown, Co E, 22d U.S.C.T has been missing since the 27 of Oct. He went into a battle on that day some where near Richmond, and has not been heard from since. Can you inform me if he had been reported as killed or prisoner." The army replied swiftly five days later, probably confirming Brown was taken prisoner near Fair Oaks, Virginia, right outside Richmond, the Confederate capital, and he was wounded. By comparison, the letters of Harris and Banks displayed less emotion and passion than those from family members whose letters revealed their yearning for any information. Regardless, months later, Mrs. Banks had to write another letter to Union officials to obtain more detailed information about the extent of Brown's wounds and his prisoner-of-war status.[15]

Quite often, letters requesting news about a soldier were sent for two purposes: first, to verify whether the soldier was dead; second, to begin the process of filing for the soldier's back pay and unpaid bounty. Often the family heard about the soldier's death but still wanted the army to verify it; army officials could have made a mistake, as with Samuel Waters, who was initially listed as dead but it turned out he was taken prisoner. At other times, the family had already received official notice about the soldier's death and simply wanted the details as to how, when, and where the death occurred. Family members wrote some of these letters, while others were written on the family's behalf by third parties hired to help the family claim any money due the soldier. On October 25, 1864, Mary Ann Nickens, of Piqua, Ohio, put her mark on a letter written for her and sent it to the Adjutant General asking for information about her son who, she worried, might have died after being sick. Mary stated, "Sir my son Robert Nickens was a soldier in the 25th U.S. Colored Troops and as I have not heard from him in the last four months I ask you would inform me about him he was sick when last heard from will you please inform me whether he is dead or alive if alive where is he if dead when and where did he die."[16] Robert was a farmer and only eighteen years old when he volunteered and enlisted in the army on January 19, 1864. Mary discovered Robert belonged to Company D, of the 27th USCT, not the 25th USCT, and he was dead. He was admitted into the hospital in September 1864 and died shortly afterwards of typhoid fever. He died having never received his pay and without receiving a $300 bounty he was entitled to for volunteering. Mary had to apply to recover these funds, which may have been what initially prompted the sending of the letter because if Robert was dead, she needed to know the date and circumstances of his death in order to file a claim for his back pay and bounty.[17]

On October 31, 1864, Jane Cable, of Lawton, New York, wrote a similar letter to the Adjutant General requesting word on her husband. She disclosed, "Dear

Sir: I am in receipt of information from a private source that my husband, Wm B. Cable, Private Co. I, 20th U.S. Colored Infantry is dead. The Regiment is in Louisiana. Will you please favor me with official notice of the time when, the place where, and the cause of his death."[18] William was a laborer and already thirty-five years old when he enlisted in the army on December 17, 1863. He was a member of Company A, not I. And Jane found out he died of dysentery on September 30, 1864, in the Corps d'Africa General Hospital in New Orleans. Like Robert Nickens, the army paymaster never paid him. He received $25 of the $75 state bounty he was entitled to for volunteering, but Jane had to apply for the back pay and remaining bounty monies. These letters reveal that, despite their sorrow over the possible or probable death of the soldiers, family members immediately began the process of getting any funds due the soldier. Those funds were gravely needed to help the family, especially given that the family had permanently lost the earning potential of their husband, father, son, or brother.[19]

A family requested the specific information on the death of the soldier because the information was necessary when applications were filed with the government to claim a soldier's back pay and unpaid bounty. By the middle of the year, the wives of black soldiers could also claim pension benefits, thanks to Congress's willingness to amend the pension laws in order to help struggling black families. This ended a discriminatory practice because white families could already claim pension benefits. Thus, as 1864 progressed, more letters from family members requested information from the army that was to be used to secure not only back pay, but also pensions due dead soldiers, something not seen in the 1863 letters. Nonetheless, laying claim to those funds could be a long and arduous process, requiring the completion of a number of official forms and affidavits to verify cause of death and sworn testimony to verify relationships and rightful heirs.[20]

Accordingly, some families were very specific in their letters about why they wanted the detailed information about their soldiers, and they preferred the documentation come from a commanding officer. George Raimer of Chambersburg, Pennsylvania put his mark on a letter written for him on November 28, 1864, regarding his son. The letter, sent to the Adjutant General, stated, "I have received information that my son Newman Raimer, Private in Company H. 54th Mass. Colored Regt. is dead. Will you please give me all the information in relation to his death, so as to enable me to make application for his Back Pay and Bounty."[21] Newman was a laborer and only eighteen years old when he enlisted on April 29, 1863. The army answered George's letter just two weeks later, on December 13, 1864, probably confirming Newman was indeed dead, having just died on December 3, 1864 in a regimental hospital at Morris Island, South Carolina. And his father now possessed the vital information he needed to apply for any funds rightfully due his deceased son. Because George was losing his sight and could no longer harvest his small piece of land, he and his wife were desperate for any funds they could obtain through their son's service to the Union. Newman, who never married and appeared to have no children, supported his parents with his wages before the war and his soldier's pay once he enlisted. In June 1868, after George lost his sight completely, his wife (and Newman's mother), Julia Ann Raimer, applied for their son's pension.[22]

Families found the process of applying for funds very difficult and confusing, and filled with bureaucratic hazards that could obstruct or derail a family's attempt to recoup back pay, bounties, and pensions. One bad or incorrect move and an opportunity could be lost forever. Therefore, families hired or depended on third parties to guide them through the process, especially African Americans who were not literate or sophisticated enough to manage their paperwork through a very difficult system. Such was the case with the wife of John Hart. On November 5, 1864, Congressman H. A. Nelson, of Poughkeepsie, New York, once again wrote a letter, this time to the Adjutant General on Mrs. Hart's behalf. "The wife of John Heart Co. "B," "20" U. S. Colored Troops," Nelson explained, "has been informed that her husband died at New Orleans, La. about two months since. Will you please inform me of the date of his death. I know her to be the proper person to receive information on this matter." John was a thirty-five-year-old laborer when he enlisted in the army on December 23, 1863. Mrs. Hart found out he died of consumption on July 8, 1864, in Jefferson City, Louisiana.[23]

Elisha C. Clarke wrote a third-party letter for the family and friends of three soldiers. The letter, written November 22, 1864, was addressed to the Adjutant General, and asked for very specific information. Clarke asked, "Can you give me any information regarding the deaths of George Lippitt, Henry J. Gardner, & Daniel Warmley all members of Co. A 11th U.C. Cold H. [Heavy]Arty late 14th RI H [Heavy] Arty. They were all residents of this place & their friends are anxious to know the particulars with the dates of their respective deaths." More specifically, "They have simply 'heard that they were dead' & can they be informed of the dates & causes of death in each case. They be very glad. Any information which you may be able to give will be thankfully received."[24] All three men enlisted in the army in August of 1863: George, a twenty-five-year-old farmer, was drafted, and enlisted on August 7, 1863; Henry, a twenty-eight-year old farmer, enlisted on August 12; and Daniel, a farmer and already thirty-eight years old, enlisted on August 6. Clarke found out all three were indeed dead. George died on

August 8, 1864 and Henry on September 24, 1864, both in the regimental hospital at Fort Jackson, Louisiana, of typhoid fever. Daniel died of a "remittent fever" on April 4, 1864, in the regimental hospital at Fort Esperanza, Texas. Additionally, all three men served without receiving any payment from the army before their deaths. Hence, their families had begun the process of applying for their soldiers' back pay, to receive any funds their soldier still had coming to him. George's wife, Elizabeth, whom he married on July 22, 1955 when he was nineteen and she was eighteen, applied for a widow's pension as early as in December 1864. It was approved in January 1865 for $8 a month, made retroactive to George's death in August 1864. Daniel's wife, Rosilla, applied and on June 17, 1865 was approved to receive $8 a month, also made retroactive to Daniel's death on April 4, 1864.[25]

Ongoing Requests for Information

Even as the war progressed and eventually came to a close, information on a soldier's whereabouts or health remained the most common requests from families. Many black families, as late as 1865, still attempted to verify the death of soldiers who they heard became casualties in battles as far back as 1863. Because of the increase in casualties every year the war continued, 1865 saw a corresponding growth in the number of letters sent to army officials. And the confirmation of more deaths generated more claims for funds families felt were rightly due them because of their war sacrifices.[26]

Some family members of African-American troops from the North who were in their third year of enlistment, such as the 54th Massachusetts Infantry, had not heard from their soldiers, or from military officials, since the soldiers were shipped to the South in May 1863. On February 3, 1865, Mary Denby, of Philadelphia, had a letter written for her and addressed to Edwin M. Stanton asking for information about her son, Alexander Robinson, a member of Company C, 6th USCT. Her son enlisted in the army on August 5, 1863, and according to Denby, "He was sent away from camp Wm Penn with the regiment to the south since which time I have never heard from him by letter or other wise." It was eighteen months later and she still had not heard from her son. Mary began to assume the worst happened. She admitted, "[it] makes me think he has had something to happen him as he was a fair writer and a good and dutiful son." She was desperate for any information, and pleaded, "This is to beg of your honor to have the record of your Department examined which may give me all the information desired." Peter Kelly wrote the letter for her.[27] Kelly may have been a Philadelphia grocer or merchant to whom Mary owed money. He wrote several letters for northern black families. On February 9, 1865, the army answered Denby, though it's not clear what information they provided to her at that time.

Equally anxious was Charlotte Harris, of Cambridge, Massachusetts, who wrote a letter requesting information about where the 55th Massachusetts Infantry was stationed. Her husband, David Harris, was a member of Company A of the 55th and she and her children had not heard from him in a year. David was twenty-seven years old and a farmer when he enlisted as a volunteer on December 10, 1863. Charlotte explained, "He left Boston Mass in January 1864 I have not Herd once I had a letter from him then he was on folly Island S C." She very much wanted to know where the regiment was, so she could write to her husband, but she realized a lot of time had passed and it was possible he was a casualty. According to Charlotte, "I should like to now where the 55 regiment is so I can wright to him . . . . I do want to here from him if is a live or dead I do want to here and my children to." She eventually found out David was still alive. He survived the war and was discharged with his regiment on August 29, 1865, in Charleston.[28] After his death of hearth disease on November 22, 1890, his widow received an $8.00 a month widow's pension commencing September 12, 1890. However, that widow was not Charlotte but instead David's second wife, Maria Harris. They married on August 29, 1867 in Massachusetts.[29] Still, Charlotte's initial letter to the military shows how not hearing anything from their soldiers for such long periods of time must have been very difficult for worried family members, as it was for Mary and Charlotte, and caused them to "assume the worst." Among the body of letters, there are many such inquiries family members initiated.

In 1865, the numbers of letters from northern African-American families inquiring whether a soldier was dead or alive increased significantly. Because black units had proven themselves as competent soldiers, they were given more opportunities to see action. That was why, in December 1864, General Grant had enough confidence in them to form the entirely black 25th Corps, and used them extensively. Now with more black soldiers in service and more of them given the opportunity to fight, more of them were certain to become casualties. In turn, families attempted to contact the military to get official notice about their troops. Ellen Brunson, of Blairsville, Pennsylvania, experienced this when she wrote a letter on April 15, 1864 to the Adjutant General begging for information about her husband. His regiment, the 127th USCT, was one of the black regiments that played a major role in the Appomattox campaign in early 1865, just before Lee's surrender. The campaign received a lot of coverage in the northern press because Lee's army was in retreat and the end of the war was near. The newspaper coverage may have caused Ellen to feel uneasy about her husband's health and prompted her to send her letter. Ellen revealed, "I am anxious to hear from my husband, Thos. Brunson in Co. 'F,' 127, Regt. U.S.C. Troops. He is reported killed. Be pleased to give me any information you may have and obligh his wife." Ellen received an answer from the army dated April 24, 1865, but it is not clear from the files what information they provided to her at that time.[30]

Matilda Dorsey was also very worried. Her husband, John, was thirty years old and a boatman when he enlisted as a substitute on October 5, 1863. He was a member of Company E, 8th USCT, and the regiment also participated in the Appomattox campaign. She had a letter written for her on April 26, 1865 in which she explained, "I am in great trouble about my husband who was wounded and sent into Hospital and afterwards sent down to front again and is said to have been killed. I would like to know the truth from your honor be kind enough to let me know."[31] After she did not receive a response to her first letter, Matilda sent another on May 3, 1865, requesting the same information about her husband, but this time it was addressed to Stanton and listed what division and corps her husband's regiment was assigned to.[32] On July 18, 1865, Matilda sent a third letter to the army, again to Stanton, and again asking for information about the reported death of her husband. The Adjutant General's office responded on August 1, 1865.[33] John was wounded on September 26, 1864, while on picket duty outside Petersburg. He was shot in the shoulder, "the ball entering near the neck passing down near the shoulder blade," and causing the loss of almost the total use of his left hand. After this incident, he spent over two months in a Union hospital at Fort Monroe, Virginia, before returning to duty on December 2, 1864. Then, in February 1865, John suffered severe frostbite while on Pickett duty outside of Fort Harrison, Virginia, and the big toe on his right foot had to be amputated. He did not require hospitalization for his foot injury and he continued to complete his military duties, according to documentation in his pension file. John eventually survived the war and was mustered out of the army with his regiment on November 10, 1865, at Brownsville, Texas. However, his wounds would limit his ability to take care of himself and his family. He was approved for a $2.00 a month pension on October 20, 1866, retroactive to November 10, 1865, the day his regiment was mustered out of service.[34]

Even more than a year after a battle, families still struggled to get accurate information about their soldier's fate. On January 9, 1865, John W. Hampton wrote a letter for Sarah and Charles Williams Sr., the worried parents of Charles Williams Jr. They were concerned their son was dead. Charles, a brick-maker and twenty years old when he enlisted on March 14, 1863, was a member of Company B, 54th Massachusetts Infantry. George E. Stephens was his first sergeant.

Hampton's letter, sent from Philadelphia and addressed to General Samuel Breck, explained, "He [Charles] was in the charge on Fort Wagner Morris Island SC and was reported kiled but we have heard that he was a prisoner at Charleston pleas Let me know if shuch is the fact."[35] Hampton made this inquiry eighteen months after the 54th's charge on Fort Wagner and it was probably not the family's first correspondence with the army about Charles's condition. The news would not be good for the Williams family. Over a year after the battle, they received confirmation their son was not killed at Fort Wagner but instead was taken prisoner in the assault and died in January 1865, as a prisoner of war for a year and a half years in Florence, South Carolina.[36]

Mary Brown, also from Philadelphia, made a similar plea for a definitive answer. She had a letter written on February 3, 1865 on her behalf and that of her neighbor, Hester White, asking for information about Brown's husband, James, who served in Company C, 25th USCT, and White's son, Daniel White, a member of the 54th. According to Mary, "I received a letter stating that my husband died in the hospital at Jacksonville Florida at Camp Leven. It would greatly relieve me if you would let me know if he has been returned dead at the War Department." She continued, "My neighbor Mrs. Hester White whose son enlisted . . . in May 1863 has never been heard of by letter from him but she has heard that he was killed on Morris Island." Stressing the importance of obtaining information, Mary added, "At the time of [Dan's] listing between eighteen and nineteen years and only child and support. I [Mrs. White] have never got a cent from him since he listed. Be so kind as to see if he is dead as I am in great trouble of mind." Mary's letters were transcribed by Peter Kelly.[37] James was a laborer and already forty years old when he enlisted as a volunteer on January 16, 1864. Mary found out he indeed was dead. On September 24, 1864, he died of scurvy at Fort Pickens, Florida. As a member of the 25th, James was not a battle casualty because the regiment did not participate in any battles in the war where it suffered casualties. However, like James, many of the regiment's men were victims of disease. Disease was the killer of most Civil War soldiers, North and South, black and white, during the war. As for Daniel White, he was a nineteen-year-old farmer when he enlisted on May 13, 1863. He was a member of Company A, 55th Massachusetts Infantry, not the 54th, and Hester was no doubt happy when she learned much later he survived the war. He mustered out with the regiment on August 29, 1865 in Charleston, South Carolina.[38]

The participation of African-American regiments in other momentous battles had the same effect at home, the sending of more letters from family members. Seven African-American regiments participated in the Battle of Honey Hill,

South Carolina, on November 30, 1864, where the regiments took a significant number of casualties in a Union loss. Two of the black regiments were the 54th Massachusetts Infantry, which had 43 casualties, and the 55th Massachusetts Infantry, which had 137 troops killed, wounded, or reported missing.[39] News of the battle and uncertainty about the safety of their men caused family members to make inquiries about soldiers who served in the regiments. Hester White's son, Daniel, as a member of the 54th, probably fought in the battle, prompting her to ask about his well-being. Patience Cain, of Piqua, Ohio, was also worried and put her mark on a letter to the Adjutant General dated February 18, 1865. George, a farmer from Ohio, was only eighteen years old when he enlisted on May 18, 1863. Only two months later, the young man was promoted to sergeant. Asking about her son, Patience stated, "Sir will you please inform me if you can, whether my son George Bazil is alive or dead he was a Sergeant in Company B 55th Massachusetts Volunteers I have heard he was wounded at the Battle of Honeys Hill in South Carolina and not hearing from him since I fear he is dead Please send answer to me."[40] Patience found out George was indeed wounded at Honey Hill, having suffered a gunshot "flesh wound" to the lower third of his thigh. Unfortunately, his wound was infected with tetanus and he died on December 13, 1864, in a military hospital in Beaufort, South Carolina.[41]

John Brunson, of Blairsville, Pennsylvania, was also worried about his son, David Brunson, and wrote to the Adjutant General on March 29, 1865, asking for information about him. David was a laborer when he enlisted on May 5, 1863 at the age of twenty. He was a sergeant in Company K, 54th Massachusetts Infantry. According to John, "When last heard from [him] he was wounded. He is my son. . . . He was a single man and has no children."[42] John found out that his son suffered a head wound at Honey Hill. It was his second serious injury since he had been shot in the leg at the charge on Fort Wagner, but he recovered from the fractured leg to serve again. This time, the head wound left David disabled, and he was eventually discharged from the army on July 10, 1865, at Beaufort, South Carolina.[43] Julia Green heard that her husband, Charles Henry Green, was reported killed at the Battle of Honey Hill, and she inquired about the accuracy of the report. The 32nd USCT also served at Honey Hill and suffered sixty-four casualties, including nine killed. Julia had a letter written for her by Peter Kelly, dated March 11, 1865, and addressed to Stanton. Charles was twenty years old and a "dealer" when he enlisted on February 24, 1864, and was assigned to Company I, 32nd USCT. He was promoted to sergeant on July 1, 1864. Julia worried: "my husband has been reported to me to be dead it grieves me much I was not prepared for it having a large family to provide and expecting to have him to help me raise them when his time would be up I hope it is not true be kind enough to let me know." With Charles's possible death, Julia suddenly found herself in a position she did not anticipate. It appears that she was in denial that he could become a casualty of the war. Luckily for her and her family, Charles was still alive and served until he was discharged with his regiment on August 20, 1865, at Hilton Head, South Carolina.[44]

As expected, many families found it very difficult to deal with the death of a soldier. The letters display the feelings of devastation many family members endured upon learning of the news. The families had to know many people were dying in the war and the risk of death or serious injury was great for their soldiers. But when they learned they had lost *their* loved one, it was still shocking and devastating. Mary Lloyd, of Philadelphia, was distraught when she received word her son, Thomas Lloyd, of Company E, 42nd USCT, might be dead. She had a letter written for her on March 18, 1865, asking for confirmation of her son's death from Stanton. She explained, "I heard he lost his arm and died in hospital." She continued, "I am in great pain of mind he was the only child I had, and only support I am now seventy years of age and it will be great relief to know if it be true." John J. Keefe wrote the letter for Lloyd.[45] On March 25, 1865, the army answered Lloyd, but it's not clear whether she was informed her son had been killed. However, when a family finally received verification of the death of their loved ones, they often found they had to deal with emotional heartbreak from their loss and the sudden realization their soldier would not return home from the war alive.[46]

The letters from northern black family members to the army and federal officials don't really discuss the actual effects of a soldier's death upon a family. Julia Green's letter is rare. African Americans more likely discussed death and the loss of a loved one in personal letters to each other rather than to government agencies. However, while grieving the death of their soldiers, family members must have had some satisfaction in knowing their troops died while fighting and "killing" in a Union uniform. Blacks troops did not join the fight just to die, but to both seek revenge for centuries of atrocities performed by the South against the race as well as to gain political victories after sacrificing for the cause and proving blacks deserved equal treatment in the country.[47]

Another consequence of the increasing number of blacks in uniform by 1865 was that families sometimes had several soldiers in the army. Thus, they had additional people whose health and whereabouts were of constant concern. Consequently, rather than sending letters requesting information about one soldier, the letters inquired about many soldiers, sometimes five, six, or seven family

members at a time. Mary Fisher, from Philadelphia, inquired about the well being of four family members in four different regiments. Her husband, Joshua, was
twenty-one years old and a laborer when he enlisted on January 6, 1864. There
are no records for her brother, Marri Davis, but her other brother, Noah, was
also twenty-one and a laborer when he enlisted on August 13, 1863 as a draftee.
On March 4, 1865, Mary had a letter written for her addressed to Stanton, stating,
"Hon Sir I am in deep distress about my husband Joshua Bowman Fisher Co D.
25th Regt U.S.C. Troop Pennsylvania not hearing from him since he left going
two years ago also my brothers Marii Davis Co C. 1st Regt U.S.C.T. Pennsylvania
who I heard was badly wounded at Fairoaks and sent to some Hospital and Noah
Davis Co B. 8th Regt U.S.C.T. said to be dead by some of my friends." Mary continued, "it would afford me great consolation if your honor would give me some
information as to their being dead or alive I have the honor to be Humbl servant.
... P.S. I forgot to mention my cousin John Denby Co I 24th Regt said to be killed
Pennsylvania Regt."[48] The letter was transcribed by John J. Keefe. Mary was no
doubt relieved to find out Joshua was not dead. He survived the war and was
discharged with his regiment on December 6, 1865, in Philadelphia. He applied
for, and on June 13, 1892 he began receiving, an $8.00 a month disability pension
due to a heart condition, rheumatism, asthma, and numerous other ailments.
For some reason, on June 30, 1896 he was dropped from the rolls for failure to
claim a pension.[49]

Unfortunately for Mary and her family, Noah did not make it back home. He
participated in and survived several battles (Olustee, where he was wounded,
Deep Bottom, Petersburg, and Fair Oaks), only to die from disease. He probably died several days after being absent due to illness on October 29, 1865 in
Brownsville, Texas. In addition, her cousin, John Demby, was a nineteen-year-
old farmer when he enlisted as a volunteer on March 7, 1865, just weeks before
the war ended. He belonged to Company G of the 24th USCT, not Company I,
and was not dead, as she earlier thought. He mustered out with his regiment on
October 1, 1865, in Richmond, Virginia, and was discharged October 29, 1865 in
Philadelphia. For his five weeks of service before the war end and seven months
of service total, he was eligible to later collect a military disability pension until
his death on January 1, 1919 in Pennsauken, New Jersey. His wife since August 31,
1876, Rachel A. Demby, and the mother of his three children (Lonella, Clearance,
and Carl) then received his pension until her death on August 2, 1935, also in
Pennsauken.[50]

In another letter inquiring about multiple family members, Jane Mares, of
Philadelphia, had a letter written for her dated April 12, 1865 and addressed

to Stanton. Jane begged for information about her husband, John Mares, and her brother-in-law, Stephen Mares. Both men were members of Company H, 25th USCT and Jane had not heard from them in over a year. She also wanted to know about a cousin, John Mares, of Company I, 25th USCT. Jane had misgivings about the well-being of her close relatives because "we suppose them to be dead, would you please give any information you may have in your power, and you will greatly relieve the anxiety that is full for them." Peter Kelly transcribed the letter for Jane. There are no records on her husband and brother-in-law. This might be because of an apparent confusion over the proper spelling of their last name. Records do exist for their cousin, John, of Company I. His name was sometimes spelled Mares, other times Maris, but most often the army spelled it Mairs. One of the documents in his service records even had two different spellings for his name. He was a thirty-four year old waiter when he enlisted on February 4, 1864. However, he died soon after Jane wrote her letter. He died of chronic diarrhea on April 26, 1865, in the general hospital in Barrancas, Florida, another member of the 25th USCT who died of disease.[51]

On April 6, 1865, another Philadelphia resident, Elizabeth Adams, had a letter written for her by John J. Keefe, asking about her husband, John Quincy Adams, of Company C, 45th USCT, and two brothers-in-law, Charles Roy and George Rico. John was a twenty-eight-year-old laborer when he enlisted as a volunteer on June 18, 1864. Charles was thirty years old and a laborer when he enlisted as a draftee on May 27, 1864, and he was a member of Company C, 45th USCT, not the 41st, as Elizabeth initially thought. Similarly, George Rico was a member of the 45th USCT, not the 41st. He was an eighteen-year-old laborer when he enlisted on July 1, 1864, and assigned to Company D. Elizabeth stated she "had two or three reports that he [John] died at Camp Casey Va," and "It was also reported that my brother inlaws . . . was also dead at Camp Casey." By the time Elizabeth sent her letter, John was already discharged from the army on February 15, 1865. According to his service records, John was granted a disability discharge because he was ruled unfit for duty owing to the effects of syphilis, a disease the army stated he contracted "not in the line of duty." How he contracted syphilis might explain why he was not in touch with his wife and had not yet made it back home. Perhaps he was ashamed to explain the circumstance of his contacting the disease. Charles, on the other hand, was dead, which Elizabeth suspected. He died on February 19, 1865, of pulmonary abscess at the hospital at Camp Casey, Virginia. George was also dead. He drowned "while bathing in the Gulf of Mexico at Brazos Santiago, Texas," on June 19, 1865.[52] With many close relatives in the army, families like the Fishers, Mareses, and Adamses were probably even more anxious not knowing the whereabouts and status of multiple family members.

Not all Union regiments, both black and white, saw action during the war, especially those regiments formed in its later stages. Many of them were held in reserve for use if the Union needed them. Some black regiments, similar to the 25th USCT, never participated in any battles. Unlike white regiments, which were used primarily for combat, they were used for fatigue duty and guard duty, and to police occupied territory in the South. These regiments experienced very few battle casualties, if any at all, but they still suffered from accidents and, more commonly, deaths by disease. That was the outcome for Mary Brown's husband, James, and Jane Mares's brother-in-law, John. Thus, their families still had plenty of reasons to worry about and inquire about their well being.[53]

Sarah Brown, of Philadelphia, described her condition in a letter she had written for her. Dated February 8, 1865, the letter was addressed to Stanton and asked for information on the possible deaths of seven soldiers—her husband, Samuel (or Sandy); his brother, Daniel; and their five cousins, Asa Miller, Daniel Horsey, George Horsey, Samuel Horsey, and George H. Washington, all of whom had not been heard from in months. The entire family appeared to be natives of Sussex County, Delaware, and, according to Sarah, all the men were members of Company C, 25th USCT. She stated, "I am in great trouble of mind about my husband it is reported that he is dead he has been over a year and I have not heard from him. . . ." Sara continued, stating the worries of the family over the soldiers: "he went with his brother and five cousins to list they are all in the same Co, and regiment but none of them have been heard from only reports that they were dead which caused their wifes great grief You will be doing charity by letting us know their whereabouts if alive so that we may write to them."[54] She also described the difficult financial condition of the families by revealing, "We have not received a cent from them since they left we are all bad off it would do us a great favor if you would give the information as soon as your time will permit." Samuel (her husband) enlisted as a twenty-year-old laborer, and George as an eighteen-year-old laborer, both on January 12, 1864. And both survived the war and returned to Philadelphia, where they were discharged with their regiment on December 6, 1865. Asa, who enlisted as a nineteen-year-old laborer on January 1, 1864, did not survive the war. He died less than three months later, on March 28, 1864, of typhoid fever while confined at Summit House Hospital in Philadelphia. He was never in the line of fire or paid for his service. It's possible Asa became ill and never completed his training. It is unclear what happened to Daniel Brown or the other cousins; Sarah might not have listed their correct regiments, or the letter writer, Peter Kelly, may have transcribed names or regiment numbers incorrectly.[55] Sarah Brown's family situation showed that even having relatives serving in a regiment that did not see action did not relieve the family of worry, grief, and pain.

Eighteen sixty-five was the first full year the wives of black soldiers could claim pension benefits since Congress's mid-1864 decision to amend the pension laws in order to help struggling black families. Financially distressed families took advantage of the opportunity to obtain needed funds, but the application process still required families to provide specific information about the exact date and nature of their soldier's death before they could lay claim to the funds. Therefore, families continued to write letters asking for specific information from Union officials, usually their soldiers' commanding officers. Victoria Covington, of Newburyport, Massachusetts, attempted to obtain this information from the army when she sent a letter dated April 7, 1865, asking about her husband's death. He was a thirty-year-old barber when he enlisted as a substitute on August 14, 1863. Victoria revealed, "My husband Evans Covington Enlisted in the 54th Regt. Mass. Vols. Co 'E' & had not heard from him for a good while until recently I had a letter informing me that he died at the Insane Asylum Oct 31 1864 but day not state where it was or the cause of his death. I have applied to the Adjt. Genl of their Comd [Command]. He inform me my husband death has not been reported in Boston." More specifically, she requested, "My object to ask the favor of knowing from you if his death has been updated at your office & if so, when, where & the cause of it all the facts that are useful for me to establish my claims for bounty."[56] Continuing with the formal process of submitting the proper documentation to claim funds, Victoria included with her letter a statement from a third-party certifying she was who she claimed to be and she was the rightful person to apply for his bounty. Victoria found out her husband was listed as having died "from insanity" on September 25, 1864, in an insane asylum in Washington. For some reason, the final statement for Evans, completed by Union military authorities for each deceased soldier, was not filed until May 15, 1865. The eventual completion of the form was probably prompted by Victoria's efforts to verify Evans' death so she could make a claim for his back pay and any other funds due her husband. Soon afterwards, on June 10, 1865, she completed a "Widow's Declaration for Pension" form, beginning what would be an arduous and lengthy process to secure Evans' pension.[57]

Families had to remain both patient and persistent as they gathered important data in order to petition for a deceased soldier's back pay and pension because getting the correct information often meant making many attempts at corresponding with army officials. Families also continued to hire, or depended on, third parties to guide them through the process. Annis E. Holland, of Canandaigua, New York, experienced difficulties when she attempted to claim funds owed her deceased husband, Adam. She had a letter to the Adjutant General written on her behalf by Gideon Granger, probably a claims agent, on February 24, 1865. In the letter, Granger stated information on Holland's death was badly needed because Annis was destitute and in immediate need of funds for her and her four young children, ages twelve, five, four, and one. Granger asked, "Can you give me information whether Adam Holland Co. E. 31st Regt. U.S.Col.T. is dead and if so when? I have conflicting accounts in reference to him and, as his family are destitute, I am desirous to find out whether he is dead that his wife may take steps necessary to secure his back pay. The different reports are so conflicting, that she can scarcely make affidavit that she believes either way."[58] Adam was a thirty-five-year-old laborer when he enlisted on December 17, 1863. It appears his wife initiated the process to claim his back pay and bounty even before she had officially confirmed his fate. She must have been confident he was dead; otherwise, she would not have hired a claims agent. She soon found out Adam was indeed dead. On October 9, 1864, he died of typhoid fever in a hospital for colored troops in City Point, Virginia. Annis could now follow through with her claim, which she officially did on April 11, 1865.[59]

Ann Eliza Palmer, of Oxford, Pennsylvania, was in the same situation when she had a letter written on her behalf by a claims agent, asking for specific information about her husband, Jacob. He was a farmer and already thirty-nine years old when he enlisted on December 30, 1863.[60] Ann's letter, written on March 13, 1865 and addressed to the Adjutant General, stated the following: "By request of Mrs Ann Eliza Palmer Alias Pammer (colored) wife of Jacob Palmer Alias Pammer (colored) I write to ask information of his fate. He was a private of Company F. 22nd Regiment U.S.C.T. under command of Captain Arthur P. Morey." "The last information his wife has had of him," explained Ann, "was 'That he was left sick at Deep Bottom Virginia when the Regiment moved from there on the 29th of September 1864. I suppose him to have gone to some Hospital' This information is from the Captains letter, to Mrs Palmer, dated Feb. 8th 1865. Any information of him will be thankfully received by her."[61] The letter was signed, "E. Chandlee MD (Claim Agent)." Similar to Annis Holland, Ann was sure her husband was dead and went ahead and obtained the service of a claims agent to obtain money owed her husband by the government. Ann received confirmation Jacob was dead. His regiment left him behind sick in Deep Bottom, Virginia, where he died on September 29, 1864. She was free to follow through with her claim, which she did, in an attempt to obtain funds to help support herself and their three children (ages twelve, four, and two). By 1868, she was receiving from the government $8 a month for herself and $2 a month for each child until they turned sixteen.[62] The persistence of Annis and Ann in eliciting the information they needed paid off, for each eventually received the official report she needed to initiate an application for her husband's pension.

By the end of the war in 1865, most of the letters to the army from northern black families were not desperate pleas for money and pay for the soldiers, so the money could be sent home to support their families, but instead, were requests for basic information about their state of health and whereabouts. More specifically, the family members, usually widowed mothers dependent on their sons for support or wives with numerous children, wanted the question answered, "Where is my soldier?" And if the soldier was dead, confirmation of that and the details of the death were paramount for applications for the soldier's back pay, bounties, and widow's or dependent pensions. Though families were devastated about the loss of their soldiers, the pay due them became even more vital for the family's long-term survival.

7

Discharge Requests

Too Late for Anything Short of a Discharge

Northern African-American soldiers and their families continued to support the Union effort. In spite of pay issues, discrimination and racism by northerners and southerners, the general hardships of military life, and the potential hardships for their families, black men continued to enlist in large numbers. Yet, for some families, financial conditions at home had become too hopeless. These families had gone on as long as they could without the financial support of their men and had reached the point where they simply wanted their soldiers home. Family members asked Union officials for the discharge of their soldiers because the family's situation was so desperate, the only resolution was for the soldiers to return home to help them.

On November 21, 1864, Jane Welcome asked Lincoln to release her son from the army. Jane could no longer support herself and wanted her son, Martin, returned home to help the family's bleak financial situation. Martin was twenty-eight years old and a laborer when he enlisted on August 14, 1863. A member of Company A, 6th USCT, he saw a lot of action and was wounded twice in battle— at the Battle of Olustee, on February 20, 1864, and at Chapin's Farm, Virginia, on September 29, 1864. Jane wrote, "I wont to knw sir if you please wether I can have my son relest from the arme he is all the suleport I have notice his father is dead and his brother that wase all the help that I had he has bean wonded twise he has not had nothing to send me yet notice." She continued, "I am old and my head is laborraming [laboring?] for the grave and if youse dou I hope the lord will bless you and me if you please insurer as soon as you can if you please tha say that you will simpathise withe the poor."[1] Jane's letter also displayed her long support for the Union because it took the death of her husband and the wounding twice of Jane's other son to get her to ask for Martin's return home. The army denied Jane's request. In a response, dated December 2, 1864, the army stated, "the interests of the armies will not permit that your request be granted." Martin served until his regiment was officially mustered out of service on November 10, 1865.[2]

Other families, knowing the heartache and suffering that would occur once their relative enlisted, tried to have them returned before they went off to do battle. Julia Rouser of Washington, D.C., found herself in such a situation when she put her mark on a letter written for her on September 24, 1864 and sent to Lincoln. She requested the release of her husband, William, from the army so he could take care of his family. William was a laborer and already thirty-eight years old when he was drafted into the Union army. He enlisted on September 23, 1864, just a day before Julia made her request, as a member of Company K, 10th USCT. Julia declared, "My husband William Rouser having been drafted on Tuesday last in the first ward in the city. I would most humbly beg to present to your kind consideration the enclosed affidavit of my physician which shows that I am totally unfit to obtain a living for my young child and myself." She continued, "Also a petition from several persons whom I have known since I have been in the city and who have known since I have been in this city and who know that it is impossible for me to go out to service or in any way provide for myself and child. Thus in the absence of my husband I am thrown upon my own exertions in order to feed and cloth us—and subject as I am to spasms and convulsions."[3] Julia pointed out she did not have some of the same options as other women, stating, "I can find no person who will give me employment, and no relative or friend to whom I can look for aid or assistance." She ended her letter explaining it was only because of her current condition she was making such a request, explaining she was "trusting that you will grant my husband a discharge for which I would not ask were I able to support myself." Julia included in her letter supporting statements from her friends, pastor, and doctor, attesting to her health problems and inability to support herself and her child. She also included a letter from her church stating the congregation would raise enough money on Julia's behalf to hire a substitute to take her husband's place in the army.[4]

On October 18, 1864, the army replied to Julia's letter with a denial of her request to have her husband discharged and replaced with a substitute, in spite of the substantial supporting documentation she submitted. The army stated, because her husband was drafted and assigned to duty, he was no longer eligible to be replaced by a substitute. William did not return home until his regiment was officially discharged from service on September 23, 1865 in Corpus Christi, Texas, exactly one year after he enlisted.[5] It appears Union officials denied most of the requests for discharge in 1864. Soldiers were required to serve until their regiments were officially discharged.

Parents who wanted to get their underage sons out of the army made other requests for discharges. From its start until its conclusion, young boys on both sides—North and South, black and white—continued to run off to join the Union and Confederate armies, usually without their parents' consent. Some served as soldiers and others as servants, cooks, and teamsters. Most served as musicians, often drummer boys. In the North, some of these boys fooled recruiters by lying about their age, while others were recruited and quickly signed up by unscrupulous recruiters and agents who knew the boys were too young but who were determined to make their recruitment quotas, and their $2 per recruit, at all cost. Unfortunately, the problem for too many recruits and their families was the financial incentives that often led to unscrupulous activities on the part of some recruiters. Although Union officials made efforts to stop the abuse through the better regulation of agents, unscrupulous recruiters and agents continued to take advantage of the system.[6]

Anxious parents of African-American boys from the North wrote letters to Union officials to get their sons discharged and returned home. This was Tabitha Thompson's situation, which she explained in a letter to the Adjutant General, requesting her son, who was a mere twelve years old, be discharged. The army believed he was eighteen years old with an occupation as a servant when he enlisted on August 26, 1864, according to his service records. A recruiting officer named James Davison enrolled him into the army in New York City, and John signed his name on the volunteer enlistment papers. John was paid a $100 bounty for volunteering, but it is unclear whether he or his family actually received the cash. From Harrisburg, Pennsylvania, on October 10, 1864, Tabitha wrote, declaring, "My son, John Alexander Thompson, a boy of but twelve years old, was enticed from his home without my knowledge or consent, taken to New York, and enlisted as a musician (drummer) in Company 'D' 26th regiment US Colored Troops. He is now at Fort Duane, Beaufort, S.C." She continued, "My husband is in the army. This boy is my only one. He is too young to endure the hardships of a soldiers life. He will be thirteen years old on the 4th July 1865 and I beg you will cause the case to be inquired into and my boy discharged and returned home to me." Thompson's letter was probably written for her because it stated that replies were to be addressed in care of an Eby Byers, who probably wrote the letter for Thompson.[7]

The army responded on October 13, 1864, with a copy of the army's rules about the enlistment of underage youth. The army also explained it was waiting for a muster roll from the regiment before a decision could be made about his discharge. They had not received the muster roll because it was requested on September 12, 1864. However, military officials must not have believed Tabitha's story and so decided to deny her request because John served until the entire regiment was finally discharged at Hilton Head, South Carolina, on August 28, 1865. In 1918, an affidavit filed in a pension application revealed John actually ran away from home with a friend, John Price, to join the army. He and his friend, like so many other boys, were lured to war by the illusions of adventure and glory on the battlefields.[8]

On December 7, 1864, another worried mother, Alicia Bass, made a similar request to have her son discharged, and she took her complaint to President Lincoln. Alicia stated her underage son, Armon, ran off from their home in Xenia, Ohio, to enlist. Worried because Armon was sickly before he left, she wrote, "I drop you these few lines concerning my son who is in the 27 Regiment 9th Army Corps Company F Colored Armur Bass of this place he was under age and ran away from me." She continued, "If he was a healthy boy I would give him up freely but the doctor sayed that he was consumption he was sunstruck on the 30th of July at the Battle of Petersburg and he has not been well since I wish you would see to him geting a discharge if you please please answer this as soon as you rec it I shall expect him."[9] Voicing her support for the Union cause, she stated, even though he was underage, she would be willing to "give him up freely" if he were not sick. According to Armon's service records, he was an eighteen-year-old laborer when he enlisted on March 7, 1864. A recruiting officer named Samuel J. Oakley enlisted him into the service in Xenia, Ohio, with Armon putting his mark on the volunteer enlistment papers. Oakley was probably motivated to earn another $2 for signing another recruit rather than checking Armon's proper age. Years after the war, one of the men who served with Armon, George Beesley, confirmed his youthful status. He stated, "While in the service, Bass was just a boy under age." It is unclear whether the army answered Alicia's letter, but the request must have been denied because Armon served until his regiment was discharged at Smithville, North Carolina, on September 21, 1865. Ironically, in spite of being "sickly" according to his mother, Armon would go on to live into his fifties. He died on May 11, 1907 in Bellefontaine, Ohio.[10]

The letter from the family of William Chandler was unusual because the soldier himself wrote it. Even though his family was surely happy to see him, having him home was probably difficult financially for the already struggling family because he was wounded and thus could not readily work to provide for the family. William was home on furlough, recovering from his battle wounds, when he wrote a letter to Lincoln. He was thirty-one years old and a farmer when he enlisted into the army on August 8, 1863, as a draftee into Company G, 8th USCT. On February 20, 1864, at the Battle of Olustee, he was wounded from a "gunshot" and never recovered from his wounds, spending a lot of time in several military hospitals before he was officially discharged from the army on December 26, 1864. In his letter of November 21, 1864, he sought Lincoln's help because he had not been paid in a year. William stated, "Dear Sir It is one year ago the 19 Aug scince I was mustered in to the U.S Service scince which I hade the misfortin to loose my left arm at the battle of Olustee, Florida on the 20 of Feb I was wounded slightly in my hip and severly im my arm and have had my arm amputated and have been in the hospital every scince." There was no sense of regret in Chandler's letter. He did not appear to be sorry for fighting for his country or for losing his arm in battle. He continued, "I am home on a furlough I have never received a cent of pay yet Necesity compells me to write to you to see if you can do anything to help me about getting my pay which is due me as a soldier." He was not asking for money just because he lost an arm; he simply wanted the pay he was already due. Chandler concluded, "My family are suffering for want of it I am a poor man and have no way of supporting my family. . . . Pleas let me know what you can do about it. . . . if you can do any thing to help a poor soldier pleas do it and oblige me."[11] Like so many of the letter writers, Chandler was proud to support his country but he needed his money because living conditions became dire for his family. It is not clear whether Chandler received a reply to his letter. However, because he was a disabled veteran who was discharged and had already returned to his home, he could apply to the government for a disability pension. He filed his application on January 6, 1865, just eleven days after he was discharged, but it was not until April 7, 1865 that he began receiving the pension, $8 a month. Until then, he and his family had to find some way to survive.[12]

Victory Is Near: Please Send My Soldier Home

By 1865, with the war coming to an end and a victory for the Union, even more families felt their financial predicament had become so acute that getting the soldier's pay or some type of temporary relief was no longer the solution. Instead, they pleaded for the discharge of their soldiers and their return home to help their families. Other requests for discharges were for the return of underage sons, who continued to enlist through deceitfulness about their age.

Rebecca Smith of Washington, D.C., pleaded financial desperation when she asked Stanton in April 1865 for a substitute to finish her drafted husband's term because he was badly needed at home to help take care of his large family. Her husband, Moses, had not been in the army long after he was drafted in February 1865 and assigned to Company G, 43rd USCT. Rebecca stated her husband was needed at home because of "having a large family of small children depending on his labor for their support." She included in her petition two statements from friends who verified her financial situation and upstanding character. One supporter, Phillip Nolan, commented, "I think she is very poor and is a sober, steady and honest woman." The other supporter, Archibald Lewis, testified, "I know them to be very poor and hard working family and if business remains in the same status it is now, I see no other alternative for her but starvation." Her mother-in-law, who lived with her, probably to conserve and share resources, which many families did during the war, was willing to sell her home in order to purchase a substitute. The Adjutant General's Office took her request into consideration and on May 1, 1865 recommended the discharge of her husband on the grounds there was a large family of small children to support and Rebecca's application was backed by statements of support. Four days later, he was discharged. Because substitutes were no longer being enlisted so late in the war, the army did not require Moses be replaced with one.[13] On the other hand, just six months previously, Julia Rouser had composed a very similar petition to the army for the discharge of her husband, William. Julia included statements of support and was willing to provide a substitute, yet the army denied her petition, and William served until his regiment was officially discharged from service on September 23, 1865.[14] By April 1865, the situation had changed considerably. The war was virtually over, new men were not being enlisted, and the army was willing to discharge some, permitting them to go home and support their families.

The family of Daniel Johnson, a member of Company H, 14th USCT, was in an even more difficult position because his wife had died. Daniel was a farmer from Ohio and already thirty-five years old when he enlisted in the army on September 26, 1864, for one year. After the death of his wife, four friends of his family wrote a letter from Niles, Michigan, to Stanton on July 10, 1865, pleading on behalf of his family for his discharge to take care of his newborn child because his wife was now dead. They stated, "About a month ago, his wife died leaving a child a few weeks old to the care of the old woman [his mother] who is unable to take care of herself, being quite old, and crippled." Members of the neighborhood attempted to assist the child's grandmother but "her situation is really pitiable," the letter explained. The friends claimed, we "suppose Daniel who is her only living relative, (except the child) is entitled to a discharge, under the exemption laws." Because northern black families were smaller, there was very little available family support when a crisis occurred.[15] Often families reached out to government officials for relief, or in the Johnson family's case, because no extended family appears to have been available, kindly people from the community reached out on their behalf. On July 19, 1865, the army responded that because Johnson enlisted for one year as a substitute on September 26, 1864, and that period would soon end, no action was needed because he would soon be home. Daniel was discharged from the army on September 29, 1865, at Chattanooga, Tennessee.[16]

While most northern blacks sacrificed their loved ones for the noble cause of defeating the Confederacy and ending slavery, others saw an opportunity to cash-in. Those seeking cash more than glory included men looking for desperately needed income to provide for their families. Some families used their underage sons as rented and leased property in order to have access to bounty payments and monthly pay from the Union government. Some of these families changed their minds and then begged for the discharge and return home of the same sons. Renting children out as laborers was nothing new during this period, but this was a war, not just a job, where many soldiers came home permanently wounded or did not come home at all due to death.

Underage soldiers usually sneaked themselves into the army in order to prove their manhood and experience what they felt were the glories of war. Or they were recruited and quickly signed up by unscrupulous recruiters who knew the boys were too young but who were determined to meet their recruitment quota and earn their commissions. However, in one case it appears the culprit was the soldier's own mother. Lyddia Ann Bartly, of Philadelphia, wrote a letter on April 6, 1865. In it she petitioned the Adjutant General to discharge her son, who she felt was enrolled into the army by men with criminal intent. Her son, Joseph, was a northern African American who was assigned to a regiment organized in the South, in Virginia. He was an eighteen-year-old farmer when he enlisted as a substitute on March 21, 1865. His mother revealed, "My son Joseph S. Bartly now in the 38th Regt U.S.C.T. at Foutress Monroe, was stolen from me and put in the army as a substitute for 1 yr for a Mr A. J. Decamp of the 1st Ward in this city the broker J. H. Joseph was the man who enlisted him as the Provost Marshals office Edwin Palmer of the city." Lyddia continued, "The boy got four hundred dollars he is only 15 years of age last March being born on the 25th of March 1850." She explained her need to have him back: "He was a great help to me and I have to beg of your honor to give him his discharge as I under stand minors are not allowed to go for substitutes and that it is unlawful to put them in as such."[17]

Lyddia was willing to return the $400 to the government but also wanted action taken against the men who wrongly enlisted her son. She explained, "I am satisfied to return the money be kind enough to tell me how to act and if the guilty parties cannot be put under arrest." On April 11, 1865, the army responded to Lyddia's letter, stating that additional evidence was needed before the army could render a decision.[18] On April 26, 1865, she had another letter written for her, which was accompanied by documents requested by the army. In the letter, Lyddia declared, "I here with enclose to you the evidence required in the case of my son," and she included witnessed, signed, and certified statements about her son's age and the provost marshal's certificate of his enlistment. She also explained, "This boy was the only child I had left out of four the other three being in the army." Lyddia appeared to have a better understanding of recruiting rules than most African-American family members. She stated, "one who takes one as such are liable to forfeit what money they may advance." Thus, she felt she would not have to return the money advanced her son. Nevertheless, she still wanted him discharged, declaring, "I hope the government will leave me one son to do for me out of the four." She ended her second letter saying she could not get any aid or financial support from soldiers' relief organizations. According to Lyddia, the relief committee denied her petition because her fourth son was too young to enlist.

There were a number of inconsistencies in Lyddia's documentation, which made it difficult to understand her intentions. First, on the initial letter she listed her son's birthday as March 25, 1850, while she certified his birthday as August 28, 1851 on one of the documents that accompanied the second letter. Whichever birthdate was the correct one, Joseph was still underage, but the inconsistency in not listing his correct date probably did not help Lyddia's credibility. Second, she admitted to letting him enlist, stating, "I was satisfied he should go as a drummer boy <u>one year volunteer</u>." It appears she let her son join the army and probably accepted the $400, but became uneasy when he was added to regular duty or when she suddenly realized she could not support herself with all four sons in the army. Her financial situation worsened when she could not get relief for her fourth son because he was too young to join. Petitioning for his discharge, she explained, "I am a Widow and the said minor my son Joseph Steward Bartley is my last son left me and taken from me and put into the army upon whom I looked to help to support me in my declining years making four of my sons now in the service. I ask his discharge on this declaration. . . ." John J. Keefe transcribed both of her letters and one of her certification statements. The army responded to Lyddia's second letter on April 28, 1864, stating, "The evidence you furnished does not meet the requirements" and "until they [the terms] are fully complied with and in due form, no further action will be taken in this case." It appears Lyddia never provided the proper documentation because Joseph served until his one-year term of service was complete on March 21, 1866. He was discharged in Brazos Santiago, Texas, where his regiment was stationed at the time.[19]

In the case of the Sands family, the illicit activities involving the enlistment of their underage son were much more obvious. Hilton Sands, of New Haven, Connecticut, had a letter written on his behalf on March 18, 1865. He wanted his son, John, discharged because his estranged wife wrongfully allowed their son to enlist. John was an eighteen-year-old teamster when he enlisted on February 18, 1865, and was assigned to Company E, 11th United States Colored Heavy Artillery. Hilton presented his version of the complicated story: "That John Sands now held in the military Service at the Conscript Camp Port and military Port at New Haven is my son—that he was born on the 12th day of August 1850 and therefore that he was fourteen years old on the 12th day of August 1864." John continued, "And that he was illegally enlisted, as I am informed somewhere in the State of Rhode Island on the day of February 1865. He has no guardian but me and I have never given any permission to his enlistment. I am fifty-five years old and am a man of color—have been by occupation a drayman in this town for seven years prior to the 8th day of December 1864 when I hired out in the town of Granly some fifty miles distant." John blamed his philandering wife for the problem, stating "and that during my absence my wife and the mother after said John Sands proceeded his enlistment and upon the bounty money was and has been living in adultery with one Joseph Freeman of this city."[20]

To support his petition, Hilton had his letter notarized by his attorney, Joseph Sheridan, who was also the person who transcribed the letter for him. In addition, Hilton included a separate letter of support from Sheridan, who referred to Sands as "a worthy man of color of this town" and his wife as "a miserable strumpet for a wife." Also included in his petition was a statement from the Provost Marshal's Office explaining that Caroline Sands, Hilton's wife, had given written consent for their son to enlist and certified he was eighteen at the time of enlistment. Hilton and Caroline had six children together and John was the second oldest son. His brother, Wallace, was six years older and already serving in Company C, 29th Connecticut Infantry. Wallace enlisted on December 4, 1863 as a twenty-two-year-old farmer. Army officials must have ultimately denied Hilton's request because his son served until his regiment was discharged in New Orleans on October 2, 1865. Once John began to receive an invalid pension in 1900, he took up where his mother left off and continued to falsify his age. Even his older brother, Wallace, did his part to help with the ruse by supplying a notarized affidavit stating John was born in 1841. Eventually, the government, needing to determine John's eligibility for an age-based increase in his pension, confirmed his rightful age using the 1860 census. The census listed the Sands family, which resided at the time in New Haven, Connecticut, and confirmed that in July 1860 he was only ten years old. Thus, he was born in 1849. This occurred in 1918, just four years before his death on September 5, 1922, at the age of seventy-three.[21] The Bartley and Sands letters demonstrate that it was sometimes a family's own unscrupulous behavior and deceitfulness, specifically parents using their sons for financial gain, that led to a family's angst, and not necessarily the army's discriminatory practices.

8   The Conclusion of the War

B y 1865 the Union could see victory in sight. But there was additional fight-ing still to be done and battles won before final victory in the war was achieved. Major Union victories in the latter months of 1864 led to the sense of optimism in the North. In September, Atlanta fell; in November, Lincoln was elected to a second term as president; and from mid-November to the end of December, General William T. Sherman led his forces on their famous "March to the Sea," cutting through Georgia and crushing the South's desire or ability to continue the war. Simultaneously, Union armies in the Virginia theater, led by General Ulysses S. Grant, continued to put pressure on General Robert E. Lee and the Army of Northern Virginia. Grant pursued the Confederates throughout the state. Still, the Confederates were not willing to end the war just yet. They scrambled to keep their morale up and their armies together and supplied with men and resources. Ironically, the Confederacy, desperate for more fighting men, contemplated using its slaves as soldiers and in the last weeks of the war eventu-ally organized one company, but it would be too little and too late.[1]

Even with victory in sight, African Americans continued to volunteer to join the Union army in 1865. In addition, because the draft was still enforced, the Union continued to form new black regiments. The majority of these regiments were organized in the South as more freedmen became available to enlist once Union armies took control of Confederate territory. These soldiers were enlisted for one-year terms, not three, because Union officials felt confident the war was drawing to an end. Some of these new recruits were motivated to serve because they wanted an opportunity to participate in the war and prove their worthiness for full citizenship before the fighting was over and the opportunity was gone. The bounty money paid to volunteers probably motivated others. Whatever the soldiers' reasons to enlist, twenty-five new regiments were completed in 1865, though only one in the North. And many of these troops, alongside veteran black regiments, participated in the major battles leading to the eventual capitulation of Confederate forces throughout the South.

In spite of the hardships black troops and their families experienced in 1863 and 1864 and would endure in 1865, Northern blacks continued to support the Union war effort. And similar to their white counterparts, the more battles they participated in, the more committed black troops became to finish the job and ensure their fallen comrades had not died in vain.[2] By the start of 1865, almost two full years since the first northern black regiment was formed, the hardships for the families, were widely known in the northern black communities through word-of-mouth and through the publication of letters from black troops in black newspapers and journals. Northern blacks knew joining the army could lead to financial hardship and anxiety about the well being of their soldiers. Yet, by enlisting and continuing to serve, northern blacks remained committed to helping the Union defeat the Confederacy and end slavery in the South, and thereby prove they fully deserved full citizenship in the United States. And with Union victory in sight, they hoped the fruits of their labor and sacrifices were also close at hand.

The Final Push

By the end of 1864, Confederate forces protecting Richmond, the Confederate capital, were badly outnumbered, starving, and almost completely surrounded by Union forces led by General Grant. At the beginning of 1865, these same Confederate forces found themselves in the same predicament. On March 9, 1864, Grant was promoted to the rank of lieutenant general, with the title of general in chief of all Union forces, and went east to confront General Lee directly. Not initially a believer in the ability of black troops, Grant still felt they could be of use in his campaign. Determined to crush rebel armies and win the war before the 1864 presidential elections, Grant refused to suspend his campaign against Lee even after horrendous and unprecedented Union casualties. However, the elections came and went, and Lee remained a formidable foe even with fewer men and resources than Grant. He continued to hold the Union army at bay, though at the cost of enormous Confederate casualties, men whom the Confederacy could not replace easily, unlike Grant and the Union army whose manpower needs could be satisfied. By the beginning of the new year, Lee found his army stretched to its limits along a line of men and trenches several miles in length protecting Petersburg, which was under siege by the Union. It was a stalemate, but it would not last, especially since the rebel army was short on food, supplies, and men. Winter set in and the armies went into winter quarters with everyone, Yankees and Confederates, knowing that the spring of 1865 would probably bring the end to the war.[3]

By the end of 1864, Grant saw black troops tested and he felt they sufficiently proved themselves in battle. He had enough confidence in them to form the entirely black 25th Corps on December 3, 1864, equaling over 13,000 men, made up of thirty-two infantry regiments, one cavalry regiment, and artillery with fifty-six guns. Assigned to the Army of the James by Grant, the 25th Corps was commanded by Major General Godfrey Wetzel, an 1855 West Point graduate who previously had been Benjamin Butler's chief engineer. The Corps's divisional commanders were Brigadier Generals Augustus V. Kautz, William G. Birney and Halbert E. Paine, all of whom were veteran commanders and supporters of black troops. Thus, well organized and well led, black troops would play a vital role as the Army of the James and the Army of the Potomac worked in tandem while Grant kept the pressure on Lee's army, which remained a formidable fighting force almost to the very end.[4]

In the warmer climate of North Carolina, Union forces continued their advances on Confederate positions early into the new year. On January 15, 1865, Major General Alfred Terry led 8,900 black and white troops in an attack on Fort Fisher. It was the largest and most important of three forts protecting Wilmington, North Carolina, the South's only remaining Atlantic seaport and the Confederacy's last trading port for blockade runners to bring in guns, ammunition, and other vital supplies from foreign countries. And only seven days after taking the fort, Wilmington itself fell to Terry's troops. Members of the 27th USCT were some of the first Union troops to enter the city.[5]

Further south, black troops played key roles in the fall of Charleston. There, the 54th and 55th Massachusetts Infantries, along with seven USCTs, were a part of the forces engaged in skirmishes against the Confederate forces protecting Charleston. Even under enemy artillery fire, Union forces continued to advance toward the city. Finally, on February 18, 1865, rebel forces, led by P. G. T. Beauregard, abandoned Charleston. The next day, Federal troops, led by the 21st USCT, an African-American regiment formed in South Carolina and composed of former slaves, marched into the burning city and worked quickly to extinguish the fires and bring order. Thus, black troops helped to capture the city in whose harbor the first shots of the war were fired upon Fort Sumter four years prior.[6]

On February 21, 1865, the 55th Massachusetts Infantry marched into the city, and six days later, the 54th Massachusetts Infantry arrived. Taking the city also had added significance for the 54th. It was the ultimate object in the Federal campaign that led to the 54th's charge on Fort Warner, on Morris Island just outside of Charleston Harbor, and now it was as if the regiment finally completed an important assignment that began with that brave charge and the death of Colonel Shaw and their comrades. Because of this history and sacrifice, the members of the regiment were happy to acknowledge the city was taken. Sergeant J. H. W. N. Collins of Company H wrote in a March 19, 1865 letter to the *Christian Recorder*: "I must say something about our regiment to let our friends know that we are on hand. . . . Although we were not allowed to remain in the city of Charleston, yet we claim the largest share in capturing it."[7] After entering the devastated city with his regiment, George E. Stephens recalled his thoughts from when the 54th sat outside the city during the fall 1864 siege: "The city I would burn to ashes. Not one stone of its buildings would I leave upon another." He must have felt some sense of great satisfaction with what he was witnessing that day.[8] The fighting in the war continued, but Confederate forces were in retreat on all fronts.

Jubilee: Final Victory at Last

When spring came in 1865, Lee found himself in a precarious position with few options. His army of 55,000 was still holding its line around Petersburg, but was almost totally surrounded by Grant's two armies totaling 120,000 men. Adding to Lee's problems, his army was disintegrating in front of him as desertions increased drastically. Some of his men simply gave up because they were too demoralized, hungry, and exhausted to fight any further. Others hustled home in response to letters of desperation, ironically, from southern mothers, wives, and other family members who needed *their* men back home to provide for their families. Lee saw no option but to abandon his position around Petersburg. The next day, Richmond fell to Union forces, and a few days later, on April 9, to avoid the annihilation of what remained of his army, Lee surrendered to Grant at Appomattox, Virginia. Following Lee's action, General Johnston surrendered his army to General Sherman on April 26 at the Bennett House in North Carolina. On May 4, Confederate forces in Alabama, Mississippi, and eastern Louisiana agreed to end hostilities. The Confederacy's last military department, the Trans-Mississippi, was terminated on June 2.[9]

The first African-American regiment formed in the North, the 54th Massachusetts Infantry, fired its last shots of the war on April 18, 1865, at Boykin's Mill. In this action, Union forces sustained few casualties as they slaughtered the Confederate forces that tried to stand their ground. The regiment's last battle casualties were "one officer killed, one enlisted man killed, one mortally wounded, and twelve wounded: a total of fifteen." One of the wounded was Private Clayton

Johnson, of Company B, the same soldier who, while refusing to follow orders, told an officer in June 1864 that he "was not going to be treated like a dog for seven dollars a month." He was wounded at Fort Wagner by an artillery shell and at Olustee when a tree hit by enemy fire fell on his head. Now, in the 54th's last action, he was a casualty again when the little finger on his right hand was nipped off by a Minié ball. One of the first recruits of the 54th, Clayton was a farmer and only eighteen years old when he enlisted as a volunteer on March 9, 1863. Two years and several battles and skirmishes later, he was a battle-hardened and tested veteran who displayed the scars of the 54th's illustrious history.[10]

Upon reaching Georgetown, the men of the 54th were satisfied by the accomplishments of their last expedition, which included the freeing of thousands of slaves the regiment encountered along the way. In an April 20, 1865 letter to the *Christian Recorder*, Private Benjamin M. Bond, of Company B, proudly explained, "We are all much gratified to inform the public that we have been instrumental in liberating about six thousand slaves, who, in spite of the President's [Emancipation] Proclamation, might have been kept in bondage for many years to come." Now with the war drawing to a close, northern black soldiers began thinking of returning home. In an April 30, 1865 letter, also to the *Christian Recorder*, Sergeant J. H. W. N. Collins, of Company H, disclosed the sentiments of the regiment when he stated, "We are now encamped at Georgetown [South Carolina], and hope we will soon be home with our friends and relatives."[11]

When the war began, African-American volunteers were initially turned away, with the reminder that "this was a white man's war," but by the war's end, 10 percent of the Union forces were made up of black men. When black soldiers were eventually permitted to participate in the war effort, they were assigned brutally rugged and inglorious duties, mostly digging ditches, clearing terrain, and re-interring of the dead, all because the Union had little faith in their ability to fight. However, by the end of the war, they had participated in major campaigns and significant battles throughout the South; they proved themselves to be brave and effective soldiers.[12] All the while, their families struggled at home with financial difficulties and the desire to know how their soldier was doing. Yet African Americans continued to support their soldiers and the Union war effort through relief services, nursing, and more importantly, by simply surviving during difficult times as their men and breadwinners were away. With the end of the war, family members expected to have their soldiers home. Moreover, the troops themselves expected to be home; however, for most black troops, these expectations would have to remain on hold because the men would not arrive home from the war for months to come.

9

After the War

A Different Kind of Battle

With General Robert E. Lee's surrender on April 9, 1865, the Civil War, after four years of fighting and the loss of over 620,000 Union and Confederate lives, was finally over. And black soldiers contributed greatly to the Union victory. From their first major battles in 1863 where they proved their ability as soldiers—Port Hudson, Milliken's Bend, and Fort Wagner—to being some of the first soldiers to enter the Confederate capital, Richmond, on April 3, 1865, to their presence at Lee's surrender at Appomattox Court House, they served with distinction and bravery, and helped the Union win the war.

Nonetheless, even with victory in hand, northern black troops and their families would have to wait longer than they imagined for their return home. Black soldiers did not anticipate the sudden shift in the Union's military plans and needs, which dashed their hopes of a speedy demobilization. While most white regiments were disbanded and their members mustered out and allowed to return home, African-American regiments remained intact because their members had not completed their three years of service. Black troops were forced to play a major role in the Union's reconstruction plans for the South, while the Union army changed from an army of war to an army of occupation. And while all the families of Union troops provided support and made sacrifices for the duration of the war, black families would have to carry on long after the war ended. White troops returned home to their families and public fanfare, while black troops worked to keep the peace in the defeated, resentful, and hostile South. In addition, black troops helped to facilitate the transition from slavery to freedom for the former slaves and were then sent even farther afield—south to Texas—to keep watch and shadow French military and political activity in Mexico.

The continued use of black regiments in the Union army meant that the families of black soldiers had to continue writing letters to Union officials to find out about the well-being of their loved ones and to obtain relief for their families. Similar to the beginning of black military participation in 1863, families wrote about their financial struggles, their lack of information about the whereabouts of their soldiers, and their need to get official notice about the condition and health of their men. What was *different* after April 1865 was the goal of a Union victory no longer made sacrifices bearable for Union families. So, they increasingly requested the discharge of their soldiers and their immediate return home.

More Letters: Desperate for Information Even After the War's End

The cessation of the shooting meant the likelihood of soldiers becoming casualties was greatly reduced. Nevertheless, northern black families continued to send letters trying to verify the status of soldiers who had participated in major campaigns, battles, and skirmishes that occurred, weeks, months, and, in some cases, years before April 1865. With the war now over, they hoped to hear from, or obtain information about, their soldiers. Maybe the soldiers, now less preoccupied with fighting battles, would have time to write home. Or maybe their commanding officers would now have time to respond to letters from families and verify the status of the soldiers. This was probably what Anna Wright, of Philadelphia, hoped when she put her mark on a letter dated April 10, 1865, one day after Lee's surrender, inquiring to Stanton about the status of her husband, Archibald, who was a member of the 54th Massachusetts Infantry. She had already heard he might be dead, but five months later she had still not received verification.[1] Archibald was a barber and already thirty-eight years old when he enlisted in the army as a substitute on August 29, 1863. He was promoted to Corporal on September 9, 1863. It was not clear whether her initial letter was ever answered, but Anna eventually found out that Archibald had died on September 29, 1864, in the battle of New Market Heights, just eight miles southeast of Richmond.[2]

Rebecca Beverly of Philadelphia hoped she would finally have her questions answered when she put her mark on a letter dated May 3, 1865, in which she inquired about the condition of her son, Richard Beverly. Maybe she would finally have her questions answered. A laborer, Richard was mustered into service in February 1864 at the age of eighteen and was a member of Company B, 32nd United States Colored Troops. Rebecca stated, "I had a letter from him dated June 21, 1864, Morris Island, S.C. and have not heard from him since and am anxious to hear respecting him."[3] Similarly, the father of Private William Lewis had a letter written for him, dated May 4, 1865, asking about the whereabouts and health of his son, William, who was a member of Company B, 8th USCT. According to his father, who was from Havana, New York, William was a twenty-four-year-old farmer when he enlisted in the army on July 25, 1863. He was at the Battle of Olustee on February 20, 1864, but had not been heard from since.[4] Both

Rebecca Beverly and William Lewis's father were requesting any information the Adjutant General could provide them about their sons. Neither had heard from them for a long time and probably hoped that with the war over they might have a better chance of finding out the whereabouts and condition of their sons. The news was good for Rebecca; Richard Beverly was still alive and was discharged with his regiment in August 22, 1865 at Hilton Head, South Carolina.[5] Unfortunately for Lewis's father, the news was sorrowful. After the Battle of Olustee, Lewis was first listed as missing-in-action and then re-categorized as killed-in-action. By April 1864, the army realized he was actually taken prisoner at the battle and was imprisoned at Andersonville, the Confederate prisoner-of-war camp. He died there on November 19, 1864. Thus, Lewis's father sought information about his son still not knowing he had been dead for six months. Ironically, the army did not know either.[6]

Likewise, May Bullett and Mary Graham, both of Philadelphia, had not heard from their soldiers for a long time. Bullett had a letter written for her dated May 10, 1865, inquiring about her husband as well as her brother. Her husband enlisted on January 21, 1864 as a twenty-eight-year-old painter and her brother, a laborer, enlisted eight days later. She explained, "My husband Henry Bullett Co E 25th Regt is mising for a long time I am in great trouble about him I am told you can give some information give it to me if in your power and also my brother Richard Quin Co F. 25th Regt who has not been heard from going two years having written numerous letters & no answer."[7] Mary Graham had a letter written May 29th to Secretary of War Stanton requesting information about her husband, James Graham, of Company A, 22nd USCT. James joined the army on July 25, 1863, at the age of thirty-three as a private and was eventually promoted to corporal. Mary revealed, "Since last Dec I much troubled about him would your honor be so kind as to give me some information about him if it be in your power and you will confer a very great favor on your humble servant."[8] At the time of her letter, May Bullett did not know her husband had died of dysentery and acute diarrhea the previous fall, on September 7, in the hospital at Fort Pickens, Florida. He and his regiment were "compelled" to drink the very bad water because it was their only option in a very unhealthy part of the state. The army commented, he was "a good and faithful soldier."[9] But there was some good news for her. Her brother, Richard, returned home and mustered out with his regiment on December 6, 1865. The news for Mary Graham was better because her husband received an early discharge on May 29, 1865 from the hospital at Fort Monroe, Virginia, and returned home, almost five months ahead of his regiment, which was not mustered out of service until October 16, 1865.[10] According to his pension records,

James was at a hospital at Fort Monroe recovering from injuries he sustained. He was losing both his sight and hearing and suffered from a "nervous affliction of the head" after an artillery shell exploded near him while performing his duties with his regiment in the trenches outside of Petersburg, Virginia. James received his pension until his death on May 22, 1899 in Sharon Hill, Pennsylvania. The very next month, June 8, 1899, his second wife, Annie, commenced receiving a widow's pension of $8 a month.[11]

Rebecca Berry of Philadelphia put her mark on a letter dated June 8, 1865, inquiring about her son, Charles H. Blake, a corporal in Company G, 22nd USCT, and her nephew, Jeremiah Cummings of Company A, 32nd USCT. Neither of them had been heard from in months and Jeremiah was believed to be gravely ill in a South Carolina hospital. Charles enlisted on December 30, 1863 at the age of twenty-five. He was a waiter before the war and regularly provided for his mother since he was her sole means of support. She had been married twice, first to Charles's father, but both husbands died. At the time of her letter, Charles had been reported sick on April 1, 1865, but since then his whereabouts were unknown by the Union army. Even worse for Rebecca was the news about Jeremiah, who was thirty years old and a laborer when he enlisted in the army on February 12, 1864. When her letter was written, Jeremiah had already been dead for over six months. He died of chronic diarrhea in the general hospital in Beaufort, South Carolina on November 20, 1864. After the war, Rebecca, with the help of a claim agent, applied to receive her son's back pay and pension. Her first application was filed on May 15, 1865, but after several years of going back and forth with the government and providing additional information, Rebecca died on December 5, 1868, having not received a cent. Pension officials continued to ask for additional "evidence" to verify the date and cause of Charles's death, in spite of the submission by her claim agents of affidavits from three former soldiers from Charles's regiment who stated they were aware he was sick and had died. According to the soldiers, Charles became ill on April 1, 1865 and was taken to Points of Rocks Hospital in Maryland, where he died of chronic diarrhea on April 4.[12]

Although the application was not rejected outright, government officials handling the case continued, for reasons that are unclear, to ask for additional evidence verifying Charles's death. On January 14, 1869, Rebecca's daughter and Charles's sister, Ellen Blake, had a letter written on her behalf requesting the unpaid funds for herself, the sole surviving child of Rebecca Berry. On January 19, 1869, the government again requested evidence as to the death of Charles, but on February 14, after pension officials decided to review the application and again decided to accept the original affidavits, the application was approved. In posterity, Rebecca, or her estate, was approved to receive $8 a month, commencing on the accepted date of Charles's death, April 4, 1865, with payments probably ending December 5, 1868, the date of Rebecca's death. In the end, the family received very little compensation for Charles's death in the line of duty and for Rebecca's loss of a son and the financial suffering that followed.[13] As with Rebecca Beverly, the Lewises, Mary Bullett, Mary Graham, and Rebecca Berry, some families would eventually receive good news about their soldiers, but for others, the weeks, months, or years of worry eventually ended with the devastating confirmation that their loved one was dead.

Occupation Duty in the South

With the end of the war came a rapid demobilization of the huge Union army. All the soldiers, black and white, were anxious to return home and the northern public demanded that they be allowed to do so immediately. At the same time, it cost a lot of money to keep the men in uniform and now, with the war over, it was hard to justify the enormous expense. Yet the government still needed a force to both maintain the peace in the South and serve as a security force as Reconstruction was implemented. These troops would guard against guerrilla attacks from the defeated but angry rebels and protect the newly freed men and women. The decision about what regiments would provide the troops for occupation duty was logical. The army would muster out most of the white troops because the majority of them had served longer, and use all of the black troops and the remaining white troops for occupation duty. When the war ended, the white troops had completed, or were close to completing, their three-year terms of duty. Because blacks were not given the opportunity to join the war effort until 1863, they had not completed their three years of service. In addition, using the black troops for occupation duty was consistent with Union policy during the war, which was to replace white soldiers, leaving black soldiers to perform duties that were considered to be undesirable, such as guard duty and police duty throughout the South.[14] Indeed, the Union had already been practicing this exact policy as it related to occupation duty when more and more Confederate land came under Union control in the final year of the war. In cities such as Charleston, South Carolina, which finally fell to Union forces on February 18, 1865, black troops were left behind to maintain the peace while white regiments moved on to continue to do battle with the Confederate armies.[15]

Thus, white troops headed home while black troops prepared for or continued with occupation duty. Ending their enlistments in fanfare and glory, thousands of white troops participated in a two-day parade up Pennsylvania Avenue in Washington, D.C., on May 25 and 26 (see Figure 7). Many of the participants in the Grand Review, as it was called, were regiments from the Army of the Potomac, equaling 80,000 troops, and black troops had fought alongside them in many battles. The other participants were those troops who accompanied Sherman to the sea, the Army of the Tennessee and the Army of Georgia, totaling 65,000 troops. His armies did not have African-American troops in their ranks, and besides, Sherman was not interested in having black troops parade with his men. Hence, because neither of these armies contained black troops, only a few contraband laborer squads that had built roads for Sherman's army were allowed to march down Pennsylvania Avenue. Approximately 870,000 white soldiers were allowed to muster out of service and return home, leaving behind 227,000 men, of whom 83,000 were black. Almost every black regiment remained in the South and were organized into 120 infantry regiments, 12 regiments of heavy artillery, 10 batteries of light artillery, and 7 regiments of cavalry, along with approximately 7,000 white officers. With this deployment, Union forces went from 11 percent black in the spring of 1865, to 36 percent black by the fall. Black troops accounted therefore for over a third of remaining Union forces.[16]

Blacks troops did not like the decision to keep them in uniform as soldiers. They felt that with the war over they had performed their duties and should have been allowed to return home and be with their families. It did not matter that occupation duty for most of them was not as dangerous and life threatening as battle. Still, the overwhelming majority of black soldiers followed orders and continued to do their duty as soldiers. However, they made their feelings known about occupation duty. Northern black troops wrote letters to black newspapers and journals in the North, describing where they were stationed, what they experienced, and what they saw developing.[17]

Black troops had to interact with a defeated group of people, the former Confederates, who viewed them with disgust and hate and resented the very existence of black soldiers. Many former Confederates were unprepared to accept the reality of the new order. They resented Union soldiers of any kind, but black troops were a visual reminder to the former rebels that the South lost the war, their independence, and their wealth, and slavery ended and southern society was changed forever.[18] Private William B. Johnson, a member of Company A, 3rd USCT, explained in a June 22, 1865 letter to a major black newspaper published in Philadelphia, the *Christian Recorder*, that local whites gave black troops a hostile reception when they arrived in Jacksonville, Florida. Johnson disclosed, "The platforms of the cars were immediately crowded with white and

Figure 7. The Grand Review of the Army was a two-day parade for the victorious Union troops. It took place on May 25–26, 1865, but no black regiments were in attendance. The black troops remained in the South to perform occupation duty. (*The Soldier in Our Civil War: A Pictorial History of the Conflict, 1861–1865,* Vol. II, 378–79)

colored persons all eager to catch a glimpse of the 'black soldiers.' Some deep-dyed citizen made the remark that all niggers should be in—(a place of not very moderate temperature)."[19] Describing the racial atmosphere in Louisiana, Private William P. Green of the 11th USCHA (formerly known as the 14th Rhode Island Colored Heavy Artillery) wrote, "The animosity existing between the United States colored troops and the conquered Southerners is so great that they cannot ever expect to live in peace together." At the time, the 11th USCHA was engaged in occupation duty in New Orleans. William was a twenty-year-old printer when he enlisted on October 8, 1863, in the first year of northern black participation in the war as soldiers. Almost exactly two years later, he must have been happy to leave the volatile environment he was serving in when the regiment mustered out on October 2, 1865, in New Orleans.[20]

While northern black troops struggled to keep the peace in the South and protect the lives and liberty of former slaves, their families continued to struggle

under desperate conditions. Inflation and the cost of living in the North continued to rise, while the army, as it had since the war's beginning, failed to pay its
soldiers on time. Most soldiers, white and black, at any given moment had not
been paid for months.[21] Nothing was different once the war ended except it was
more inexcusable because regiments were no longer on the move as they had
been during the war. However, while the soldiers at least had food, clothing, and
shelter, their families were without sufficient funds and they continued to struggle to meet their basic needs for survival. And as they did during the war, they
sent letters, or letters were sent on their behalf, to Union officials requesting help.
John Wilson was a musician when he enlisted in the army on October 23, 1863 at
the age of twenty-five. For some reason afterwards, his wife had problems getting
family relief from the Michigan authorities, which made it very difficult for her
to provide for her family. She wrote to Stanton asking about her husband's pay, a
furlough for her husband, or transportation so she could travel to see him. In the
letter dated May 27, 1865, she wrote, "Sir I have the privilege of writing to you asking a favour of you if it is in your power to grant that is to give my husband John
Wesley Wilsom a furlough. My husband belongs to the 102d U.S. Colored regiment and is the leader of the regiment band now Staation at Beaufort S.C." She
continued, "or will you please to give me Transportation to Beaufort S.C. if I had
money I would not ask you for a Pass. John Wesley Wilson has not received any
pay from the government for nine mounths and it leaves me compleatly dititute
of means for my support."[22] Mrs. Wilson made clear her disgust with her state for
not providing what she felt was proper support for black families whose men had
gone off to fight. She stated, "Michigan has no respect for her colored Soldiers or
their families. My Husband has benn in the army one year and half and I am very
anxous to see him and by giving me transportation to Beaufort S.C. you would
confer agreat favour on your well wisher."[23] John was not discharged from the
service until October 3, 1865, four days after his regiment was demobilized. His
discharge was delayed because he had been in the hospital since August 1865.[24]
Nonetheless, he was lucky to have survived long enough to be discharged because the army had a habit of losing track of soldiers, black and white, who had
to spend long periods of time in army hospitals recovering from battle wounds
or sickness. Often, these men remained in the hospital, and sometimes died, long
after their regiment was mustered out of service and returned home.[25]

African-American troops were there to implement and uphold the government's post-war policies, including helping former slaves adjust to life as free
men and women. Black troops were the representatives of the Union. This was
a difficult task because the former rebels created a very hostile environment.

African-American soldiers still worked closely with the Freedmen's Bureau, which was at the center of the North's reconstruction program. Congress established the Freedmen's Bureau (formally called the Bureau of Refugees, Freedmen, and Abandoned Lands) on March 13, 1865, less than a month before the war ended. The Bureau attempted to secure for blacks equal access to improving their lives and providing for themselves, specifically as paid laborers. The Bureau's duties included dispensing rations—clothing, food, and fuel—to white and black refugees, or anyone in a distressed state and in need of relief in the South. There was a close arrangement between the black regiments and the Freedmen's Bureau because the Bureau operated under the War Department and many USCT officers served as agents for the Bureau. The former slaves logically viewed the USCT as the government representatives who protected their well being.[26]

Consequently, black troops became targets for the rage of the former rebels. Southern whites regularly cursed and insulted black troops but their most common and effective weapon was to tarnish the reputation of the troops with false accusations. Black soldiers were accused of malicious acts such as plundering white homes and property and inciting trouble among freedmen. And southern whites also reverted to violence to drive out black troops or to intimidate them and the people they protected. Officers were also victims of scorn and violence. On occasion, the violence resulted in the death of an officer at the hands of former rebels. Such violence continued as black troops and their officers became fair game for former rebels and terrorists. Whites instigated disputes and provoked black troops into brawls against hostile whites.[27]

Southern whites were not the only people who abused black soldiers during occupation duty. Also unsettling to blacks was the harassment they received at the hands of their fellow Union soldiers in the white regiments also completing their terms of enlistment by performing occupation duty. No longer under enemy fire and in the trenches together, idle time and unappealing occupation duty gave white Union soldiers the opportunity to forget whatever respect they might have acquired toward their black comrades or bonds they might have formed with them. Black soldiers became the target for their anger and frustration for not being able to return home themselves.[28]

Occupation duty for black troops also meant laboring in very remote and unhealthy places where food supplies were limited and where they were assigned terrible work details. The troops were camped in towns and in the countryside with bad living conditions, poor medical care, and limited supplies. Many soldiers came down with illnesses because of the unhealthy conditions. Private Johnson, a member of Company A, 3rd USCT, formed in Philadelphia in August

1863, explained in a July 27, 1865 letter to the *Christian Recorder* that "Sickness has made a fearful havoc in this regiment. I wrote to you some time ago that we were ordered to Tallahassee, the capital of the State of Florida. While there the men suffered—fevers raged throughout the camp, and out of 800 men there were not 300 fit for active service."[29] Receiving late and limited supplies made it even more difficult for the soldiers to remain fit and healthy because many Confederates scattered in all directions with all their food and livestock when learning Union forces were arriving in an area. Chaplain George W. LeVere of the 20th USCT, in an August 30, 1865 letter to the *Weekly Anglo-African*, described the situation. The 20th, formed in New York City in February 1864, was assigned to occupation duty in Milliken's Bend, Louisiana. According to LeVere, "We have been endeavoring to find out for which of our many sins we have been sent here to be punished. It is going on the third week since we landed here, and we have yet to get the first mouthful of fresh meat. The rebs, when they went to Texas, did not only drive their slaves with them, but everything else that could be driven."[30] Along with executing orders from Freedmen's Bureau agents, occupying forts, and keeping the general peace, black troops were assigned duties such as the re-interment of the dead from major battles in the region. All these factors and duties, performed while enduring physical and verbal harassment from whites, made occupation a difficult assignment for black troops. In addition, their pay rarely reached them on time, making it even harder for the troops to help their struggling families. All of these hardships would only worsen when black troops were reassigned even farther south to Texas.

Post-War Demands for Discharges

Occupation duty continued for northern black regiments, while one white northern regiment after the other was mustered out of the army and returning home. For white families, the letter writing stopped or decreased drastically because most white soldiers who survived the war were home with their families. On the other hand, black families continued to write; while the war was over, they felt they were being unfairly treated because their men were still on duty. With the Union preserved and slavery ended, what family members wanted was simply for their soldiers to be discharged. While some families had their desperate pleas answered favorably, others received further disappointments.

Martha Douglass, of Washington, D.C., desired the discharge of her husband so she sent a letter to the War Department dated July 6, 1865. Martha was desperate for her husband to return home because she found it very difficult to provide for the family in his absence. She explained in detail her situation: "Sirs as I am in distress I know no way but to make it known to the war department and my distress is this My husband was taken to the war when my Baby was six weeks old and I have two children besides and no support and it seems impossible to get along withe my children and pay rent." She continued, "I have tried to get on without troubling you but I cant help it so I thought I would appeal to you for my husband discharge so I can have his assistance my husband had been very sick when he was drafted so had nothing to leave me and bing sick myself that now I am quite a strait."[31] Martha's husband, Lewis Douglass, was a member of Company H, 43rd USCT. He was a thirty-six-year-old laborer when he was drafted into the army on February 28, 1865. He must have been an effective leader because by May 1 he was appointed a corporal and by July 19 he was promoted to sergeant.[32] The regiment was sent to Texas on May 30, 1865 and was stationed there when Martha's letter was mailed. The army denied her request. The July 15, 1865 letter from the army stated, "the reasons presented are not sufficient to justify favorable action on your request."[33] Martha, like so many other black families after the war, had to continue to struggle to support herself and her family for three more months because she would not see her husband again until after he was mustered out with his regiment on October 20, 1865 in Brownsville, Texas, and then discharged from service in Philadelphia on November 20, 1865.

Isleanor Burke was just as desperate and in a similarly precarious financial situation. In her letter, dated June 17, 1865, she pleaded to Stanton to discharge her husband, David M. Burke, so he could return home and provide for his family. David did not belong to a regiment formed in the North, but he and his family resided in the North, in Washington, D.C. He was a twenty-five-year-old laborer when he was drafted into the army on February 21, 1864.[34] Isleanor explained the family's distress and homelessness when she made her request: "I most respectfully asks you to discharge my husband from the Army—I would not be so hasten but I am out of a home and expecting to be sick in a few days, and one of my children am sick. I have no one to depend on. I am living from one friend to the other. It would be a great favor indeed, as I am in great need."[35] Isleanor also pointed out her husband was sickly, suffering from scrofula, which was another reason he should be discharged.[36] The Assistant Attorney General, C. W. Foster, responded to the request in an interoffice note on June 19, 1865. David, a member the 38th U.S.C.T., was currently a patient in the hospital at Fort Monroe and Foster agreed to discharge him "in view of the indigent and helpless condition of his family."[37] It appears the order was given on June 22nd for David to be released from duty but for some reason it did not take effect until August 2, when he was officially discharged from duty at Fort Monroe, Virginia, because of a disability. This meant he was able to avoid going to Texas with his regiment. Because it was a black regiment formed in the South, the 38th USCT did not muster out of service until as late as January 25, 1867.[38] Considering the equally desperate situations of both Martha Douglass and Isleanor Burke, it is unclear why Martha's plea was denied while Isleanor's was approved. It may have been because Douglass was still useful to the army as a soldier and Burke was not.

Rachel Batties of Philadelphia had three sons in the Union army and she needed one of them home immediately. All three sons were members of the 24th USCT, which at the time was stationed in Richmond, Virginia, performing occupation duties, distributing government supplies to needy inhabitants, and keeping order. In her letter, dated September 13, 1865, she explained she was straining to provide for herself and her family since her husband died. It is not clear from the letter whether he died while in Union service. She appealed to Stanton for help: "I would respectfully ask your kind attention to the following statement. I have three sons, Charles, John and Edward in the service of the US. In 24th Regt. U.S. Colored troops. My husband died about four weeks since leaving me with four small children depending on me. I have no means of supporting them and myself and children are on the brink of starvation."[39] Rachel wanted one of her three adult sons, Charles, discharged "in order that he may help support myself and his younger brother and sisters." All three brothers were laborers and enlisted in the army in 1865. Charles, the oldest, was twenty years old when he enlisted on February 2 and by February 23 he was already appointed a corporal. John was nineteen years old when he enlisted on February 25 and Edward was also nineteen years old when he enlisted on March 8.[40] The army responded to Rachel's letter on September 20, 1865, denying her request because "the regiment mentioned is under orders to be mustered out of service."[41] Indeed, just eighteen days after her letter was sent, the regiment was in fact mustered out in Richmond. And Charles and his brothers were mustered out with them, and now available again to find work and help their mother and other siblings. Thus, Rachel and her large family had a happy ending to the war. The family had sacrificed at the front, with the boys serving in the army, and at home as Rachel struggled to provide for herself and young children without her older boys or her husband.[42]

On other occasions, friends or close associates who knew the plight of a family wrote to military officials on behalf of family members. They requested the return home of the family's soldier so he could provide for them. In a letter dated July 11, 1865, R. W. Downey requested the discharge of Martin Clayburn. Clayburn was twenty-four years old and a molder when he enlisted in the army on

February 27, 1864.[43] Downey revealed, "Clayburn has been in the service about 16 months. He left at home a wife and two children, aged father and idiot sister all of whom were dependent on him for assistance and support." He stressed that Clayburn's services and bravery were no longer needed because the war was over. According to Downey, "He has served his country well and says so long as fighting was to be done he was anxious and willing to 'go in' but 'peace' has come and he wishes to be at home."[44] At the time, Clayburn was with Company G, 32nd USCT, performing garrison duty in South Carolina. The army responded July 19, 1865, requesting additional information and affidavits.[45] In the end, Clayburn was not discharged early and he did not return home until after the entire regiment was mustered out of service on August 22, 1865.

In a comparable situation, several friends wrote a letter on behalf of Mary Anderson, of Washington, D.C., requesting the return of her husband so he could provide for his destitute family. Robert was thirty-eight years old and a laborer when he was drafted into the army on November 24, 1864.[46] He was assigned to Company I, 6th USCT, and the regiment was in North Carolina performing occupation duty when the letter, dated July 19, 1865, was sent stating, "We the undersigned do certify that Mary Anderson wife of Robt Anderson who was drafted in the U S Service November 18th 1864 in this city has not received any of his pay and is in need of his help to take care of a family of 4 small children. She has done for them alone until now, but being in delicate health she finds it impossible to do for them."[47] As if Mary Anderson was not burdened enough, trying to care for her children with her husband away, the letter writers listed additional responsibilities that accentuated the need for her husband's discharge. They stated, "Besides this she has had to bear burial expenses of her aged Mother and Brother who died in her house within the last few months. You would be doing an act of Charity if you could possibly get his discharge for her."[48] To help support Mary's appeal to have her husband discharged, her friends included letters of affidavits. One was from J. H. Hilton, dated July 14, 1865, in which he referred to Mary as "a hard working and worthy woman" and corroborated that she and the children were on the verge of starvation. In another affidavit, dated July 15, 1865, Mrs. F. M. Hartwell stated she was "confident that she [Mary] needs the aid which she will ask of you."[49] Despite what appeared to be a desperate situation, the army denied the request, stating in a letter dated July 26, 1865 "that in view of his short time which Private Anderson has to serve it is not deemed expedient to take any action in the matter."[50] Robert had to stay in the army another two months performing occupation duty in Wilmington, North Carolina, until his regiment was mustered out on September 20, 1865 and he was able to return home to his family. He was not discharged early because his regiment was only a couple of months away from mustering out of service.

In the case of Ruben Mann, nine members of the community where his family lived wrote a letter to have him discharged and sent home. His family was experiencing severe financial difficulties and needed him home immediately. Spelled out by A. J. Fox and others, "We the undesigned of Steuben Co [county], New York do most respectfully petition you for the discharge from service of Sergt Ruben Mann 8th Regt of Co B U.S. Colored Troops. He is the only support of a large & very worthy family who will be obliged to depend on charity for maintenance unless he is discharged." The letter writers revealed Mann had been in the army since July 1963, when he was drafted—few northern black soldiers entered the service sooner—making him a relative old-timer in comparison to most black soldiers. Moreover, he participated in "several" battles.[51] They also stated "A brother [of Mann's] William Mann of Co L 14th Regt U.S.C.T. died in the service, another brother died at home since he entered the service the only remaining brother is unable to work or do anything to contribute to the support of the family." The letter writers stated the family's financial situation was worsened because Mann enlisted before blacks were considered to be eligible for bounties and for relief funds for their families. The community members explained, "He has never received any state or local bounty which has made his family in worse circumstances than those who have since enlisted & received large bounties."[52] The army responded in a June 9, 1865 letter, stating "no reasons are presented that will justify favorable action upon" the request.[53] Mann's family had to continue to endure the best way they could without him. He was forced to stay in the army until he was discharged with the rest of his regiment on November 10, 1865, in Brownsville, Texas.

Even if there was a possibility of a discharge, there was no guarantee the soldier would make it home to be with his family. For example, Lidy Johnson, of Blainsville, Pennsylvania, knew where her husband, John M. Johnson, was stationed, knew he was sick, and she hoped and expected he would be discharged from the army. Lidy was responding to a June 22, 1965 letter from John in which he told her of his precarious health, which he hoped would lead to his release. A laborer, John was twenty-five years old when he enlisted in the army on July 13, 1863 as a substitute. He was a member of Company A, 6th USCT. John appealed to Lidy to come and pick him up and take him home, but she needed help to get to him. She wrote a letter dated June 26, 1865, requesting funds to pay for transportation to pick up her husband. She was unable to pay for her transportation to Fort Monroe, where he was hospitalized. Lidy made her appeal to the army, explaining, "Your humble servant Mrs. Lidy A. Johnson, solicits you to get a transportation to go to her husband he is sick and not able to come home by himself and I am not able to pay my fare to home. and I want a transportation to fortress Monroe. and back. I will have to go for him as he is not able to come by himself. and if you can give me a transportation please let me know."[54] The army responded in a letter dated July 1, 1865, in which it denied Lidy's request, stating, "that there is no appropriation" to cover such a cost.[55] John remained in the hospital even after his regiment was mustered out of service in North Carolina on September 20, 1865. With Lidy and his family unable to get to him, John died in the hospital on October 30, 1865.[56] One can only imagine how Lidy Johnson felt, having sacrificed to help the Union win the war, only to have her husband die months after the war was over, while she was unable to get to him and provide what could have been lifesaving care.

Post-War Requests for Information

Even after the end of the war and during occupation duty, the most common request from northern black families was for information on the well being of their soldiers. Many family members wanted to know specifically whether their soldier was sick, wounded, or dead. Angeline Jacobs, of Philadelphia, had a letter written for her asking about the whereabouts and condition of her husband, Noah B. Jacobs, and her brother, John S. Driver. Noah was thirty-five years old when he enlisted on February 12, 1864, and John was nineteen years old when he enlisted on July 27, 1864; both men were laborers. However, Noah was born in Delaware, a northern slave state, and was one of the few northern black soldiers who was a slave and then given his freedom specifically to enlist. His former owner, William F. Jones of Georgetown, Delaware, signed an oath of loyalty to the United States and executed a "Deed of Manumission and Release" of all claims toward Noah, at which point Noah was allowed to enlist in the army on February 12, 1864.[57] This occurrence was more common in the border states, such as Missouri, Kentucky, and Maryland, where a large population of slaves were owned by masters who remained loyal to the Union. And most of those former slaves ended up serving in regiments formed in the South, with other former slaves, not regiments formed in the North. Jones was probably compensated by the government for freeing Noah so he could join the army. He may also have received the bounty Noah would have been entitled to in exchange for enlisting. Both Noah and John were in the 32nd USCT, Noah in Company A and John in Company I. In her letter, dated June 3, 1865, Angeline explained, "My husband has not been heard from since December, he was in a big fight at Hilton Head S.C. last Christmas I am afraid he is dead. . . . It would relieve my troubled mind if you would give me some tidings of them."[58] Angeline was later relieved because both of her soldiers were mustered out of service along with their regiment on August 22, 1865.

Likewise, Sally Davis, of Philadelphia, had a letter written for her, dated May 5, 1865, inquiring about two sons and a neighbor's husband. and addressed to Stanton. Her son, William E. Davis, enlisted in the army on April 11, 1864 at the age of thirty-three, while her other son (probably her stepson), Adam, who was also thirty-three, enlisted in the army on August 10, 1864. Adam enlisted as a substitute and, like his brother, he was a laborer in civilian life. He must have been a very able soldier because during his service time he was promoted to corporal and then to sergeant. Sally worried her sons and her neighbor's husband were all dead. She revealed the following: "My son Wm Davis is said to have died at the Louverture Hospital in Alexandria Va he belonged to Co G. 43rd Regt U.S.C. Troop I wrote to Hospital and got no answer from the Surgeon In Chief I would be thankful to know the truth." Sally continued, "also my son by my first husband is a longtime mising Adam Willet Co I. 45th Regt U.S. Colored Troop. My neighbor Mrs Price has had a report that her husband is dead that he died at Point of Rocks Hospital Va he belonged to Co C. 41st Regt U.S. Colored Troops. be kind enough to give all the information in your power."[59] She eventually received the good news that William did not die at L'Ouverture General Hospital. He was a patient there but was discharged from the hospital and the army on June 21, 1865, probably because of poor health, four months before the regiment was mustered out of service.[514] Sally also received good news about Adam. He was mustered out of service with his regiment on November 4, 1865.[60] Unfortunately for her neighbor, Mrs. Price, the news was not favorable. Her husband, William C. Price, died on June 22, 1865. William, a farmer, enlisted as a twenty-seven year old substitute on September 17, 1864 and survived the war, only to die while performing occupation duty in Brazos Santiago, Texas. He died from a "hemorrhage of the bowels."[61] William was just one of hundreds of black soldiers assigned to Texas who would survive the war and combat, only to die of disease while performing occupation duty.

When families asked whether their soldier was dead or alive, they frequently revealed the financial significance to the family if their soldier was killed. These soldiers often were the main or only financial provider for the family. That was the reality for Mary Fitzgerald of Philadelphia. She had a letter written for her, dated July 18, 1865, in which she inquired about her son, Joseph Fitzgerald, of

Company K, 32nd USCT. She had not heard from him since the previous October. In the meantime, she heard he was killed during a three-day battle near Charleston, South Carolina. Mary disclosed, "It gives me great grief as he was my only support being a widow."[62] Her only son was a twenty-five-year-old laborer when he enlisted on March 7, 1864. He began providing for his mother at a very early age, soon after his father died in 1847, when Joseph was hired out as a farm hand and "he gave to his mother all the money he earned." Joseph's financial support continued long before and after he joined the army, having never married and continuing to live with his mother. Unfortunately for Mary, her financial struggles would worsen because her son was killed on November 30, 1864, at the Union defeat at the Battle of Honey Hill in South Carolina. She filed an application for a mother's pension on July 25, 1866, which was approved on June 15, 1867, for $8 a month, retroactive to the day Joseph died. Also, according to the pension records her name was actually Francis Ann Fitzgerald, not Mary. The letter writer of her initial inquiry to the army might have made the mistake, or Francis escaped slavery years before and was using an alias until slavery was finally abolished with the 13th Amendment.[63]

Northern black families continued seeking out news or tidings about their soldiers as occupation duty proceeded, hoping at least to confirm they were still alive, especially so late after the war's conclusion. In a letter dated July 25, 1865 and addressed to Stanton, Edmund H. Anderson, of New Port, Delaware, asked for information about his son, also named Edmund, asking whether he was dead or alive. Edmund volunteered at the age of 19 and was in the military for two years. His father declared, "I am at a loss to gain information; and having endeavored in vain, I appeal to you, Sir I wish Sir you will inform whether The 3d Regiment U.S.C. Troops Are still at Jacksonville Florida, yet or have they moved, if so Their present destination. . . ." The elder Edmund continued, "I have a son in the Company I cannot hear whether he Is living or dead. heretofore he Has written very regular. . . . my son volunteered on the 20th of July 1863 mustered into the service on The 27th. Is he entitled to a bounty."[64] He eventually received good news about his son. He was alive and later discharged, as a corporal, along with his regiment at Jacksonville, Florida, on October 31, 1865.[65]

D. B. Booth wrote a similar letter, dated August 15, 1865, for the family of John M. Coley. The letter was from Danbury, Connecticut, and requested information about John, who was not heard from "for a long time." An older soldier, John enlisted in the army at the age of thirty-nine on December 23, 1863, and was a member of Company E, 29th Connecticut Infantry. He was a farmer. The family feared he was dead, since the last they heard about him was that he was in a hospital.[66] They found out he was dead since the previous year. He was hospitalized on November 13, 1864, and on December 14 he died of chronic diarrhea at Point of Rocks hospital in Virginia.[67] Margaret Lewis, of Philadelphia, had not heard from her son, who wrote regularly, and she feared he might be dead. In a letter written on her behalf, addressed to Stanton and dated August 16, 1865, she not only asked if her son was dead or alive, but she also reminded the army why he went off to fight for the Union. Her son, John Lewis, was a twenty-five-year-old laborer when he enlisted as a substitute on October 12, 1864.[68] He was a member of Company H, 41st USCT. In her inquiry Margaret disclosed, "It has been reported to me that my son is dead my only child who went in the hour of danger to assist in sustaining this glorious Union of ours. . . . I have not heard from him since March last as he was very punctual in writing to me every week I am afraid it may be true."[69] She also reminded the army her family was concerned for the well-being of "this glorious Union of ours." Their love of the Union led to her son's enlistment and her willingness to sacrifice her only son. Lucky for Margaret, she did not have to sacrifice his life; her son was alive. At the time of the letter, he was with his regiment in Texas. The regiment did not muster out of service until November 10, 1865, from Brownsville, Texas. He did not make it home until after the regiment was disbanded in Philadelphia on December 14, 1865.

Quite often, families, or their friends or associates, still had to send several letters to army officials to get their questions answered. Even with the war over, it remained difficult for families to obtain the information they needed. Examples of such struggles were evident with the families of Clayton Johnson and Obediah Cromwell. Mary Ann Johnson, of Philadelphia, had a letter written for her, dated July 15, 1865 and addressed to Stanton, requesting information about the well-being of her husband. Clayton was a thirty-five-year-old laborer on August 3, 1865 when he enlisted as a substitute in Company C, 6th USCT.[70] According to Mary, "I have not heard from my—husband . . . since two week before assassination our best and beloved friend President Lincoln I was in receipt of a letter every two weeks from him up to that point and his silence makes me fear that something has befallen him. . . . I would take it as a great favor if your honor would let me know something about him as I am in great trouble. . . ."[71] The very next month, Mary had another letter written for her, dated August 22, 1865 and again addressed to Stanton. She stated she learned just three days earlier Clayton was dead. Since she had not received any official notice from the army she wanted to know if the news was true. According to Mary, "I am not in receipt of any letter but it has been so stated to me it grieves me much having a large family would you be so kind as to give me the truth."[72] After sending at least two letters she finally found out her fears were valid when she was informed Clayton took ill and died at Goldsboro, North Carolina on June 28, 1865, two weeks after she failed to receive her usual letter from him.[73]

Obediah Cromwell was a twenty-one year old farmer when he enlisted on November 21, 1864. In a letter dated July, 8, 1865, Henry Fletcher wrote to Stanton on behalf of Fletcher's sister, Livinia, requesting information about her husband, Obediah Cromwell, a member of Company B, 6th USCT. Cromwell enlisted on November 18, 1864 but had not been heard from since March 22, 1865, when his regiment was sent to Wilmington, North Carolina. Henry described the family's situation in the letter: "Now, Obediah Cromwell, has a wife and two little children, And his wife depends upon me for Brains and advice In naviagting along through this pretty rough & Interesting world. . . . She' is now very much troubled about her husband, she has wrote to him herself, and several of her Big white friends have written to some of the Big army folks . . ." He continued, "and she & thay can not get any answer or Information concerning at all. . . . Day In & Day out, Obes poor wife is after me to try my <u>hand</u>, and see if I can not get some Information of his whereabouts, even if he is dead it would be some satisfaction to know it."[74] Henry requested that any answers be directed to him at the Collections Office, Custom House, New York, where it appeared he was employed. He clearly felt confident and very sure of himself and his abilities. Since he was literate and in government employment, it is not surprising that his family would turn to him to make inquiries.

Henry wrote another letter to the army on August 21, 1865, stating that he received an answer informing him his brother-in-law was "absent sick." As instructed in the response from the army, explained Henry, he sent a letter to Obediah, but did not get a response. Thus, in the August 21st letter, he again asked the army if Obediah was dead or alive.[75]

Just a few days later, on August 24, the family sent still another letter requesting a response to news Obediah was reported sick on June 30. This time, however, the letter was not sent by Henry on his sister's behalf, but instead sent by Livinia herself, though it was written by a Dr. Gilford.[76] After three letters from two family members, she still did not have any answers. It had to be a frustrating process for families like Mary Ann Johnson's and Livinia Cromwell's that it was such a hassle to get information from army officials about the status of their husbands. They had to continue to correspond with the military as the year progressed and the regiment remained in service. Eventually, Thomas's family found out he died of chronic diarrhea on June 26, 1865, in the General Hospital in Wilmington, North Carolina. Obediah had been mistakenly listed as a James Cromwell in the hospital where he died, which likely led to the communication problem. The military could not account for Obediah after he was admitted into the hospital on June 12, 1865. Two years after the war, Livinia applied for Obediah's pension as his widow. Her application was approved, at which point she began receiving a monthly pension for her and her two dependent children.[77]

Even with the war over, the military still struggled to get information to families about the possible death of their loved ones. It was particularly difficult to keep track of soldiers as their regiments moved around from one city or town to another, or from one region to another. The federal government's procedure required officers complete specific paperwork confirming a soldier was a casualty and his pay stopped. However, with soldiers in and out of hospitals and regiments on the move, it was difficult to get the proper paperwork completed about a soldier's changed status, whether he was infirm or dead. If a soldier's death was confirmed, an inventory was made of his belongings so they could be shipped to his family. Additional paperwork was required to record whether the soldier was owed any bounties or back pay, and in most cases, the soldier was actually owed months of back pay. All of this was difficult to carry out if a soldier was left in a hospital when his regiment moved away.

Rather than sit and wait for confirmation, families took things into their own hands and continued to make inquiries, or have inquiries made for them. Eliza Lukens, of Philadelphia, had a letter written on her behalf dated August 9, 1865. In the letter, addressed to Stanton, she requested information about the possible death of her son and her brother-in law. Eliza explained, "I have not heard from my son for over three months his name is Charles Lukens Co H. 45th Regt U.S. Colored Vol it is reported that he died I would be much indebted if your honor could give me some account him." In addition, stated Eliza, "My sister Mrs Augustus has not heard from her husband Benjamin Augustus Co G. 127th Regt U.S. Colored Vol for the last nine months it is reported that he is dead she is anxious to know if it is true."[78] Benjamin, Mrs. Augustus's husband, enlisted in the army on August 25, 1864 as a twenty-two-year-old laborer. His wife had not heard from him for months because he was killed on October 21, 1864 at Dutch Gap, Virginia. He was struck by pieces of a mortar shell while guarding prisoners of war. Benjamin died before he received any pay as a Union soldier. And ten months after his death and almost four months after the war had ended, his family still did not know he had been killed.[79]

Charles was a laborer and was just eighteen years old when he enlisted as a substitute on August 5, 1864. At the time of Eliza's letter, his regiment was stationed in Edinburg, on the Texas border with Mexico, but he was sick in a hospital in Alabama, where he had been since June 6, 1865. The regiment was mustered out of service on November 4, 1865, without Charles in attendance. The family found out from the captain of Company H that Charles had been left behind in the hospital at Ft. Gaines in Mobile Bay, Alabama. Upon receiving this news, George Lukens, Charles's father, sent a letter on December 6, 1865, also addressed to Stanton, asking for any information about his son. He wanted to know if Charles was still alive. Charles suffered the same fate as Charles Blake (Rebecca Berry's son): He probably died in the hospital with no one in his regiment around to complete the final paperwork verifying the date and the cause of his demise. With no one around to complete the necessary paperwork, Eliza and Charles had to wait before they found out that Charles was dead.[80] Even after the war ended, the army had a habit of losing track of soldiers, black and white, who spent long periods of time in army hospitals recovering from sickness.[81]

In the case of Augustus Thomas, the incorrect reporting on his status in the hospital had listed him as dead rather than alive. A member of the Company D, 43rd USCT, it was initially believed by the military that he had died in the hospital. When the 43rd mustered out of service on October 20, 1865 in Texas, he was "reported as having 'Died in Hospital'" on the regiment's muster roll. It took a letter dated December 18, 1865 from Lieutenant Colonel W. B. Lane, the Chief Mustering and District Officer in Philadelphia, to verify Augustus was still alive. The letter, addressed to the Adjutant General's Office in Washington, stated that Augustus reported to his office looking to be discharged since his regiment, the 43rd, was no longer in service. The regiment was discharged on November 30, 1865 in Philadelphia. Augustus's identity was verified by one of his former Company D officers, 1st Lieutenant Jacob C. Hankey, and he was officially mustered out of service. If his family members were worried about his whereabouts and health, they surely were relieved to know he was not dead as reported when the regiment first returned home.[82]

10

Even Farther Away
from Home

Occupation Duty Continues

Texas

While some black regiments remained throughout the South performing occupation duties, others were sent to Texas to perform a combination of duties. They were keeping the peace and helping freedmen and women with their transition to freedom, but they were also sent to Texas to counter French aggression in Mexico. In Texas, the troops would have to endure being even farther away from their families, in more remote and difficult terrain and in disease-ridden conditions. With the war over, General Ulysses Grant sent Major General Phil Sheridan with a large force to Texas to defeat any remaining Confederate troops in the state and to provide a show of force to Napoleon III of France. France invaded Mexico and seized control of the government, which was an action in conflict with the Monroe Doctrine, while the United States was preoccupied with the Civil War. In 1864, the French installed Archduke Maximilian of Austria as emperor of Mexico.[1]

In Texas, the army stationed a total force of about 52,000 men, of which 25,000 were black. A severe and debilitating outbreak of scurvy broke out among the men because the remoteness of Texas made it more difficult for the army to provide fresh food, supplies, and proper health care to the soldiers. In addition, homesickness, the terrible conditions, and the increase in idle time and boredom because there was little to keep the men busy, all led to a breakdown in order and professionalism among the officers and the men. This in turn led to an increase in tension between the two groups.[2]

Black troops reacted negatively to being sent to Texas. Many African-American troops from the North were among them because many of these units had been stationed in Virginia as members of the 25th Corps. The soldiers' discontent arose from knowing that, while white troops continued to get mustered out of service and return home, they were headed to Texas. They were also upset about being farther away from their families, and because many of them had not been paid in months, they did not like being even farther away from the paymaster. Their lack of pay directly affected the ability of their families to endure their absence. Especially disgruntled were black soldiers from the South. Many of them were former slaves who enlisted after escaping with their families toward Union lines. While the soldiers served in the army, their refugee families were allowed to follow the regiments and were provided with rations. But with the regiments sent far away to Texas, the army decided to discontinue the rations, causing wives, children, and other family members to have to fend for themselves.[3]

Some black troops, from the North and South, reacted violently to being sent to Texas. Members of the 1st U.S. Colored Calvary mutinied while in route to the southwest and refused to obey orders. The regiment was disarmed by other troops on the transport and order was restored. In a separate incident, the men of the 29th Connecticut (Colored) Infantry mutinied, though the root of their problem was bad communication between the enlisted men and their officers. The mutiny ended when some of them were arrested for insubordination. Still, other black soldiers found other ways to show their dissatisfaction with the army's decision to send the troops farther South, for they simply deserted. Right before their regiments were scheduled to leave for Texas, these men disappeared. For example, the 29th USCT saw six men desert right before it departed for Texas. But as in wartime, the desertions among black troops remained no higher than among whites.[4]

Beginning with regiments in the 25th Corps, African-American troops were dispatched to Texas in late May and early June 1865. They immediately experienced difficulties on their journey, some coming from as far away as Virginia, a three-week trip, only to get another jolt upon their arrival at their new posts. The regiments traveled by sea to Texas but, because of poor planning and preparation by the army, the soldiers suffered from fever, cramped space, poor sanitation, strictly rationed water, and spoiled and insufficient food. Consequently, troops who had managed to survive several years of the deadliest war in American history now became very sick and in some cases died on what should have been a simple and routine journey to Texas. The voyage of the 29th USCT illustrated how dreadful the journey was. Three members of the 29th died on the voyage from Virginia, another died of diseases made worse by the voyage, and it cannot be determined how many of the regiment's men arrived at Brazos Santiago, Texas, too sick for duty.[5]

Some regiments landed at Brazos Santiago, only to find preparations were not made for their arrival, and others were sent to Brownsville; both places were desolate, barren, sandy, and very much like deserts. As bad as the conditions were for these men, the beach did give them the opportunity to swim, to cool off from the heat, and to fish. That was not the case for the men who landed at Brownsville. Life there was horrendous. Brownsville did not have a beach to provide simple relief. And because there were no fish to catch, as in Brazos Santiago, the resulting food shortages meant that the men had to go on half rations. Brownsville was also infested with tarantulas, rattlesnakes, mosquitoes, and a host of hazardous wildlife.[6]

Some family members sent letters of concern about their soldiers who they heard were sick or maybe dead in Texas. Families of the deceased eventually received confirmation their soldiers were not killed in action and did not die of wounds received in battle, but instead, they died from disease long after combat had ended. William J. Kauffman, of Coatesville, Pennsylvania, sent a letter to the army dated November 16, 1865. He wrote on behalf of a soldier's children. He requested information about the whereabouts and health of Private William B. Peterson of Company I, 127th USCT. Peterson was just months from being forty years old when he enlisted on September 3, 1864. Kaufman explained, "The last heard of him by his children he was in the hospital at New Orleans. By giving the desired information, you will confer a favor on his children."[7] Kaufman probably wrote to help the children because Peterson's wife, Margaret, died on October 18, 1864, just weeks after his enlistment, leaving behind five young children ranging from two to eight years old. At the time of the letter, the 127th was stationed in Brazos Santiago. It was there Peterson became sick and was admitted into the hospital on August 27, 1865. By September 14, 1865, he was dead, of chronic diarrhea and scurvy. Having survived the war, he died from disease just a month away from being mustered out of service with the regiment, and going home to take care of his children. His children, having lost both parents during the war, would have to apply for their father's military pension.[8] Peterson was just one of hundreds of black soldiers assigned to Texas, who would survive the war and combat, only to die of disease while performing occupation duty.[9]

Black family members continued to appeal to the army for early discharges while their soldiers were assigned occupation duty and then relocated to Texas in the summer of 1865. They wanted their soldiers to return home, not go farther south. In the unique case of George Broden, a private in the Company C, 5th Massachusetts Cavalry, *he* himself requested a discharge on behalf of his family. In a letter dated August 14, 1865 and sent from Clarksville, Texas, he explained to Stanton why he needed to return and help his family. Broden declared, "As the war is over and I don't see that I can be any more service to you and my family very very sickly and my health being very bad since I have been here I would thank you very much if you would give me my discharge and you will be doing me a great kindness and my family also."[10] Broden's attitude was very similar to other black soldiers in Texas. Their first thought was of returning home and helping their families. For Broden and his family, their problems—sickness and possible financial difficulties—may have been offset by the achievement of their primary objective, a Union victory. But once the war was over and victory achieved, Broden and other soldiers wanted to go home to rebuild their civilian lives and help provide for their families.

Mothers, wives, and children, as well as sisters, brothers, and fathers wanted their relatives back home, not farther south. They wanted them home again to take up their familial roles, especially their roles as breadwinners and providers for families that were struggling financially. They no longer understood the need for their soldiers to still be in uniform and any further away from them. This was the reality for Maria Herbert of Washington, D.C., who had a letter written on her behalf by a Mrs. S. E. Draper, possibly a family friend or acquaintance. The letter was dated August 22, 1865, and requested government relief for the destitute Herbert family who had a soldier in the Union army. The letter was addressed to Major General Oliver O. Howard, the Freedmen's Bureau Commissioner and stated, "I desire to be pardoned for troubling you—in asking whether there is any mode of relief for the families of such soldiers, provided by Government? In this case there are an aged, rheumatic parent—an epileptic sister and three small children—all dependent upon the $8. Per month—earned by the wife at service." He continued, "She is a most excellent woman and is not even able to send her little ones to the Sunday School for need of clothes. I could provide these, if there were some money for the daily necessities of the family—now—I believe— crowded into one room."[11] Draper could "vouch for the worthiness of the woman [Maria]."[12] The Freedmen's Bureau routed the letter to the Treasury Department, which then routed it to the army. The Assistant Adjutant General referred the case to a military official in D.C. who was to inform Draper "what can be done in this case." The military official in D.C. probably referred Mrs. Draper to local relief services that could help Maria, maybe one of the black-run organizations such as the Freedmen and Soldiers' Relief Association of Washington or some local chapter of the USSC.[13]

The troops experienced long hours of boredom and idleness performing re- construction and occupation duty throughout the South. And these experiences were hazardous to the well being of African-American regiments, especially on the desolate Texas border with Mexico. When black regiments were first formed, the daily life of a soldier was new to the troops and they accepted its rigors and tediousness with pride. They were especially satisfied to finally be in uniform and working for a Union victory. But with the war finally over victory at hand, the circumstances were different. Military life now became a joyless, laborious chore and idleness became dangerous as troops searched for other ways to occupy their time. The idea of what they could be doing at home with their families only frustrated and reduced the morale of the men. An end result was a rise in public drunkenness, gambling, and other sorts of trouble. The white officers were similarly affected by the idle time, consuming large quantities of alcohol themselves. They also felt the war was over and so were their duties as officers. The most unscrupulous of them spent their free time swindling black troops of their money, at times getting away with the entire savings of their men, who had entrusted them to look after it. This was soldiers' money that would not make it home to help their families. These acts further increased the mistrust of black troops toward their white officers and heightened the regiments' internal tensions. It did not help that many of the officers with whom they fought and bonded during the war had served out their terms of duty and returned home. Their replacements were neither abolitionists nor men committed to the welfare of the black troops. Nor were they familiar to the soldiers or trusted by them.[14]

Other officers, usually the new ones who were less abolitionist in sentiment, attempted to keep order and control in the regiments by increasing the discipline (with rigorous physical drills and harsh punishments), which in turn prompted black troops to use their newfound sense of freedom and equality to display their disfavor.[15] Hardened veterans who fought and won the war, they felt they deserved better treatment while meeting their service requirements before returning home. They were no longer willing to accept the harsh punishments and strict treatment they once endured during the war (see Figure 8). They protested their treatment and what they felt was abuse at the hands of uncaring officers. And they wrote letters to newspapers and government officials. African-American troops wrote to leading officials, just like they had with previous problems, such as unequal pay. The troops wrote to Secretary of War Stanton and made him aware of their discontent. They had already proved their bravery as men and soldiers, fought and won the war, and were ready to take full advantage of the fruits of their victory. More importantly, they were ready to get back to their families and their regular lives.[16]

An Opportunity to Teach and to Learn

One positive outcome of occupation duty for black troops was their greater access to literacy programs. Blacks, men and women, and many of their white offi-

Figure 8. This was a common form of punishment for both black and white soldiers during the Civil War. (Library of Congress)

cers had a mutual interest in their education. Black troops, from both the North and South, who could not read, write, or calculate arithmetic were very anxious to learn, improve themselves, and go beyond just putting their mark (or an "X") on documents, such as the official army documents they marked when they enlisted. They wanted to be able to write their own letters. Some of the more ambitious troops thought an education would help them rise to the rank of sergeant, clerk, or quartermaster. Most saw the ability to go to school as an experience of liberty and believed education would enable a person to function successfully in a free society. Moreover, they equated freedom and citizenship with education. In addition, abolitionist officers in black regiments saw an opportunity to better prepare African Americans, especially those from the South, for their new roles as free men in American society. They were particularly interested in educating blacks in order to better prepare them to function successfully, not just as good soldiers, but also as responsible and self-reliant citizens once they left the army and returned home.[17]

It was black troops who were the driving force behind the effort to get educated, though they received help from abolitionist-minded and supportive commanders. Before the war, education was denied to slaves, while in the North access for northern blacks was limited, but the war brought an opportunity to become literate. And many blacks knew how to take advantage of this opportunity while they wore the Union blue, and they did so, by the thousands.[18]

The teaching was done in a variety of places and by a variety of people, both white and black, depending on who organized it and what resources were available in terms of people and materials. And because there were no War Department guidelines or regulations for the education of African-American soldiers, the teaching was very localized and varied, and the schools sprang up haphazardly. Success depended on the talents, generosity, and commitment of those involved. Northern benevolent associations, or the families of white officers, provided the elementary textbooks, pens, slates, and blackboards. Black troops learned outside, in tents, or if the regiment was in one place long enough, in wooden buildings, often paid for when they could gather up enough funds, and built by the troops themselves.[19]

In most cases, it was the regimental chaplain who headed and organized the literacy program because his official position encouraged him to take responsibility for educating soldiers. He was the logical choice, especially given that many chaplains believed education and religion went hand-in-hand, leading to a more moral and capable soldier. The chaplains first lined up sympathetic white officers to teach, but then literate black soldiers, who proved to be the most effective teachers, did the bulk of the teaching.[20] Sergeant James M. Trotter, of the 55th Massachusetts, was one of these literate black soldiers. Trotter revealed, "Let it not be supposed for a moment that only officers and men of another race were engaged in this noble work of school-teaching in our colored army. Not a few of the best workers were colored chaplains, . . . while many non-commissioned officers and private soldiers cheerfully rendered effective service in the same direction."[21] Literate black troops saw an opportunity to better prepare their brethren for what they hoped and expected to be a better life with greater opportunities to succeed in the North and South. In addition, black teachers understood the culture and could communicate better with other black troops. Furthermore, because they were more numerous than those white officers who were supportive, they could do more one-on-one teaching, which was the most effective approach. Also, with black troops as teachers, learning could take place both in the classroom and outside it while troops were performing routine and less time-consuming duties together.[22]

Because troops who belonged to regiments in the North tended to be better educated than those from the South, many of these men, specifically the noncommissioned officers, served as teachers. For example, in the 127th USCT, formed in Philadelphia in September 1864, sixty-one percent of the noncommissioned officers had some degree of literacy. Elite African-American regiments such as the 54th and 55th Massachusetts Voluntary Infantries had to have had an even higher literacy rate. The northern regiments were more literate because many more of the troops received a formal education as children. For example, Sergeant George E. Stephens, of the 54th Massachusetts Infantry, was probably educated at one of several primary schools in Philadelphia founded by blacks or one of several schools organized by Quakers, benevolent societies, or the Pennsylvania Abolition Society (PAS) to educate blacks. He very likely used his education to teach fellow soldiers in his regiment.[23]

Sergeant James Monroe Trotter, of the 55th Massachusetts, was actually employed as a teacher before the war. He was born into slavery in Mississippi but, when he was a young child, his mother escaped to the North with him and his brother through the Underground Railroad. They then settled in Ohio. In Cincinnati, he attended the Gilmore School, a college preparatory school established for blacks by a Methodist minister, Hiram S. Gilmore. He then attended the Albany Manual Labor Academy in Athens County, where he trained as a teacher. Upon graduation, he taught at schools for black students in Muskingum, Pike, and Ross Counties in Ohio. He was twenty-one years old when he joined the army as a volunteer on June 11, 1863 and was assigned to Company K. By July 30 of the same year, he was promoted to first sergeant, and by November 19 to sergeant major, most likely due to his high literacy. While in the army, he used his teachers training and experience to instruct other soldiers whenever time permitted. In an article titled "The School-master in the Army," he described his efforts: "Of the many interesting experiences that attended our colored soldiery during the late war none are more worthy of being recounted than those relating to the rather improvised schools. . . . One would naturally think that the tented field, so often suddenly changed to the bloody field of battle, was the last place in the world where would be called into requisition the school-teacher's services. . . ." He continued, "Yet in our colored American army this became not only possible but really practicable. . . . Books were used at times, of course, but quite as often the instruction given was entirely oral."[24] Trotter was so capable and talented as a soldier that he was promoted to second lieutenant on June 6, 1865, becoming only the second African American to reach that rank.[25] Stephens, Trotter, and other educated men in northern black regiments were an invaluable resource in the effort to educate black soldiers.

Chaplains also used their connections to missionary and relief organizations to secure learning material and supplies and to obtain teachers from the North.

Thus, civilian teachers also played major roles in educating black troops. Though the symbol of Civil War and Reconstruction teachers is the white "schoolmarm," many of the teachers were black women. Some civilian teachers were the wives of staunch abolitionist commanders, such as Colonel James Beecher, whose wife, Francis Beecher Perkins, was a teacher in her husband's regiment.[26]

Most teachers, however, were from northern missionary organizations and freedmen's aid societies. The United States Christian Commission (USCC), which was formed in New York in November 1861 to provide for the needs of Union soldiers and sailors, issued food, clothing, and religious material to soldiers, and also organized elementary education programs in the camps they visited. The Freedmen's Aid Society and the American Missionary Association (AMA) also provided teachers. The AMA was a Christian organization founded by white and black abolitionists on September 3, 1846 in Albany, New York. The organization's goals were to eliminate slavery, to promote racial equality, to promote Christian values, and to educate African Americans. The AMA missionaries and teachers followed Union armies and established freedmen schools wherever they could. The organization provided the most educators to the South, many of them black, and of the black educators most were female. In addition, African-American organizations also sent black teachers to the South. The African Civilization Society, which was founded and led by blacks, hired only black teachers. It established six schools from 1864 to 1867 and employed 129 teachers and assistants. The focus of civilian teachers was the education of the freed men, women, and children. However, many of them performed double duty because they believed education was essential to the race's success; they taught the children of freedmen and refugees in nearby contraband settlements in the day, and the adult freedmen and black soldiers at night. Civilian teachers hired to teach the troops were paid from regimental funds.[27]

Just like black male teachers in the army, black female teachers believed education was the key to full citizenship and saw an opportunity to better prepare their brethren, who were freedmen and illiterate black soldiers, for what they hoped and expected to be a better life with greater opportunities to succeed. Sallie L. Daffin, of Philadelphia, was a graduate of the Institute of Colored Youth, in that city and, like so many black female teachers, she was a graduate of Oberlin College in Ohio because it was one of the few colleges that accepted both women and African Americans. In addition, she taught locally before heading to the South. Assigned by the AMA to a school in Norfolk, Virginia, in early 1864 and inspired by her pupils, she stated, "There is, I think, abundant evidence of an increasing desire on the part of *our* people to become educated; and I hesitate not to affirm that if we have the same advantages afforded us as the whites, we will convince those who deny the fact that we are inferior to none." Similar to Daffin, these women tended to be from the North, and they were freeborn, middle-class, well educated, and already teachers. Teaching was a natural progression for many of them because it was very similar to the service and work many of them did in black soldiers' relief and freedmen's relief organizations, where they helped to provide funds and resources for black soldiers, for their families, and for refugee freedmen families. Daffin also found time to care for sick and wounded black troops as they convalesced in a local military hospital. It was in the hospital that many of them learned to read as they convalesced, thanks to her efforts.[28]

Many black female teachers had male relatives in the Union army, their sense of dedication and commitment must have been heightened, knowing they were doing their duty to elevate the race, as were their loved ones in blue uniforms. They felt obligated to help teach the same people their men fought and died to free. Charlotte Forten, of the wealthy and activist Forten family of Philadelphia, taught black refugees in Port Royal, South Carolina, from 1862 to 1864, under the auspices of the Philadelphia Port Royal Relief Association (later the Pennsylvania Freedmen's Relief Association). She also served as a nurse and hurried to the nearby African-American hospital when wounded members of the 54th began arriving there immediately after their July 1863 charge on Fort Wagner. She was concerned about the care of the valiant black troops and her "much loved friend," Colonel Shaw, whom she felt "really affectionate admiration for" and in a short time had grown to know. Similar to Sallie Daffin, Charlotte also taught wounded soldiers how to read and write while she nursed them back to health. She did all this while her father, Robert B. Forten, served in the 43rd USCT and her cousin, Charles Purvis, served as a physician in the army. Forten, already forty years old, enlisted at Camp William Penn as a private on March 2, 1864. He was assigned to Company A and only a month later was promoted to Sergeant-Major. He was transferred to Maryland to help recruit black troops, but he became ill and died of typhoid fever on April 18, 1864, while on sick leave in Philadelphia. He became the first African American to receive a military funeral in Philadelphia.[29]

Edmonia G. Highgate, the daughter of ex-slaves, was from Syracuse, New York, where she was educated. Very bright, strong willed, and committed, she was already serving as a nineteen-year-old school principal in Binghamton, New York, when she applied to the AMA for a teaching appointment in the South in January 1864. She strongly believed it was the responsibility of African Americans to educate the freedmen. Working for the AMA, and then after the war for the Freedmen's Bureau, she served in Norfolk, Virginia, and Darlington, Maryland, as well as New Orleans and rural Louisiana, and Enterprise, Mississippi. Because she taught throughout the South, she must have encountered black troops she also instructed. And as Edmonia worked diligently as a teacher in the South, her brother, Charles, served in the army. He was killed in a battle at Petersburg just before the war ended. Sarah Swails was from New York, and her husband, Lieutenant Stephen Atkin Swails, was originally from Columbia, Pennsylvania, and was a member of the 54th Massachusetts Infantry. Because she taught freedmen in South Carolina, it was very likely she taught black troops stationed nearby.[30]

Like black troops, black teachers in the South overcame obstacles imposed on them by the racist policies and habits of whites. And like black troops, they fought discrimination on two fronts, against white female and male teachers, as well as southern whites who despised their existence, as they did black troops. Black teachers were even discriminated against while working within or alongside white organizations. They were given inferior accommodations and segregated from the white teachers, many of whom had no problem spending the day teaching blacks but had no intention of sharing their living quarters or dining space with their fellow black teachers, not even temporarily. Very similar to black troops, they received unequal pay while performing the same duties as their white counterparts and having given up more lucrative and less demanding positions in the North. Black and white teachers were supposed to receive the same pay, anywhere from $10 to $15 per month, depending on experience, but often that was not the practice. Male teachers were paid more, with $25 a month as starting salaries. Black women protested this insidious treatment to white leaders of these organizations, usually males, but to no avail. Southerners cursed and insulted them in the streets and, in extreme instances, because they were hostile to blacks becoming educated, southerners attacked teachers physically, shot at them, and burned down homes and schoolhouses. Yet in spite of the racism, hardships, and dangers, these courageous black teachers continued to teach and educate.[31]

There appeared to be much success during the war in improving the literacy of black troops, but the demands of military duties, including fatigue duty, the constant troop movements, and the time commitment required to fight the war, limited the efforts and successes of officers and black troops. However, occupation duty provided a unique opportunity. Although black troops would have preferred to be home with their families, occupation duty enabled all interested parties to take the process of education blacks much further, especially in Texas. The key was time. Occupation duty, and its long periods of daily inactivity for soldiers, provided the stretch of undisturbed time needed for the project. That is why in almost all back regiments, formal education became a part of the daily routine during occupation duty.[32]

Although it is hard to assess the overall success of the programs and efforts of both teachers and students, black regiments as a whole, those formed in both the North and the South, were more literate when they mustered out. When the 1st USCT, the only regiment organized in Washington, D.C., was mustered into service in May and June of 1863, about 100 of its 1,000 enlisted men could read and write, but by the time it mustered out, the figure had increased threefold. The 43rd USCT had only seventy men who could read when the regiment was organized in Philadelphia in March and June of 1864. However, after just seven months of work, five of those while serving in Texas, over one-half the regiment could read. Many of the newly literate began handling their own letters and correspondences. By the time black troops left the service, their reading and writing skills probably surpassed the rest of the black population in the United States (see Figure 9).[33]

Sergeant Trotter praised the efforts of the teachers when he stated, "And so we say, all honor to teachers and taught in the Grand Army that made a free republic, whose safe foundation and perpetuity lies in the general education of its citizens." But as important as a teacher's role was, it was the students—the soldiers—and their hunger to learn that made possible the improvement in the literacy

Figure 9. Members of a black regiment using downtime to learn how to read. (Library of Congress)

rate of African Americans. Trotter explained, "[It was] those earnest, ambitious soldier pupils who, when finding themselves grown to man's estate, having been debarred by the terrible systems of slavery from securing an education, yielded not to what would have been considered only a natural discouragement." He continued, "But, instead, [they] followed the advice and instruction of their comrade teachers, and, bending themselves to most assiduous study, gained in some cases great proficiency, and in all much that fitted them for usefulness and the proper enjoyment of the well-earned liberty."[34] And when they returned home to the North and South, they used their new skills, and the confidence gained from the process of acquiring them, to take advantage of new political and economic opportunities and to make life better for themselves and their families.

The Beginning of the End: Homeward Bound

By September 1865, Union policy shifted against the continued use of black regiments. Union officials, including General Ulysses S. Grant, determined it was best to release all northern-raised black troops from military service. This was partially because of complaints throughout the South that these troops were instigating racial disturbances, such as the Charleston race riot, and inhibiting the ability of former masters to reach labor agreements with the freedmen. Surely, it did not make whites happy that the presence of the black troops from the North meant that former slaves were becoming educated and more confident in pressing their new rights. The constant complaints of former slaveholders eventually pressured federal officials to quicken the pace of demobilization. Many of these same officials, including President Johnson, were just as interested in pressuring the former slaves back to work in order to get the South's economy up and running again, and they felt black troops, especially from the North, hindered this process. Johnson approved the removal, and on September 9, 1865, the army ordered all black troops in regiments formed in northern states to be mustered out of the service immediately. That meant northern black troops received early discharges; they were no longer obligated to complete their initial three years of service. Some regiments had already been sent home by late August, such as the 54th and 55th Massachusetts. The remaining northern black regiments exited the South by the end of the year.[35]

Regardless, letters from family members continued to arrive in the offices of Union officials even as one northern black regiment after the other was mustered out and discharged from the army. Families carried on their efforts to have their soldiers released even sooner. Northern black families first had to experience seeing the majority of white troops come home immediately after the war ended to revelry and praise while their soldiers continued to serve. Now with northern black regiments beginning to return home, families hoped their soldier's regiment would be next. However, while the remaining northern white regiments were mustered out of service in a short period of time, northern black families had to anticipate the release of their soldiers as they were mustered out and discharged over a period of several months.

Family members in the most desperate of financial straits were motivated to write to the army after seeing other black soldiers discharged and return home. Indigent families at this point felt the return of their soldier to home and to work was the only way their lot could improve. Elizabeth Conrad, of Zenia, Ohio, wrote to Stanton in a letter dated November 18, 1865, requesting the release of her husband, Thomas A. Conrad, who was a member of Company B, 5th U.S. Colored Heavy Artillery, which was stationed at Vicksburg, Mississippi. He was a twenty-nine-year-old plasterer when he enlisted in the military on February 23, 1865, for a one-year term. According to Elizabeth, she needed Thomas home because the family could not make it through the winter without him. She declared, "Owing to my poor health, and very scanty circumstances, also with two little children to take care of, I am forced to fear the worst results during the coming winter, without my husband's being home to provide."[36] "Also my husband," she explained, "has been in very feeble health, for some time, and has had the fever, and feel as though he may not recover unless he is at home, where I can give him my attention."[37]

Thomas served in the army earlier in the war but had to leave because of bad health, explained Elizabeth. It is not clear why he rejoined the army, particularly a regiment formed in the Deep South; maybe he did so to obtain the bounty, which could be used to support his family. It is clear Thomas's ailments were acquired after he enlisted, including an incident where he was "severely bruised and injured" after getting thrown from a horse. Several of his regimental mates stated that when he joined "he was a stout healthy robust young man" who was "free from disease of the body," but his health became consistently poor afterwards. Elizabeth finished her letter with a more personal appeal to Stanton: "I now appeal to you as a father, and as a husband, one who alone can have any idea of the anxiety of a wife for the health of her husband. You have the power to have him discharged, and in the name of the God of the widow and the orphan I beseech you to grant me this favor, by letting my husband home."[38]

Elizabeth probably saw, or at least was aware, members of the two regiments formed in Ohio had mustered out of service. The 5th USCT mustered out of service on September 20th and the 27th USCT on the very next day. Also, black men from Ohio who joined regiments in Massachusetts and Pennsylvania, before the Ohio black regiments were organized, returned home even earlier. Either seeing or reading about these men returning to their homes may have prompted Elizabeth to appeal for her husband's release. The army responded to her in a letter dated November 28, 1865, stating the issue was forwarded to the commanding general in the Department of the South "for such action as the circumstances of the case and the interests of the service may seem to require." It appears the request was eventually denied because the army could find "no physical reason why this man should be discharged."[39] In the end, Thomas completed his full term. He served until February 22, 1866 when he was mustered out of service in Vicksburg, Mississippi. The remaining members of the unit were not mustered out until May 20, 1866, also at Vicksburg, because it was not considered a northern regiment. Ironically, he would out-live Elizabeth, who died in Zenia on December 31, 1874. Though Thomas suffered from hearing problems, rheumatism, lung disease (probably bronchitis), and other ailments as a result of his service in the war, he went on to live another fifty years, dying at the age of eighty-eight on September 17, 1824 in Dayton, Ohio.[40]

Like Elizabeth Conrad, Sarah Odrich of Washington, D.C., probably saw, heard, or read about the return of black soldiers who served in other northern regiments, as well as those who served in the 1st USCT, which was mustered out of service on September 29, 1865. However, Sarah wanted her husband released from the army for different reasons. He was sick and she could take care of him better than an army hospital; she probably heard the horror stories of men dying of diseases in army hospitals or the horrendous care they were given. Like Thomas A. Conrad, Joseph Henry Odrich was another soldier from the North who served in a regiment formed and organized in the South. He was a member of Company I, 10th USCT and was a thirty-year-old farmer when he was drafted on January 14, 1865, for a one-year term. In a letter dated October 11, 1865, and addressed to Stanton, Sarah requested Joseph's discharge. She revealed, "He has been sick four months, confined in Hospital at Key West, Florida. . . . I wish to have him Home with me so that I could nurse him myself. . . . I Know they would soon be discharged If I waited, but he is of no use and I should be very grateful if you would take the trouble to release him now."[41] Unfortunately for Sarah, her letter to the army arrived—or was acted upon—too late. The army responded on January 10, 1866, stating Joseph died in the hospital in Florida. According to his service records, Joseph was already dead when Sarah sent her letter. On September 8, 1865, he died of "inflamation of the bowels" in a hospital in Key

West, Florida. They advised her she should apply for his pension.[42] Just like other soldiers mentioned before, such as Charles Lukens of the 45th USCT, neither he nor his family received a single monthly payment before he died while serving his country.[43]

Elizabeth Conrad's and Sarah Odrich's letters showed that, even as northern black troops were headed home and their service coming to a conclusion, appeal denials and death notices often were the responses from army officials. At other times, the answer to inquiries had more joyous outcomes for family members. In a letter dated October 22, 1865, George B. Clark, of Washington, D.C., made a plea on behalf of the family of William F. Miner, a native of D.C., and a member of Company F, 38th USCT. The Miner family probably saw the return of black soldiers who served in other regiments, as well as those who served in the 1st USCT. Miner was twenty-eight years old and a laborer when he was drafted into the army on March 12, 1865, for a one-year term. Clark requested Miner's discharge because his wife, Mathilda, and children were in great need financially and could not provide for themselves. Clark illustrated the family's situation in his letter to Stanton: "That said Miner has a family consisting of a wife and four small Children. The eldest being but Eight years old and the youngest at the breast. The three eldest Children are now sick and the only means the Mother has of earning a livelihood is by putting the children to bed Leaving them in the house and going out to seek employment."[44] According to Clark, Mathilda received letters from her husband stating he sent money to her but she never received the money. If Miner were discharged, explained Clark, he "could readily get employment that would enable him to support his family."[45] The army responded in a letter dated November 1, 1865, approving Clark's request for Miner's discharge.[46] Since June 1865, the 38th USCT was performing occupation duty in Texas, at Brownsville and at various points on the Rio Grande and at Brazos Santiago, Indianola, and Galveston. For reasons not explained in his service records, Miner was discharged "by way of favor" on November 26, 1865 in White Ranch, Texas, and left for the North soon afterwards. The rest of the regiment, primarily made up of southern blacks, did not leave until January 1867, and were not mustered out until January 25, 1867.[47]

The family of John W. Adams also received a joyous ending to their inquiry. However, in Adams's case, a complete stranger who happened to have seen a person in need made the request for information. Adams was especially lucky because he was recuperating in the hospital where he easily could have been forgotten about. Robert T. Seagrave, a non-military white man, wrote a letter, dated October 16, 1865, on behalf of Adams, a member of Company K, 8th USCT. It is unclear what Seagrave was doing in Virginia at the time or why he involved himself in the situation, but he wrote the letter to a friend of his, Miss D. L. Dix, of Salem, New Jersey, requesting her assistance in getting Adams discharged. Seagrave's friend was almost certainly Dorothea Lynde Dix, the prominent and influential social reformer and political lobbyist. She also worked closely with civilian relief organizations such as the U.S. Sanitary Commission, where she had experience helping wounded soldiers and their families. Adams was a twenty-five-year-old farmer when he enlisted on December 4, 1863, but since then, he and his family's lives had become imperiled, which was what Seagrave described: "There is a Colored man in Ward No 16 General Hospital Fortress Monroe who was wounded in the battle near Jacksonville Florida It appears that he has been moved around from one hospital to another and has been of no service to the Government and was to have been discharged long ago but from some cause unknown to me has not." He continued, "He left a wife and two children when he enlisted His wife has since died and his children are exposed to the roughs of the world. If he was home he could be put in a way to provide for them. If you could have him discharged I think it would serve the cause of humanity. . . ."[48] In February 1864, while the regiment was in Florida, Adams was both wounded in battle and contracted a severe cough and cold. He was shot in the left hand at the Battle of Olustee, and one of his fingers eventually had to be amputated. However, it was the severe cough and cold that kept him in and out of hospitals for the next year and a half, which Seagrave referred to.[49]

It looks as if Adams was eligible for a discharge on September 8, 1865 because he was unable to perform his duties as a soldier. But none of his officers were around to process his paperwork because his regiment left for Texas in May 1865, while he was in the hospital recovering. He finally recuperated enough to leave the hospital and was allowed to return to Philadelphia, where he was discharged. His regiment was mustered out on November 10, 1865 in Texas and the regiment returned to Philadelphia where the men were discharged on December 12, 1865. Adams was originally from New Jersey, where his wife and children resided, but made Philadelphia his home after he left the army. Evidently, he recovered from his illness, for he remarried in 1866.[50]

Letters about the location and health of their soldiers continued to be the prominent subject of correspondence from black northern families, even while 1865 came to an end and northern troops headed home. And because disease was the most prominent killer in the war, families had good reason to continue to worry about their soldiers, even long after the fighting ended. Families also had good reason to request information about soldiers who were hospitalized because the army continued to forget about those who were admitted to hospitals, as may have happened to John Adams. If they lived, they were overlooked and not properly discharged. If they died, they were often not properly recorded. Frequently, such soldiers were left to themselves to seek out the right army officials who could straighten out their status and provide proper discharge certificates, or their families had to do it, often hiring agents to handle the process of finalizing their soldier's status in the army.[51] But first the families had to determine where their soldiers were and whether they were dead or alive.

A letter dated September 16, 1865, and written on behalf of Willis Clark, requested information about Willis's son, William Elbridge Clark. The letter was written by B. M. Albany of Columbus, Ohio, and was addressed to Stanton. Albany explained, "a Poor Colored man . . . he [Willis] has not heard from him—his time was out last August and his father is much distressed about him." Albany also asked for the location of the 25th USCT so he could find information about the wellbeing of William.[52] William was a farmer and only eighteen years old when he volunteered to enlist on August 18, 1864. It appears Albany did not get a response to his first letter and so he sent another letter to Stanton, dated December 2, 1865. In the second letter, Albany described William as a member of Company D, 23rd USCT, his actual regiment. Again, he requested information on the location of the regiment but, this time, Albany also provided more details about William and about his father's needs. Albany stated, "He is a Boy only or perhaps under the age of 18 years and is the only help of his Father. He is enlisted in August 1864 for one year and his time has been out for some time and the Father has heard nothing from him for a long time and has become Very anxious about him and is using and has used all endeavors to find out if he is living or dead."[53] Albany also asked what back pay or bounty Willis was entitled to if his son was, in fact, dead. Albany may have been a pension agent hired by Willis to help him get any back pay or pension he was eligible for upon his son's death. According to William's service records, he was entitled to a $300 bounty he had not yet been paid. The regiment was mustered out of service on November 30, 1865, just two days after Albany sent his second letter. However, because William was absent sick in the general hospital at the time the regiment was mustered out, he was never officially discharged from service and it is unclear if he was alive or dead. Very similar to black soldiers mentioned before, Charles Lukens and Charles Blake, he may very well have died there because no one from his regiment was around to process his paperwork and notify his family.[54]

Of all of these predicaments brought to light by these letters of inquiry, there is one unique situation where a soldier either tried to use to his own advantage the army's inability to keep track of its troops, or that incapacity worked against him when he could not prove his own whereabouts when he was away from his regiment. A. B. Hutchinson, of Bellefourte, Pennsylvania, wrote a letter on behalf of Rachel Witten, requesting information about her son's well being. Joseph W. Witten, a member of the Company K, 8th USCT, was nineteen years old and a laborer when he enlisted as a substitute on November 28, 1863. Dated October 31, 1865, Hutchinson's letter asked for "any information which may be on file regarding his fate, as no tidings of him have reached his mother for above a year." Witten was not mustered out of the service with his regiment on November 10, 1865. The army first stated in his service records that, at the time the regiment was mustered out of service, he had been in the hospital since August 18, 1864. But when his service records were updated on September 24, 1888, twenty-three years after the war, it was acknowledged he was admitted on September 3, 1865 to the army corps hospital at Point of Rocks, Virginia, for jaundice and then on the same day admitted to the general hospital near Petersburg, Virginia, for diarrhea.[55]

Not done yet with his records, on December 20, 1890, the army included with his muster records a Memorandum From Prisoner of War Records form, stating that no record was available.[56] It appeared Joseph was another soldier who was in the hospital recovering and the army had lost track of him. However, some time after 1864, Joseph returned to his regiment and, according to his account, he became a prisoner of war. He stated he was captured by the Confederates, sold into slavery, and sent to Cuba. He was there, he claimed, for four years before escaping and returning to America. Unfortunately for him, the army did not believe his story. When he applied for an invalid pension in 1888, which is what prompted the government to begin updating his service records, the army rejected his application because he was deemed to have been a deserter. Joseph may have been telling the truth for several reasons. First, as early as the fall of 1862, the Confederate government threatened to sell captured black troops into slavery. Second, Joseph proved his loyalty to the Union by fighting and spilling blood for the nation at the Battle of Olustee on February 20, 1864, where he was shot on the right side of his body and received a broken left arm and leg after getting run over by artillery. And, third, a black person was more likely to have been forced to go to Cuba as a slave rather than to have deserted to Cuba because slavery was still legal and flourishing in the country. Nevertheless, pension officials continued to reject his applications, even as late as 1895 when his petitions stopped. It probably did not help Joseph that he did not have any affidavits from regimental mates and officers to corroborate his story. It is unclear whether his mother, Rachel, ever heard from him again.[57]

All the northern regiments were home by the end of 1865, but the new policy was not applied to the regiments formed in the South. They were forced to complete their full three-year terms and were not discharged until 1866 or 1867. Similar to how black troops responded when the majority of the white troops were mustered out immediately after the fighting ended and they were ordered to begin occupation duty, regiments from the South resented having to complete their terms while their northern black brethren returned to their homes. Sergeant-Major Thomas Boswell, of the 116th USCT, must have been upset to see other regiments around his own getting mustered out and returned home to northern states, while his Kentucky regiment remained in Texas. He was twenty-two years old and a barber when he enlisted on July 12, 1864. Based on information in his service records, he was probably a former slave. On November 6, 1865, writing from Roma, Texas, he sent a letter to the *Weekly Anglo-African* stating how he felt. He explained, "We were in high hope of being mustered out soon, but it seems that they have slighted us. Our [25th] Corps is pretty much all gone home." Thomas felt that troops from the South were being discriminated against because they were "slave State troops" and for some reason were not worthy to receive equal treatment. He reminded readers, "We are Kentucky boys, and there is no regiment in the field that ever fought better. We can boast of being the heroes of eight hard fought battles, and this we deem a sufficient recommendation for our discharge." He was right because his regiment performed siege operations against Petersburg and Richmond from October 23, 1864 to April 2, 1865 when Petersburg fell to Union forces. The 116th also participated in the pursuit of General Lee's army, from April 3 to 9, and was there when Lee surrendered at Appomattox Court House on April 9. Speaking for his fellow troops, he declared, "We earnestly hope that the Government will not be guilty of this great wrong toward us, as we have tried to do our duty." In spite of what they desired, he and his regiment were not mustered out until January 17, 1867, in Louisville, Kentucky.[58]

In January 1866, after all the northern black regiments were demobilized and sent North, Sherman's forces in Texas still numbered 6,500 white soldiers and 19,768 black soldiers. The African-American troops were from regiments organized in the South, such as the 116th USCT, Sergeant-Major Boswell's regiment. By October 1866, the total number of all-black regiments who remained in service in all of the former Confederate states, including Texas, was reduced to 12,985 men and officers. Still, General Sheridan appeared to have no misgivings about keeping so many black soldiers in uniform. He incorrectly believed blacks preferred military life rather than civilian life. It did not seem to occur to him that maybe these men would prefer to go home to their families and enjoy the fruits of their hard-fought Union victory, similar to white soldiers. Sheridan was not compelled to muster out of service the remaining USCT soldiers until he received a direct order from Grant in January 1867. The 125th USCT was the last black regiment discharged in the South. The regiment finished its service on December 20, 1867. At the end, nearly 200,000 black soldiers served in the Union forces, 178,975 in the army and the remainder in the navy. Over 37,000 black men from the North and South lost their lives. Black troops participated in 449 fights and battles against Confederate forces and sixteen African-American soldiers were awarded the Medal of Honor. Four black sailors also received the award.[59]

Northern black soldiers began arriving home as their regiments were mustered and then discharged out of service. But now they were armed with the experiences and knowledge they had obtained as soldiers as well as a newfound confidence gained from obtaining a higher level of education and demanding and achieving equal treatment as soldiers, as in their victory in getting equal pay. These were all attributes they would use to press their demands for change in northern society. They wanted full equality and citizenship; more than anything, they wanted the right to vote. This was especially so for northern black troops.[60] They already had the basic rights of a free man before the war started. They fought for a Union victory to end slavery, a system they knew diminished the entire race in the eyes and minds of whites.

They also fought to prove their worth as men, while their families proved their worth as committed and supportive citizens. Writing from Texas on August 28, 1865, in a letter to the *Christian Recorder*, Private Henry Carpenter Hoyle of Company F, 43rd USCT, reminded readers that blacks proved their worth and now deserved equal rights. Hoyle declared, "We know of what value we have been to the Government, and I guess our officers know our bravery, and of what metal we are. And we defy any one to dispute our rights as soldiers and men." In addition, northern blacks fought for economic opportunity, legal equality, and civil rights through the vote, and Hoyle expressed what he wanted in return for his sacrifice when he was back home in Philadelphia. He stated, "May we be an honor to our race, and may our future conduct be such as to please a most noble and generous public. We want the right of suffrage, that we may be free and equal as other men. . . . and I have no doubt we will get our rights as men and citizens of the United Sates."[61]

On September 19, 1865, Chaplain Garland H. White of the 28th USCT displayed a similar attitude in the *Christian Recorder* when he wrote, "The Government has a right to the service of men, when and where it [needs them] and we calmly submit to it. But we soldiers ask the nation to grant us the right to vote, that we may, by that bestowment, be enabled to protect our families from all the horrors that prey upon the disfranchised people."[62] Black troops strongly felt the government was obligated to meet their demands because military duty helped them to hone the skills they needed to work and function effectively within the political and governmental system.[63]

For most white soldiers, the war was truly over and victory, the end to the rebellion, was achieved. For blacks, it was a much different experience. Only a partial victory was achieved with the ending of slavery and the capitulation of the slave-owning regime. Now, northern blacks wanted full equality and economic opportunity, which they felt they deserved and would focus on after contributing to the Union.[64]

11   Home Again

B y the end of 1865, all twenty-six of the northern black regiments were mustered out of service and returned home to their families. The first to return was the first black regiment formed in the North, the now legendary 54th Massachusetts Infantry, which was mustered out on August 20, 1865, and discharged in Boston on September 1. Next were the 32nd USCT, which was formed in Philadelphia and mustered out on August 22, and then the 55th Massachusetts, mustered out on August 29. The last regiment was the 25th USCT, also organized in Philadelphia, and the only northern regiment to serve as late as December 1865. Depending on the means of transportation and the distance they had to travel, it took the regiments anywhere from two weeks to a month to return to their city of origin. Regiments returning home from Texas on average took the longest, often several weeks, due to the distance and the means of travel. The regiments stationed in Texas usually had to travel first by boat to New Orleans and then by boat and train to the regiment's home state. Once back where the regiment was organized and initially mustered into service, the regiment settled their final business with the paymaster and then officially disbanded as a regiment. These were probably emotional and climatic moments filled with memories of months or years passed together as a fighting unit, reflections of battles won and lost, and thoughts of fallen comrades who did not make it home. The soldiers then went home to their families who were either local or in another state.[1]

The reception once they arrived home was one of exuberance and joy for most northern black regiments. Large crowds of admirers welcomed them home. Government leaders and local communities throughout the North held parades, banquets, and celebrations to honor their returning heroes. African-American communities turned out in large numbers to greet and honor their heroes.[2] Thus, these events marked the end of their historic service to their country.

The first welcome-home celebration was held in Boston, where the first regiment formed in the North was organized. On September 2, 1865, the 54th Massachusetts landed in the morning at Commercial Wharf, where many admirers, including a marching band, greeted them. Large crowds of people greeted the veterans with flags waving and cheering. Now participating in their final parade as a regiment, they marched down the same streets that they marched down as new soldiers. This time however, they returned as "seasoned" veterans who had defended their country and won a war.[3]

After the parade, Brevet Brigadier-General Hallowell, who had taken command of the regiment after Colonel Shaw was killed at Fort Wagner on July 18, 1863, thanked his officers and then the enlisted men for their brave service and wished them well in their future lives. After the regiment ate a light meal provided in their honor, they disbanded for good and the soldiers were free to go their separate ways.[4]

In terms of fanfare, the 1st USCT's homecoming in Washington, D.C. was very similar to the 54th's homecoming. However it occurred over several days, October 8–10, 1865, and included a review by the President in front of the Executive Mansion, a rare honor for any regiment, white or black.[5] In other northern states, including as far west as Springfield, Illinois, the homecoming celebration for black troops was very similar to what occurred in the Boston and Washington, D.C.[6]

Once soldiers arrived at their own homes, they received an even warmer welcome from their families. If a family did not meet their soldier at the regiment's point of disembarkation, and many did not, they did not see him until he arrived at the family's doorstep. Such was the case of Alexander H. Newton of the 29th Connecticut Infantry. After the regiment was discharged in Hartford on November 24, 1865, he left by train for New Haven, where he arrived at 7:00 A.M. At home "[I] found my wife and children, my father and mother, ready to give me the most hearty welcome and greeting which I receive with a glad heart."[7] Thus, Newton described another scene repeated thousands of times over throughout the North. The family members the soldiers left behind, who had struggled to survive in their absence, were overjoyed to see their soldier finally home safe and to stay.

Of course, the return of the regiment was not the same for all families because not all the soldiers returned home. More than 37,000 black soldiers died in Union uniforms. Thousands more black troops returned home severely injured or disabled. Hence, family members whose soldiers did not return from the war, or who came back as invalids, would have to deal with the emotional challenges of losing a loved one or having to provide for a severely wounded former soldier. Additionally, families were burdened with the permanent loss, as well as the loss in income, that accompanied a soldier's death. That is why back pay and pensions became so very important to these families, who were already struggling financially, or even destitute.

Upon their return to civilian life, black men were not the same men who went to war. When they entered the war, their nation was under attack and slavery existed. Now northern black soldiers went home with a tremendous sense of accomplishment. They successfully defended their country against rebellion, helped to put an end to slavery, showed both skill and bravery, and proved their worth to their country. They saw different places and things, which made them more worldly and experienced. In addition, many of them returned better educated than when they left home. Many of them had become experienced and skilled administrators who, as non-commissioned officers, knew how to give orders, follow through with assignments, hold important responsibility, and keep records. Just as important, they learned how to be committed and loyal members of the Union. In return for their loyalty, blacks felt that their actions justified equal treatment in American society. Thus, with their chests stuck out with pride and with greater expectations of the society from which they departed a few years earlier, these black soldiers went back home to the North (see Figure 10).[8]

Black men and women were optimistic and continued to strive for better lives as they settled into their post-war lives.[9] After the war, James Trotter went on to become the first African-American employee in the Boston branch of the United States Post Office. In 1887, President Grover Cleveland appointed him to a position in the Recorder of Deeds Office. He was one of the first blacks to hold a position in that office.[10]

Charles R. Douglass, Frederick Douglass's eldest son, convalesced at home in Rochester, New York, after his discharge from the army on September 17, 1864. He stayed there for two months while recovering from a fever that affected him even before leaving the army. Moving on with his post-military life, he relocated to Washington, D.C., taking a position as a property steward at what became the Freedman's Hospital. He married Elizabeth Murphy in September 1866, and their son was born on July 3, 1869. Also in 1869, he became a clerk at the Treasury Department, and in 1874, he was appointed U.S. Consulate to Santo Domingo. His first wife died on September 19, 1878, and he remarried Laura Antoinette Haley on December 30, 1980. Charles and Laura had six children but only one, the youngest, lived to adulthood. Charles retired as a clerk because he lost his hearing as a result of an injury sustained during the war. He remained in Washington until his death on November 23, 1920.[11]

Many of the former USCT soldiers from the North felt the need to help the freedmen and returned to the South. A year after returning home from the war,

Figure 10. "Be Citizens in Peace" was on the regimental flag and the motto of the 24th USCT. The motto best represented what northern black troops and their families fought and sacrificed for, full citizenship once the war was over. (Library of Congress)

George Stephens returned to the South and opened a school for freedmen in Liberty Hill, outside of Port Royal, Virginia. He continued to teach in Virginia for over three years, with his wife, Susan, joining him there as a teacher in 1869, before they both returned to Philadelphia in early 1870. Soon after they returned, Susan died, and in 1873 George relocated to Brooklyn, New York, where he opened an upholstery business. He began a relationship with an Irish laundress, Catherine Tracy, and on April 14, 1875 they were married and she bore him a son,

George E. Stephens, Jr., on May 28, 1876. George was involved in politics as well as veterans' organizations, and on August 15, 1881, he applied to the federal government for disability payments as a result of the reoccurrence of a nerve injury that affected the muscles in his hands. He sustained the injury at Fort Wagner in July 1863. His application was approved, and he received a monthly invalid pension until April 24, 1888, when he died of hepatitis.[12]

Some former northern black troops moved to the South and remained. Stephen Swails and his wife, Sarah, returned to South Carolina to teach freedmen. Both of them had previously taught there when the 54th was stationed there during the war. Stephen also worked as a Freedmen's Bureau agent. He was later elected a state senator, worked as a clerk for the Treasury Department, and served as a member of the University of South Carolina board of trustees.[13] Marcus Dale and his wife, Mary, having survived the 1863 Detroit Riot and his service in the 102 USCT, also permanently relocated to the South soon after the war. In August 1867, they moved to New Orleans where they made a new life for themselves. Marcus served as a minister and elder at the Methodist Episcopal Church and worked as a teacher. They also resided for a time in Water Valley, Mississippi and Greensburg, Louisiana, before Marcus died in 1892. The effects of the riot would continue to influence the lives of the Dale family long after the Detroit Riot ended. After the war, Marcus received a pension because of the chronic rheumatism he suffered as a result of his military service. After he died on December 7, 1892, Mary applied for his pension as his widow. She had difficulty proving they were legally married because their marriage certificate was destroyed when their home was destroyed by fire during the riot; a second copy of the marriage certificate, held by the African Methodist Church where they had been married, was also destroyed when the church burned down in the riot. She was forced by pension officials to provide notarized affidavits from friends and acquaintances who could verify she and Marcus were married on September 29, 1854 and remained so until his death. Her application was approved and she received pension funds as Marcus's widow until her death in 1900.[14]

Similar to Marcus Dale, Charles Jackson survived a race riot, the New York draft riots, *and* the war. He never applied for a military pension, but for eight years after his death, his widow, Eliza, struggled to obtain pension payments for herself because he was listed in the army under two other names, Charles Clark and William S. Brown. He was probably a former escaped slave and used the aliases to conceal his real identity, as Charles Clark, from potential bounty hunters looking to capture him and return him to slavery and the South. It also did not help that the army had listed him as a deserter on May 30, 1865. However, his name was cleared and the desertion removed from his record on March 2, 1888, two years before he died on August 4, 1890 in New York City. The military realized he was actually sick and in the hospital when they thought he had deserted, another sick soldier they had lost track of once the regiment marched away. Eliza worked as a laundress and "janitress" until she could not anymore due to bad health; she died penniless on June 12, 1898 in New York City, in the midst of her extensive effort to prove her eligibility for Charles's military pension. Charles and Eliza's daughter, Matilda Spencer, took care of her in her last years of life and paid the expenses for her burial, for which the government never reimbursed her.[15]

The voices of the women became more silent as women were no longer writing letters to military officials. The exceptions were the more prominent women such as Sojourner Truth, Mary Ann Shadd Cary, and Harriet Tubman, who continued to be leaders within their communities. Truth continued to work to help freedmen as an employee of the Freedmen's Bureau in Arlington, Virginia. Cary returned to Washington D.C., where she taught school, attended Howard Law School, and became the second black female lawyer in 1883. Tubman returned to Auburn, New York, where she cared for her aging parents and opened up her home to care for elderly and indigent African Americans. She also helped to promote the women's suffrage movement.[16] After the war, Charlotte Forten Grimke continued to serve the black community as secretary of the teachers committee of the New England branch of the Freedmen's Union Commission in Boston and as a teacher in Charleston, South Carolina. She returned to the North and settled in Washington, D.C., where she continued to work as a teacher. In 1878, she married Francis Grimke, and supported his ministry and work as a civil rights advocate in Washington, D.C. Later in her life, she became a founding member of the National Association of Colored Women.[17] Edmonia Highgate and her mother and two sisters also remained in the South teaching after the war. Edmonia first taught in New Orleans before she left there to establish a school in Vermilionville, Louisiana, two hundred miles from New Orleans. By 1869, all four of them were teaching in Mississippi. Edmonia returned to New York in the fall to recover from exhaustion. While there, she raised money for the schools where her mother and sisters were teaching. However, a year later, Edmonia was dead after attempting to end a pregnancy. She had become pregnant with the child of a former Union officer, John Henry Vosburg, to whom she was married. They kept their marriage a secret because, having been crippled in the war, Vosburg was dependent on the financial support of his family, who would have disowned him had they known he married a black woman.[18]

Though their voices were quieter, working-class black women were just as visible to the public. Most still had to work as laborers (such as laundresses and maids) to support their families.[19] However, now their men were back to help, so together they toiled to better their lives, those of their children, and of their community. Yet these women must have felt a sense of accomplishment, having singly provided for themselves and their families while their men were away, in some cases for years. And they did this in a northern society hostile to blacks, while receiving little to no pay for their soldiers-. Yes, the soldiers who made it back home were not the same people that went off to war, but neither were the women the same people they left behind. The war and desperate circumstances forced the women to use their wits and resourcefulness to survive.[20]

But now their families were complete again. And with the sense of accomplishment that came with the victory in war, the few legal gains mentioned before, and the right to vote—at least for black men through the ratification of the Fifteenth Amendment—northern black families moved forward better prepared to achieve greater gains and accomplishments as Americans.[21]

Appendix: Northern Black Regiments

(*continued*)

Regiment	Organized or Muster-In Date	Muster-Out Date	State Where Organized
32nd USCI	February 7 to March 7, 1864	August 22, 1865	Pennsylvania
41st USCI	September 30 to December 7, 1864	November 10, 1865	Pennsylvania
43rd USCI	March 12 to June 3, 1864	October 20, 1865	Pennsylvania
45th USCI	June 13 to August 19, 1864	November 4, 1865	Pennsylvania
54th Massachusetts Infantry	May 13, 1863	August 20, 1865	Massachusetts
55th Massachusetts Infantry	June 22, 1863	August 29, 1865	Massachusetts
60th USCI (formerly the 1st Iowa Volunteers—African Descent)	March 11, 1864	October 15, 1865	Iowa
79th USCI (formerly the 1st Kansas Colored Volunteers)	January 13, 1863	October 1, 1865	Kansas
83rd USCI (formerly the 2nd Kansas Colored Volunteers)	August 11 to October 17, 1863	October 9, 1865	Kansas
102nd USCI (formerly the 1st Michigan Colored Volunteers)	February 17, 1864	September 30, 1865	Michigan
127th USCI	August 23 to September 10, 1864	October 20, 1865	Pennsylvania

National Park Service, The Civil War Soldiers and Sailors System at http://www.nps.gov/civilwar/soldiers-and-sailors-database.htm.

Acknowledgments

This is a section I have been looking forward to writing for some time now. Not only does it signify that I have completed my project but also that I have not traveled the weary path and journey toward completion alone.

I have benefited from the nurturing and guidance of the history department faculty at the University of Illinois at Chicago (UIC). Thank you for what you contributed to my early intellectual and professional development as a historian. I am especially indebted to Michael Perman for years of excellent advice about how to become a better writer, researcher, and historian. Also, he has set a high standard for research, writing, and thinking that I have tried to live up to. More importantly, I thank him for being a dedicated and supportive mentor. Though he is now emeritus, I still hear his voice guiding me in whatever scholarly work I do.

A special thank you goes out to the competent, dedicated, and hardworking people at various libraries, historical societies, and archives where I conducted my research: the staff at Massachusetts Historical Society; the staff at Newberry Library in Chicago; the staff at UIC's Richard J. Daley Library; the staff at my home institution, Loyola University Chicago Health Sciences Library; Leslie Rowland and the staff at the Freedmen and Southern Society Project, which is housed at the University of Maryland, who graciously hosted me for several days as I used their facilities in my initial research for this project; and the entire staff (security personnel, secretaries, cafeteria workers, research specialists, and so on) at the National Archives in Washington, D.C., who made my numerous research visits to the archives fruitful and productive. Additionally, a special thank you to all those who have worked to preserve the history of African-American participation and sacrifice in the Civil War.

I thank Fordham University Press for seeing potential in this work as a contribution to the *North's Civil War* series. I'm especially grateful to Andrew Slap, whose invaluable suggestions greatly improved the manuscript.

My family, especially my son, James, and my daughter, Kellie, may not have always understood what I was doing or what was taking me so long, but without their love I would not have been able to complete this project. I am thankful for my parents, James and Larisla Mendez. They instilled in me the discipline and commitment to hard work that have enabled me to finish this project. In addition, they have always been proud and supportive of me.

Finally, I want to thank my beautiful and loving wife, Katrina. While I question whether I could have finished this project without the help of others, I know I could not have done it without you, and I am forever grateful. I love you dearly!

Any inadequacies in the book are my sole responsibility and are present despite, not because of, the input, support, and guidance of the people mentioned here.

Notes

Introduction

1. Mattild Burr to Abraham Lincoln, January 18, 1864, B-132, 1864, Letters Received, series 360, Colored Troops Division, Record Group 94; Charles Burr Service Records, 3rd USCT; Charles Burr Pension Files, 6th USCI, Records of the Veterans Administration, Record Group 15. It is unclear whether Mattild received a response to her letter, but Charles survived the war and was discharged October 31, 1865. Upon his death on March 9, 1888, Mattild began receiving an $8 per month widow's pension, commencing July 22, 1890 until her death in New Brighton, Pennsylvania, on July 20, 1920.

2. The 25th USCT, organized in Philadelphia, was the last northern black regiment to return home. Its muster-out-date was December 6, 1865.

3. Black women in the South had to take up the extra workload if their men left and were able to enlist in the Union army. For additional information about the dynamics of slave families, male and female roles, and their ability to function under the stresses of slavery, see Amy Dru Stanley, *From Bondage to Contract: Wage Labor, Marriage, and the Market in the Age of Slave Emancipation* (Cambridge: Cambridge University Press, 1998); Noralee Frankel, *Freedom's Women: Black Women and Families in Civil War Era Mississippi* (Bloomington: Indiana University Press, 1999); Herbert G. Gutman, *The Black Family in Slavery and Freedom, 1750–1925* (New York: Vintage Books, 1977); Eugene D. Genovese, *Roll, Jordan, Roll: The World the Slaves Made* (New York: Vintage Books, 1976); John W. Blassingame, *The Slave Community: Plantation Life in the Antebellum South* (Oxford: Oxford University Press, 1979), Chapter 4; Nancy Bercaw, *Gendered Freedoms: Race, Rights, and the Politics of Household in the Delta, 1861–1875* (Gainesville: University Press of Florida, 2003), 1–93; Alicia P. Long and Lee Ann Whites, eds., *Occupied Women: Gender, Military Occupation, and the American Civil War* (Baton Rouge: Louisiana State University Press, 2009), 137–54.

4. The families of southern black soldiers, left behind with their masters, had to endure reprisals from masters who were upset about their former slaves joining the Union, usually after running away. For information about the struggles of black families in the South during the war, see Richard Reid, *Freedom for Themselves: North Carolina's Black Soldiers in the Civil War* (Chapel Hill: University of North Carolina Press, 2008), 215–53; Paul David Escott, *Paying Freedom's Price: A History of African Americans in the Civil War* (Laham, Md.: Rowman & Littlefield, 2016), 8–9; Wilma A. Dunaway, *The African-American Family in Slavery and Emancipation* (Cambridge: Cambridge University Press, 2003); Christopher Hager, *Word by Word: Emancipation and the Act of Writing* (Cambridge: Harvard University Press, 2013), 164–67; Long and Whites, eds., *Occupied*, 137–54. After the war, the threat of violence through race riots became prevalent. One of the first and worst was the three-day riot in Memphis, Tennessee, that began on May 1,

1866; see Hanna Rosen, *Terror in the Heart of Freedom: Citizenship, Sexual Violence, and the Meaning of Race in the Postemancipation South* (Chapel Hill: University of North Carolina Press, 2009), 47–49, 54; Stephen V. Ash, *A Massacre in Memphis: The Race Riot That Shook the Nation One Year After the Civil War* (New York: Hill & Wang Books, 2013).

5. Historian Christopher Hager argued that the act of writing displayed a "political representation" and a "national consciousness" not experienced before by most African Americans in their interaction with the government; see Hager, *Word by Word.*

6. Gregory P. Downs, *Declarations of Dependence: The Long Reconstruction of Popular Politics in the South, 1861–1908* (Chapel Hill: University of North Carolina Press, 2011), 1–14. In his study, Downs's primary sources were letters from southern family members to local and federal Confederate governments.

7. For an analysis of letters from southern blacks during and immediately after the Civil War, see Hager, *Word by Word.*

8. Immediately after the American Revolution northern states began amending their constitutions to ban slavery: Vermont, 1777; Pennsylvania, 1780; Massachusetts and New Hampshire, 1783; Connecticut and Rhode Island, 1784; New York, 1799; and New Jersey, 1804. In 1887, the Northwest Ordinance banned slavery in the Northwest Territory (from which became the states of Ohio, 1803; Indiana, 1816; Illinois, 1818; Michigan, 1837; and Wisconsin, 1848). For additional information about the transition from slavery to non-slavery in the northern states, especially for African-American women, see Erica Armstrong Dunbar, *A Fragile Freedom: African American Women and Emancipation in the Antebellum City* (New Haven: Yale University Press, 2008).

9. Based on the 1860 U.S. Census, Delaware had an African-American population of 19,829 free blacks and only 1,798 slaves. It was the only slave state with more free blacks than slaves within its borders. In comparison with what would become the other Union slave states, Kentucky had 10,684 free blacks and 225,483 slaves, Maryland 83,942 free blacks and 87,789 slaves, and Missouri 3,572 free blacks and 114,931 slaves. See *Population of the United States in 1860; Compiled From the Original Returns of the Eight Census* (Washington: Government Printing Office, 1864). I excluded three other Union states because geographically they are far western states: California, Nevada, and Oregon. In addition, their African-America population was minuscule in comparison to the northern and Midwestern states.

1. Life in the North: Before the War

1. Escott, *Paying Freedom's Price*, 8.

2. Based on the 1860 U.S. census, there were 46,150 black men in the North between the ages of eighteen and forty-five. See Ira Berlin and Leslie Rowland, eds., *Families & Freedom: A Documentary History of African-American Kinship in the Civil War Era* (New York: The New Press, 1997), 79; Ira Berlin, Joseph P. Reidy, and Leslie S. Rowland, eds., *Freedom: A Documentary History of Emancipation, 1861–1867*, Series 2, *The Black Military Experience* (New York: Cambridge University Press, 1982), 12.

3. Escott, *Paying Freedom's Price*, 8; Edward A. Miller, Jr., *The Black Civil War Soldiers of Illinois: The Story of the Twenty-Ninth U.S. Colored Infantry* (Columbia: The University

of South Carolina Press, 1998), 4–5; Ira Berlin, *Slaves Without Masters: The Free Negro in the Antebellum South* (New York: The New Press, 1974, reprinted 2007), 136; Campbell Gibson and Kay Jung, *Historical Census Statistics on Population Totals By Race, 1790 to 1990, and By Hispanic Origin, 1970 to 1990, For The United States, Regions, Divisions, and States*, Population Division, U. S. Census Bureau, Working Paper Series No. 56 (Washington, D.C., 2002), http://www.census.gov/population/www/documentation/twps0076/twps0076.html. For information on the antebellum and Civil War lives of African Americans in a small Indiana county, see Nicole Etcheson, *A Generation at War: The Civil War in a Northern Community* (Lawrence: University Press of Kansas, 2011).

4. Julie Winch, *Philadelphia's Black Elite: Activism, Accommodation, and the Struggle for Autonomy, 1787–1848* (Philadelphia: Temple University Press, 1988), 1; James Oliver Horton and Lois E. Horton, *Black Bostonians: Family Life and Community Struggle in the Antebellum North* (New York: Holmes & Meier Publishers, Inc., 1979), xi; R. J. M. Blackett, ed., *Thomas Morris Chester, Black Civil War Correspondent: His Dispatches from the Virginia Front* (New York: Da Capo Press, 1989), 6–8; Stephen Kantrowitz, *More Than Freedom: Fighting for Black Citizenship in a White Republic, 1829–1889* (New York: The Penguin Press, 2012), 2.

5. Robert L. McCaul, *Soldiering for Freedom: The Black Struggle for Public Schooling in Nineteenth-Century Illinois* (Carbondale: Southern Illinois University Press, 1987), 11–12 15–16, 20. Horton, *Black Bostonians*, 86; Blackett, ed., *Thomas Morris Chester*, 6–8; Kantrowitz, *More Than Freedom*, 2, 5.

6. For additional information about African-American activism in the North before the war, see Patrick Rael, *African-American Activism Before the Civil War: The Freedom Struggle in the Antebellum North* (New York: Routledge, 2008).

7. Horton, *Black Bostonians*, xi, 25, 15–16, 18; Stephen Kendrick and Paul Kendrick, *Sarah's Long Walk: The Free Blacks of Boston and How Their Struggle for Equality Changed America* (Boston: Beacon Press, 2004), 25.

8. Horton, *Black Bostonians*, 19–20; Jane Rhodes, *Mary Ann Shadd Cary: The Black Press and Protest in the Nineteenth Century* (Bloomington: Indiana University Press, 1998), 19.

9. Horton, *Black Bostonians*, xi, 25, 38; Kendrick, *Sarah's Long Walk*, 30.

10. Horton, *Black Bostonians*, xi, 25, 27–28, 30-31; Kendrick, *Sarah's Long Walk*, 33.

11. Sterling, ed., *We Are Sisters*, 105–10, 112; Harris, *In the Shadow of Slavery*, 202; Horton, *Black Bostonians*, 31–32.

12. Horton, *Black Bostonians*, 39, 43–45, 52; Kendrick, *Sarah's Long Walk*, 31.

13. Rhodes, *Mary Ann Shadd Cary*, 7; Horton, *Black Bostonians*, 39–42, 44–45, 51.

14. Horton, *Black Bostonians*, 66.

15. Leslie M. Harris, *In the Shadow of Slavery: African Americans in New York City, 1626–1863* (Chicago: University of Chicago Press, 2003), 222; Horton, *Black Bostonians*, 86; Winch, *Philadelphia's Black Elite*, 130, 134–36; James McPherson, *The Negro's Civil War: How American Blacks Felt and Acted During the War for the Union*, (New York: Ballantine Books, 1965, reprint 1991), 3; Nell Irvin Painter, *Sojourner Truth: A Life, A Symbol* (New York: Norton, 1996), 64; Milton C. Sernett, *North Star Country: Upstate New York and the Crusade for African American Freedom* (Syracuse: Syracuse University Press, 2002), 9; Rhodes, *Mary Ann Shadd Car*, 20.

16. Horton, *Black Bostonians*, xii; William Wells Brown, *The Negro in the American Rebellion: His Heroism and His Fidelity* (Athens: Ohio University Press, 2003 [originally published 1867]), xix–xx; Harris, *In the Shadow of Slavery*, 170–71, 210; Judith Giesberg, ed., *Emilie Davis's Civil War: The Diaries of a Free Black Woman in Philadelphia, 1863–1865* (University Park: Pennsylvania State University Press, 2014), 7; Philip S. Foner, ed., *The Life and Writings of Frederick Douglass*, Vol. 3, *The Civil War, 1861–1865* (New York: International Publishers, 1952), 246. For additional information on the kidnapping of free blacks see Carol Wilson, *Freedom at Risk: The Kidnapping of Free Blacks in America, 1780–1865* (Lexington: University Press of Kentucky, 1994).

17. Horton, *Black Bostonians*, 93; Berlin and Rowland, eds., *Families*, 79. For a discussion of the reasons why northern blacks chose to participate in the war, see Wilbert L. Jenkins, *Climbing Up to Glory: A Short History of African Americans During the Civil War and Reconstruction* (Wilmington: Scholarly Resources Inc., 2002), 45–47. Also see Dudley Taylor Cornish, *The Sable Arm: Black Troops in the Union Army, 1861–1865* (1956, reprint, Lawrence, University of Kansas Press, 1987), xiii; Joseph T. Glatthaar, *Forged in Battle: The Civil War Alliance of Black Soldiers and White Officers* (New York: Free Press, 1990), 79–80; John David Smith, ed., *Black Soldiers in Blue: African American Troops in the Civil War* (Chapel Hill: University of North Carolina Press, 2002), 7; Keith P. Wilson, *Campfires of Freedom: The Camp Life of Black Soldiers during the Civil War* (Kent: Kent State University Press, 2002), 4; Kantrowitz, *More Than Freedom*, 32.

18. McPherson, *The Negro's Civil War*, 10–13; Foner, ed., *Frederick Douglass*, Vol. 3, 100.

2. A Grand Opportunity: 1861 and 1862

1. For a better understanding of the initial reaction to the war by northern blacks, see Sernett, *North Star Country*, 222; Hondon B. Hargrove, *Black Union Soldiers in the Civil War* (Jefferson, N.C.: McFarland & Company, 1988), 2; Donald Yacovone, ed., *A Voice of Thunder: The Civil War Letters of George E. Stephens* (Urbana: University of Illinois, 1997), 14; Glatthaar, *Forged in Battle*, 3; McPherson, *The Negro's Civil War*, 19; Brown, *The Negro in the American Rebellion*, 30; Foner, ed., *Frederick Douglass*, Vol. 3, 97; David W. Blight, *Frederick Douglass' Civil War: Keeping Faith in Jubilee* (Baton Rouge: Louisiana State University Press, 1989), 148–49. *Frederick Douglass's Paper* was published in Rochester, New York, from 1851 to 1859. In 1859, Douglass began publication of *Douglass' Monthly*, a supplement to *Frederick Douglass's Paper*. Even after ending publication of *Frederick Douglass's Paper*, he continued publishing *Douglass' Monthly* until 1863.

2. Peter Clark, *The Black Brigade of Cincinnati* (New York: Arno Press, 1969), 5. Horton, *Black Bostonians*, 135.

3. The offer by northern blacks to help in the war effort was uniformly rejected throughout the North: See Yacovone, ed., *A Voice of Thunder*, 14–15; Benjamin Quarles, *The Negro in the Civil War* (New York: Da Capo Press, 1989, originally published 1953), 27–29; Brown, *The Negro in the American Rebellion*, 30; Sernett, *North Star Country*, 238; McPherson, *The Negro's Civil War*, 21–22; Cornish, *The Sable Arm*, 6–7; Clark, *The Black Brigade of Cincinnati*, 4–5; Rhodes, *Mary Ann Shadd Cary*, 137.

4. Quarles, *The Negro in the Civil War*, 30–31; C. R. Gibbs, *Black, Copper & Bright: The District of Columbia's Black Civil War Regiment* (Silver Spring, Md.: Three Divisional Publishing, 2002), 5–6; Sernett, *North Star Country*, 223, 234; Hargrove, *Black Union Soldiers*, 10–15; James P. McPherson, *Battle Cry of Freedom: The Civil War Era* (Oxford: Oxford University Press, 1988), 497; McPherson, *The Negro's Civil War*, 22, 166; Berlin, et al., eds., *Freedom*, 6; Glatthaar, *Forged in Battle*, 3; Miller, Jr., *The Black Civil War Soldiers of Illinois*, 1; Cornish, *The Sable Arm*, 10–11.

5. The reasons why, at its onset, the war was not about ending slavery have been well articulated by historians: See Yacovone, ed., *A Voice of Thunder*, 15; Foner, ed., *The Life and Writings*, III, 151–54; Blight, *Frederick Douglass' Civil War*, 149; McPherson, *The Negro's Civil War*, 29, 31–32, 33–35. The *Pine and Palm* was an emigrationists newspaper that was published in both Boston and New York. It was funded by the Haitian government in its effort to promote emigration of black Americans to Haiti. See Quarles, *The Negro in the Civil War*, 152–53; and Edwin S. Redkey, ed., *A Grand Army of Black Men: Letters of African-American Soldiers in the Union Army, 1861–1865* (New York: Cambridge University Press, 1992), xi.

6. Joseph T. Wilson, *The Black Phalanx: African American Soldiers in the War of 1812 & the Civil War* (Cambridge, Mass.: Da Capo Press, 1994), 103; *The War of the Rebellion: A Compilation of the Official Records of the Union and Confederate Navies*, 30 volumes (Washington, 1874–1922), series 1, vol. 6, 252; Giesberg, ed., *Emilie Davis's Civil War*, 35. For information about the African-American experience in the Union navy, see Steven J. Ramold, *Slaves, Sailors, Citizens: African Americans in the Union Navy* (DeKalb: Northern Illinois University Press, 2002); and Joseph P. Reidy, "Black Men in Navy Blue," *Prologue Magazine* 33, no. 3 (2001), https://www.archives.gov/publications/prologue/2001/fall/black-sailors-1.html.

7. McRae, *Negroes in Michigan*, 48–49; Miller, Jr., *The Black Civil War Soldiers of Illinois*, 10; McPherson, *The Negro's Civil War*, 35. According to Joseph T. Wilson, blacks passing as whites were scattered throughout northern white regiments, and some held prominent positions within their regiments; see Quarles, *The Negro in the Civil War*, 31–32, 128; Wilson, *The Black Phalanx*, 179–80. George probably easily passed for white since his father was white and his mother had a very light complexion herself. Elizabeth's father was also white, having been her mother's master. Elizabeth applied for, and was approved to receive, a pension after her son's death. As his surviving mother, she received the pension from August 10, 1861 until her death in 1907; see Jennifer Fleischner, *Mrs. Lincoln and Mrs. Keckley: The Remarkable Story of the Friendship Between a First Lady and a Former Slave* (New York: Broadway Books, 2003), 29, 87–89, 222; and Elizabeth Keckley, *Behind the Scenes in the Lincoln White House: Memoirs of an African-American Seamstress* (Mineola, N.Y.: Dove Publications, 2012 (originally published in 1868). George W. D. Kirkland Pension Files, 1st Missouri Volunteers, Records of the Veterans Administration, Record Group 15. Ironically, some southern blacks, loyal to the Confederate cause, passed for white and joined the Confederate army as well.

8. Yacovone, ed., *A Voice of Thunder*, xi–xii, 15–16; Redkey, ed., *A Grand Army of Black Men*, x–xi.

9. Yacovone, ed., *A Voice of Thunder*, 15–16.

10. Fleischner, *Mrs. Lincoln and Mrs. Keckley*, 248.

11. Ibid. "Contraband" was a term coined by General Benjamin F. Butler to classify fugitive slaves who escaped to Union lines. The fugitives were considered captured property of the Confederacy (equated to horses, mules, and other livestock) that the Union chose to not return to their masters. Categorized as contraband, the fugitives were considered to be property of war and the Union could now use the property to its own advantage to win the war. Until the Second Confiscation Act and Militia Act in July 1862, when all captured and fugitive slaves of rebels were declared free, the contraband label was used to justify the non-returning of runaway slaves by Union forces to their masters. See Berlin et al., eds., *Freedom*, 3–4, 7; Escott, *Paying Freedom's*, 14–15; Glatthaar, *Forged in Battle*, 4; McPherson, *Battle Cry of Freedom*, 355–56; William Dobak, *Freedom by the Sword: The U.S. Colored Troops, 1862–1867* (Washington: U.S. Government Printing Office, 2011), 3–5. Another result of the contraband interpretation is that it motivated even more slaves to run away toward Union lines, as they became aware that they would not be returned to their masters; Hargrove, *Black Union Soldiers*, 13.

12. See Fleischner, *Mrs. Lincoln and Mrs. Keckley*. Nina Silber, *Daughters of the Union: Northern Women Fight the Civil War* (Cambridge: Harvard University Press, 2005), 166–67, 224, 232, 234–35; Quarles, *The Negro in the Civil War*, 128–29; Rhodes, *Mary Ann Shadd Cary*, 155; Painter, *Sojourner Truth*, 203–4; Ella Forbes, *African American Women During the Civil War* (New York: Garland Publishing, 1998), 66–72; Dorothy Sterling, ed., *We Are Sisters: Black Women in the Nineteenth Century* (New York: Norton, 1984, reissued 1997), 245–47, 248–51; McPherson, *The Negro's Civil War*, 138–40.

13. Sterling, ed., *We Are Sisters*, 119–26, 188; Horton, *Black Bostonians*, 20–21; McPherson, *The Negro's Civil War*, 141; Quarles, *The Negro in the Civil War*, 176. Charlotte's grandfather was James Forten, Sr., a wealthy black businessman, sail maker, and one of the nation's first abolitionist leaders. Her paternal grandmother and namesake, Charlotte Forten, was also an active abolitionist in Philadelphia, as was her father, Robert Bridges Forten, and her uncle Robert Purvis, Sr., who was married to her aunt, Harriet Forten, an activist in her own right. Purvis was an influential member of several anti-slavery organizations and he helped organize the first underground railroad group in Philadelphia, helping many fugitive slaves gain their freedom. She was a well-educated woman. And Charlotte involved herself in similar protest activities as well as efforts to improve the lives of people in her community, with the blessings of her family. During the Civil War, Charlotte even took her activism south, where she taught black refugees in Port Royal, South Carolina, from October 1862 to May 1864. After the war, she married Francis Grimke, a prominent black minster and civil rights advocate in Washington, D.C. For additional information on Charlotte Forten Grimke, see Brenda Stevenson, ed., *The Journals of Charlotte Forten Grimke* (New York: Oxford University Press, 1988); see also, Julie Winch, *A Gentleman of Color: The Life of James Forten* (Oxford: Oxford University Press, 2002); Margaret Hope Bacon, *But One Race: The Life of Robert Purvis* (Albany, N.Y.: SUNY Press, 2007).

14. McPherson, *The Negro's Civil War*, 140; Forbes, *African American Women*, 68, 110; Sterling, ed., *We Are Sisters*, 250–51; Jeanie Attie, *Patriotic Toil: Northern Women and the American Civil War* (Ithaca: Cornell University Press, 1998), 93–94.

15. Berlin et al., eds., *Freedom*, 1, 8; Quarles, *The Negro in the Civil War*, 107, 157–58; Brown, *The Negro in the American Rebellion*, xxii; Hargrove, *Black Union Soldiers*, 23–25. It must be also noted that even though Lincoln proclaimed to free slaves in rebel territory once those territories came under the control of Union armies, freedom was only a temporary status. In reality, these blacks were no longer under the control of their rebel masters, but legally they were not *free* and would not be until slavery was officially abolished after the war with adoption of the Thirteenth Amendment on December 6, 1865. Also, historically, many slaves had freed themselves by running away from their masters. Those numbers increased drastically during the war because slaves saw an opportunity with Union armies nearby and many male masters away from home. For additional information about self-emancipation, see David Williams, *I Freed Myself: African American Self-Emancipation in the Civil War Era* (New York: Cambridge University Press, 2014).

16. Quarles, *The Negro in the Civil War*, 161; Glatthaar, *Forged in Battle*, 9; Hargrove, *Black Union Soldiers*, 35; Noah Andrea Trudeau, *Like Men of War: Black Troops in the Civil War* (Boston: Little Brown, 1998), 18–19. Lincoln felt he could not move against slavery until the North achieved a major battlefield success. His Secretary of State, William H. Seward, advised him to wait until a Union victory so the bold move did not appear as if the government was acting out of desperation. That victory came with the defeat of Lee's forces at the battle of Antietam on September 17, 1862. Though it was not a decisive victory, it was good enough after the string of Union defeats that began in the spring of 1862. For a more detailed account of the battle and its aftermath, see James McPherson, *Antietam: The Battle That Changed the Course of the War* (Oxford: Oxford University Press, 2002).

17. Brown, *The Negro in the American Rebellion*, 62, 69; Quarles, *The Negro in the Civil War*, 164, 170–76; Blight, *Frederick Douglass' Civil War*, 106.

18. Brown, *The Negro in the American Rebellion*, 72.

19. Brian Taylor, "A Politics of Service: Black Northerners' Debates over Enlistment in the American Civil War," *Civil War History* 58, no. 4 (December 2012), 451–80.

3. The Forming of Black Regiments and Success in Battle

1. See Cornish, *The Sable Arm*, xiii; Yacovone, ed., *A Voice of Thunder*, 321n2; McRae, *Negroes in Michigan*, 31–32. Norwood Hallowell, *Papers of the Military Historical Society of Massachusetts: Civil and Mexican Wars, Vol. XIII, Chapter VIII*, "The Negro as a Soldier in the War of the Rebellion," Read before the Society on January 5, 1892 (Boston: Military Historical Society of Massachusetts, 1913), 291. For additional information about the role of blacks in the American Revolution, see Michael Lee Lanning, *African Americans in the Revolutionary War* (New York: Kensington Publishing, 2000); Benjamin Quarles, *The Negro in the American Revolution* (Chapel Hill, University of North Carolina Press, 1996, first published 1964). For additional information about the role of blacks in the Mexican-American War, see Robert E. May, "Invisible Men: Blacks and the U.S. Army in the Mexican War," *Historian* 49, no. 4 (August 1987), 463–77.

2. Ira Berlin, *Families*, 79. See the obituary of Sgt. Alexander Atwood in the Philadelphia *Christian Recorder*, November 5, 1865. According to historian Bell I. Wiley, most

Civil War soldiers were between the ages of 18 and 29, with an average age of 26, but many black regiments had men far beyond that age. Anxious to participate as soldiers, men joined who were far beyond their twenties. The 54th Massachusetts, for example, had men who were in their forties and even fifties. See Bell I. Wiley, *The Life of Billy Yank: The Common Soldier of the Union* (Indianapolis: Bobbs-Merrill Co., 1851, 1952), 296, 298–303. Yacovone, ed., *The Voice of Thunder*, 26, 33.

3. Berlin, et al., eds., *Freedom*, 75; Cornish, *The Sable Arm*, 105–6; *The War of the Rebellion: Official Records of the Union and Confederate Armies*, 128 Volumes (Washington, 1880–1902), series 3, vol. 3, 20–21; Trudeau, *Like Men of War*, 71; Glatthaar, *Forged in Battle*, 37; Yacovone, *The Voice of Thunder*, 29.

4. Cornish, *The Sable Arm*, 107–8; Berlin et al., eds., *Freedom*, 75–76; Blight, *Frederick Douglass' Civil War*, 158. For more information on the formation of the 54th Massachusetts Infantry, see Luis Emilio, *A Brave Black Regiment* (1894, reprint, New York: Bantam Books, 1992), 11; Peter Burchard, *One Gallant Rush: Robert Gould Shaw and His Brave Black Regiment* (New York: St. Martin's Press, 1965), 84–86; Yacovone, ed., *The Voice of Thunder*, 222–23.

5. Charles R. Douglass Service Records, 54th Massachusetts Regiment; Lewis H. Douglass Service Records, 54th Massachusetts Regiment. Lewis applied for an invalid pension in 1904, at the age of sixty-three. His application was approved and, on November 21, 1905, he began receiving $8.00 per month, which he received until his death on September 19, 1908, in Washington, D.C. Afterwards, his wife, Helen Amelia Douglass, received a widow's pension until her death on June 21, 1936, at the age of ninety-three, also in D.C.; see Lewis H. Douglass Pension Files, 54th Massachusetts Regiment, Records of the Veterans Administration, Record Group 15.

6. Norwood P. Hallowell, colonel of the 55th Massachusetts and brother of Edward M. Hallowell, compiled statistics on the 55th, which he felt was a typical northern regiment. According to Hallowell, "Of the 961 enlisted men in the 55th, the largest number (222) were born in Ohio, followed by Pennsylvania (139), Virginia (106), Indiana (97), Kentucky (68), Missouri (66), and Illinois (56). The remaining 207 men were born in eighteen states (including eleven slave states), the District of Columbia, Nova Scotia, Canada, Africa, and places "unknown." See Hallowell, *Papers of the Military Historical Society of Massachusetts*, 294.

7. Forbes, *African American Women*, 44. Mary Ann Shadd Cary was a leader within the black community in the United States and Canada. She was an abolitionist, educator, newspaperwoman, suffragist, and emigrationist. Cary came from a remarkable free-born activist family, the Shadds. Born in Delaware and raised both there and in Pennsylvania, Mary Ann emigrated to Canada in 1851. In Canada, she became the first black woman, in either country, to publish and edit a newspaper when she started and operated the *Provincial Freeman*, first published on March 24, 1853 in Windsor. See Rhodes, *Mary Ann Shadd Cary*; and Sterling, ed., *We Are Sisters*, 164–75.

8. Jenkins, *Climbing Up to Glory*, 25. Mary Shadd Carey personally recruited a number of men from Canada, many of them ex-slaves who escaped to there. See Norman McRae, *Negroes in Michigan During the Civil War* (Lansing: Michigan Civil War Centennial Observance Commission, 1966), 47; Forbes, *African American Women*, 43, 195; also

see Rhodes, *Mary Ann Shadd Cary*, 152–57. For a short period of time, Abraham was relieved from regular duty and, like his sister, served as a recruiter for the Union army, working directly with Martin Delany; Abraham W. Shadd Service Records, 55th Massachusetts Infantry. After serving only one year, Gabriel was discharged for a physical illness (chronic rheumatism) on June 24, 1864, at Folly Island, South Carolina; Gabriel Jackson Shadd Service Records, 55th Massachusetts Infantry; Gabriel Jackson Shadd Pension Files, 55th Massachusetts Infantry, Records of the Veterans Administration, Record Group 15. Gabriel Jackson Service Records, 55th Massachusetts Infantry; Toussaint L'Overture Delany Service Records, 54th Massachusetts Infantry; Toussaint L'Overture Delany Pension Files, 54th Massachusetts Infantry, Records of the Veterans Administration, Record Group 15. Later in life, when Delany found it necessary to apply for a military pension due to a disability, he verified his birthday as February 28, 1848. Thus, he had just turned sixteen when his father actually enlisted him in the Union army.

9. Glatthaar, *Forged in Battle*, 121–22; Smith, ed., *Black Soldiers in Blue*, 4–5; Cornish, *The Sable Arm*, 110; Hallowell, *Papers of the Military Historical Society of Massachusetts*, 293–94.

10. Cornish, *The Sable Arm*, 110; Burchard, *One Gallant Rush*, 84–86; Blight, *Frederick Douglass' Civil War*, 158–59; Yacovone, ed., *The Voice of Thunder*, 29–33; See Hallowell, *Papers of the Military Historical Society of Massachusetts*, 294; Taylor, "A Politics of Service," 451–80. For additional information about the new regiment's initial training at Readville, see Russell Duncan, ed., *Blue-Eyed Child of Fortune: The Civil War Letters of Colonel Robert Gould Shaw* (Athens: University of Georgia Press, 1992), Chapter 11.

11. *Official Records*, series 3, vol. 3, 100–1; Trudeau, *Like Men of War*, 47–48; Glatthaar, *Forged in Battle*, 10, 38; Smith, ed., *Black Soldiers in Blue*, 25–28; Hargrove, *Black Union Soldiers*, 104; Cornish, *The Sable Arm*, 112–14, 130–31; Berlin et al., eds., *Freedom*, Series 2, 407. As the head of the Bureau for Colored Troops, it was Major Charles W. Foster's signature that was on many of the letters the Union army sent responding to requests from northern black families.

12. Dobak, *Freedom by the Sword*, 13–19; Ira Berlin, Joseph P. Reidy, and Leslie S. Rowland, eds., *Freedom's Soldiers: The Black Military Experience in the Civil War* (Cambridge: Cambridge University Press, 1998), 26–29; Glatthaar, *Forged in Battle*, 36; Wilson, *Campfires of Freedom*, 109–10; Smith, ed., *Black Soldiers in Blue*, 36.

13. Glatthaar, *Forged in Battle*, 35, 83–84. Quarles, *The Negro in the Civil War*, 116–20; Hargrove, *Black Union Soldiers*, 48–58; Cornish, *The Sable Arm*, 63, 65–68, 88–93; Trudeau, *Like Men of War*, 3–7, 13–14, 26–28, 46; James G. Hollandsworth, Jr., *The Louisiana Native Guards: The Black Military Experience During the Civil War* (Baton Rouge: Louisiana State University Press, 1995), 16–18, 70; *Official Records*, series 1, Vol. XIV, 377–78. These regiments were formed under the Second Confiscation Act and the Militia Act, both enacted in July 1862, which authorized the mobilization of African Americans into military units. Other regiments formed were the 1st South Carolina Colored Volunteers, mustered into service on November 7, 1862, and the 1st Kansas (Colored) Volunteer Infantry, which was mustered in on January 13, 1863, and would later be designated the 79th United States Colored Troops. For additional information about the 1st South Carolina Infantry, later designated the 33rd USCT, see Stephen V. Ash, *Firebrand*

of Liberty: The Story of Two Black Regiments that Changed the Course of the Civil War (New York: Norton, 2008). For additional information about the 1st Kansas (Colored) Volunteer Infantry, later designated the 79th USCT, see Ian Michael Spurgeon, *Soldiers in the Army of Freedom: The 1st Kansas Colored, the Civil War's First African American Combat Unity* (Norman: University of Oklahoma Press, 2014).

14. See Hollandsworth, Jr., *The Louisiana Native Guards*, 16–18, 20, 70; *Official Records*, series 25, vol. 1, 539; Trudeau, *Like Men of War*, 27, 46; Cornish, *The Sable Arm*, 142; Glatthaar, *Forged in Battle*, 123; Redkey, ed., *A Grand Army of Black Men*, 137–38; Smith, ed., *Black Soldiers in Blue*, 82.

15. Needing every available regiment for the campaign, Banks included the 1st and 3rd Louisiana Native Guards in his forces. The 1st had already lost its black officers but not yet the 3rd. The 2nd Louisiana Native Guards was not available at the time because it was performing garrison duties elsewhere. See Trudeau, *Like Men of War*, 34–43; Glatthaar, *Forged in Battle*, 123–27; Redkey, ed., *A Grand Army of Black Men*, 137–38; Smith, ed., *Black Soldiers in Blue*, 84–91; Wilson, *The Black Phalanx*, 212–19.

16. Wilson, *The Black Phalanx*, 212–13.

17. Trudeau, *Like Men of War*, 43–46; Glatthaar, *Forged in Battle*, 127–29; Smith, ed., *Black Soldiers in Blue*, 91–97; Wilson, *The Black Phalanx*, 212–17.

18. Trudeau, *Like Men of War*, 45; Cornish, *The Sable Arm*, 143; Glatthaar, *Forged in Battle*, 129–30; Smith, ed., *Black Soldiers in Blue*, 97–98; Hollandsworth, Jr., *The Louisiana Native Guards*, 62–64; *Official Records*, series 1, vol. 26, 45; Wilson, *The Black Phalanx*, 217–19.

19. Trudeau, *Like Men of War*, 46–59; Cornish, *The Sable Arm*, 144–45; Glatthaar, *Forged in Battle*, 130–35; Smith, ed., *Black Soldiers in Blue*, 55; Wilson, *The Black Phalanx*, 203–7. For more details about the performance about black soldiers at Milliken's Bend, see Smith, ed., *Black Soldiers in Blue*, 107–35. The 9th was organized on May 1, 1863, the 1st on May 16, and the 11th on May 23. The 1st was not armed until the day before the battle. As a result, its men received only two days of target practice. The Confederate soldiers under the command of Major General John G. Walker's Texas Infantry Division were nearly as inexperienced as the black soldiers they faced at Milliken's Bend. Though they had more experience marching, they had virtually no experience under fire and had received no target practice with their antiquated weapons. See Richard N. Current, ed., *Encyclopedia of the Confederacy* (New York: Simon & Schuster, 1993).

20. Burchard, *One Gallant Rush*, 90–95; Yacovone, ed., *The Voice of Thunder*, 35–37; Cornish, *The Sable Arm*, 147–48; Kantrowitz, *More Than Freedom*, 1. Crispus Attucks is considered the first American killed in the American Revolutionary War. He was of African-American decent and was shot by British troops on March 5, 1770 during the Boston Massacre.

21. Yacovone, ed., *The Voice of Thunder*, 37; Cornish, *The Sable Arm*, 148.

22. Duncan, ed., *Blue-Eyed Child of Fortune*, 384; Burchard, *One Gallant Rush*, 122–26; Trudeau, *Like Men of War*, 74–76. For additional information about the treatment of black soldiers by Confederacy, including after they were captured, see Cornish, *The Sable Arm*, Chapter 9.

23. Burchard, *One Gallant Rush*, 133; Trudeau, *Like Men of War*, 76; Bob Luke and John David Smith. *Soldering for Freedom: How the Union Army Recruited, Trained, and*

Deployed the U.S. Colored Troops (Baltimore: Johns Hopkins University Press, 2014), 1. It has been well recorded by historians that Strong and Shaw saw an opportunity for the 54th to shine, but in question were the intentions of Major General Truman Seymour, the division commander, who approved the request to have the 54th head the attack. It is not clear whether he gave the approval because he saw the planned assault as an opportunity to get rid of the well publicized regiment once and for all or, as he was quoted as saying afterward, the 54th was chosen because they were as "efficient as any body of men." See Cornish, *The Sable Arm*, 151–53; Glatthaar, *Forged in Battle*, 136–37.

24. Burchard, *One Gallant Rush*, 120–21; Glatthaar, *Forged in Battle*, 137–38; Trudeau, *Like Men of War*, 76, 77; Redkey, *A Grand Army of Black Men*, 29; Yacovone, ed., *The Voice of Thunder*, 42–43.

25. Burchard, *One Gallant Rush*, 134–41; Cornish, *The Sable Arm*, 153–54; Trudeau, *Like Men of War*, 78–86. Aware that he might not survive the charge, Shaw had earlier given some of his personal papers to a friend to give to his family in case he died. See Glatthaar, *Forged in Battle*, 138–40.

26. Cornish, *The Sable Arm*, 55–56; Redkey, *A Grand Army of Black Men*, 27–28. Yacovone, *The Voice of Thunder*, 45–46; Burchard, *One Gallant Rush*, 141. For number of casualties also see Frederick H. Dyer, *A Compendium of the War of the Rebellion. Compiled and Arranged from Official Records of the Federal and Confederate Armies Reports of the Adjutant Generals of the Several States, the Army Registers and Other Reliable Documents and Sources* (Iowa, 1908), 1237; William F. Fox, *Regimental Losses In The American Civil War, 1861–1865, A Treatise On The Extent And Nature Of The Mortuary Losses In The Union Regiments, With Full And Exhaustive Statistics Compiled From The Official Records On File In The State Military Bureaus And At Washington* (New York, 1889), Chapter 10. Congress first authorized the Medal of Honor in the navy in December 1861 and the army in July 1862. It is "the highest decoration for valor" in all U.S. branches of the military. See Mark M. Boatner, ed., *The Civil War Dictionary* (New York: Vintage Books, 1991), 541–42. For additional information about the history of the 54th Massachusetts Infantry, see Virginia Matzke Adams, ed., *On the Altar of Freedom: A Black Soldier's Civil War Letters from the Front* (Amherst: University of Massachusetts Press, 1991).

27. Burchard, *One Gallant Rush*, 149; Trudeau, *Like Men of War*, 356. Fort Wagner did not come under Union control until after the Confederates abandoned it and nearby Fort Gregg on September 7, 1863, at which point Gilmore's guns freely fired upon Fort Sumter and Charleston.

28. Glatthaar, *Forged in Battle*, 32, 141; Dyer, *Compendium*, 1718; Smith, ed., *Black Soldiers in Blue*, 8, 99; Yacovone, ed., *The Voice of Thunder*, 58; Berlin et al., eds., *Freedom's Soldiers*, 16–17.

29. The Enrollment Act of March 1863 allowed wealthy draftees to buy their way out of military service by employing a substitute to take their place. This provision upset other draftees who felt it unfairly allowed the rich to avoid service. Protests over the provision helped to cause the riots in Detroit and New York City in 1863. In February 1864, Congress revised the Enrollment Act, eliminating many of the inequities that led to violent protests. See Berlin et al, eds., *Freedom's Soldiers*, 14; McRae, *Negroes in Michigan*, 34.

30. Cornish, *The Sable Arm*, 235; Hargrove, *Black Union Soldiers*, 105.

31. Glatthaar, *Forged in Battle*, 65–66, 76; McRae, *Negroes in Michigan*, 46. Recruits who were not yet eighteen could enlist as musicians in the army if their parents agreed and signed the required paperwork.

32. Mary Ann Douglas to Edwin Stanton, August 6, 1863, Colonel John H. Holman (commander 1st USCT) to Lorenzo Thomas, September 16, 1863, D-29, 1863, Letters Received, series 360, Colored Troops Division, Record Group 94; Daniel Douglas Service Records, 1st USCT; Daniel Douglas Pension Files, 1st USCI, Records of the Veterans Administration, Record Group 15.

33. Daniel's ailments, which had become chronic, were the basis of his February 19, 1891 pension application. In addition, after his death, his two youngest children were eventually approved to receive minor pensions; see Daniel Douglas Pension Files, 1st USCI, Records of the Veterans Administration, Record Group 15. Most Civil War regiments were mustered out of service while still in the field. The regiment was then allowed to return to the regiment's home, where the soldiers were officially discharged. During the Civil War, regiments were mustered out of service when they were brought together for final inspection and registered for final payment and discharged from military service. Individual soldiers were discharged from service when they were officially relieved of duty and the regiment disbanded. See Edward Samuel Farrow, *A Dictionary of Military Terms* (New York: Thomas Y. Crowell Company Publishers, 1918); Thomas Wilhelm, *A Military Dictionary and Gazetteer: Comprising Ancient and Modern Military* (Philadelphia: L. R. Hamersly, 1881).

34. Charles B. Smith to Abraham Lincoln, November 27, 1863, Charles B. Smith to Abraham Lincoln, November 28, 1863, Charles B. Smith to Abraham Lincoln, December 25, 1863, S-334, 1863, Letters Received, series 360, Colored Troops Division, Record Group 94.

35. Ibid.

36. Ibid; Richard Smith Service Records, 3rd USCT; Richard Smith Pension Files, 3rd USCI, Records of the Veterans Administration, Record Group 15. Richard Smith provided the government with signed physician statements and several other notarized documents as a requirement to prove his eligibility for a disability pension.

37. Hester Ann Laws to Lorenzo Thomas, October 27, 1863, F-70, 1863, Letters Received, series 360, Colored Troops Division, Record Group 94.

38. Hester Ann Laws to Lorenzo Thomas, October 27, 1863, F-70, 1863, Letters Received, series 360, Colored Troops Division, Record Group 94; Daniel Laws Service Records, 6th USCT; Joshua Laws Service Records, 43rd USCT.

39. Hester Ann Laws to Lorenzo Thomas, October 27, 1863, F-70, 1863, Letters Received, series 360, Colored Troops Division, Record Group 94; Daniel Laws Service Records, 6th USCT; Joshua Laws Service Records, 43rd USCT; Glatthaar, *Forged in Battle*, 67–68. Hester later filed and was awarded a dependent mother's pension for her son's service and death for his country. She received it monthly until her death on March 20, 1894. See Daniel Laws Pension Files, 6th USCI, Records of the Veterans Administration, Record Group 15.

40. Dobak, *Freedom by the Sword*, 310–12. Beginning with the 3rd USCT, which graduated in late July 1863, a total of eleven black regiments, equaling 10,940 men, were

trained at Camp Penn, more than any other camp for black troops. Many of them were from Philadelphia. For additional information about Camp Penn and the recruitment of black troops in Philadelphia see Jeffry D. Wert, "Camp William Penn and the Black Soldier," *Pennsylvania History* 46, no. 4 (October 1979), 335–46; Andrew T. Tremel, "The Union League, Black Leaders, and the Recruitment of Philadelphia's African American Civil War Regiments," *Pennsylvania History* 80, no. 1 (Winter 2013), 13–36; James M. Paradis, *Strike the Blow for Freedom: The 6th United States Colored Infantry in the Civil War* (Shippensburg, Pa.: White Mane Books, 1998), 5–31. James Elton Johnson, *A History of Camp William Penn and its Black Troops in the Civil War, 1863–1865* (Philadelphia: University of Pennsylvania, 1999), dissertation; and Donald Scott, Sr., *Camp William Penn: 1863–1865* (Atglen, Pa., Schiffer Publishing, 2012). Because of the camps' close proximity to a large African-American community, the troops in training were visited often by northern black female family members, friends, and supporters, stated twenty-three-years-old Philadelphian Emilie Davis. Giesberg, ed., *Emilie Davis's Civil War*, 54, 88, 98.

41. Glatthaar, *Forged in Battle*, 71; Berlin et al., eds., *Freedom's Soldiers*, 16, 22; Cornish, *The Sable Arm*, 255; Smith, ed., *Black Soldiers in Blue*, 8.

4. The Unequal Pay Issue

1. Cornish, *The Sable Arm*, 188; Yacovone, ed., *The Voice of Thunder*, 58–59.

2. Berlin and Rowland, eds., *Families & Freedom*, 84; Cornish, *The Sable Arm*, 184–85; Hallowell, *Papers of the Military Historical Society of Massachusetts*, 302; Wiley, *The Life of Billy Yank*, 48–49; Yacovone, ed., *The Voice of Thunder*, 58. As a part of their monthly pay, Union troops were given a three-dollar allowance for uniforms. Troops in white regiments received the three dollars as a part of their salary, giving them control and flexibility as to how to use the funds, whereas black troops never saw their three-dollar allowance because it was taken out of their monthly pay from the start.

3. Berlin and Rowland, eds., *Families & Freedom*, 84; Burchard, *One Gallant Rush*, 115; Cornish, *The Sable Arm*, 184–86; February 12, 1863 diary memoranda, Records of the 54th Regiment (Captain Luis F. Emilio, of Salem), 1863–1915, Civil War Correspondence, Diaries, and Journals at the Massachusetts Historical Society, 1754–1926, reel 13; Emilio, *A Brave Black Regiment*, 109; Glatthaar, *Forged in Battle*, 169–70; Smith, ed., *Black Soldiers in Blue*, 49–50; Wilson, *Campfires of Freedom*, 44–45.

4. Redkey, ed., *A Grand Army of Black Men*, 230–31; Yacovone, *The Voice of Thunder*, 58–59. One of the reasons given for the New York Draft Riots was competition between blacks and newly arrived immigrants for the same menial employment opportunities. See Iver Bernstein, *The New York City Draft Riots: Their Significance for American Society and Politics in the Age of the Civil War* (New York: Oxford University Press, 1990), 27.

5. Aaron Peterson to Edwin Stanton, October 29, 1863, Hiram A. Peterson to Aaron Peterson, October 24, 1863, P-29, 1863, Letters Received, series 360, Colored Troops Division, Record Group 94; Hiram Peterson Service Records, 2nd USCT.

6. Aaron Peterson to Edwin Stanton, October 29, 1863, Hiram A. Peterson to Aaron Peterson, October 24, 1863, P-29, 1863, Letters Received, series 360, Colored Troops Division, Record Group 94.

7. Berlin et al., eds., *Freedom*, 365–66; Berlin et al., eds., *Freedom's Soldiers*, 30; Glatthaar, *Forged in Battle*, 170–71; Hallowell, *Papers of the Military Historical Society of Massachusetts*, 302–3; Wilson, *Campfires of Freedom*, 47; Redkey, ed., *A Grand Army of Black Men*, 231, 234–35.

8. Redkey, ed., *A Grand Army of Black Men*, 234–35.

9. Glatthaar, *Forged in Battle*, 171; Wilson, *Campfires of Freedom*, 47–49; Redkey, ed., *A Grand Army of Black Men*, 231–48; Taylor, "A Politics of Service: Black Northerners' Debates over Enlistment in the American Civil War," 472.

10. Yacovone, ed., *The Voice of Thunder*, 259.

11. Redkey, ed., *A Grand Army of Black Men*, 235–36.

12. James Henry Gooding to Abraham Lincoln, September 28, 1863, H-133, 1863, Letters Received, series 360, Colored Troops Division, Record Group 94. In his letter, Gooding was referring to Lincoln's July 30, 1863 statement to the Confederacy proclaiming the Union would "give the same protection to all its soldiers [black and white]" and would severely punish any offenses by Confederate troops upon any Union soldiers. See *Official Records*, series 2, vol. 6, 163. From March 3, 1863 to February 22, 1864, the *Mercury* published one of Gooding's letters almost every week. See Adams, ed., *On The Altar of Freedom*, xxxiii, 118–20. According to Adams, there is no evidence that Lincoln ever saw the letter.

13. James Henry Gooding Service Records, 54th Massachusetts Regiment; James Henry Gooding to Abraham Lincoln, September 28, 1863, H-133, 1863, Letters Received, series 360, Colored Troops Division, Record Group 94; Redkey, ed., *A Grand Army of Black Men*, 232–33, 235–36; Wilson, *Campfires of Freedom*, 47–51, 75; Yacovone, ed., *The Voice of Thunder*, 59–60, 62, 241.

14. Cornish, *The Sable Arm*, 188; Glatthaar, *Forged in Battle*, 171–72; Yacovone, ed., *The Voice of Thunder*, 63–64. According to Yacovone, Stephens was probably given the month-long furlough specifically to deal with his family's situation and to move his family, who according to city directories, moved three times between 1860 and 1865.

15. Cornish, *The Sable Arm*, 192–95; Glatthaar, *Forged in Battle*, 174–75; Yacovone, ed., *A Voice of Thunder*, 78–79; Redkey, ed., *A Grand Army of Black Men*, 231.

16. Smith, ed., *Black Soldiers in Blue*, 52, 55, 136.

17. Trudeau, *Like Men of War*, 122–28; Emilio, *A Brave Black Regiment*, 148–50; Redkey, ed., *A Grand Army of Black Men*, 30–31; Yacovone, ed., *A Voice of Thunder*, 64–65; Smith, ed., "The Battle of Olustee," *Black Soldiers in Blue*, 136–37. Seymour was a West Point graduate with some degree of success in a number of battles in Virginia, but was known for being both vain and impulsive, if not reckless, in battle. The 55th Massachusetts Infantry and the 3rd USCT also arrived in Florida, but too late to participate in the battle so they were held in reserve at Jacksonville, performing picket and guard duty.

18. Emilio, *A Brave Black Regiment*, 157; Yacovone, ed., *A Voice of Thunder*, 65–67; Adams, ed., *On the Altar of Freedom*, 108–9; Smith, ed., *Black Soldiers in Blue*, 137–38; Trudeau, *Like Men of War*, 132–37.

19. Trudeau, *Like Men of War*, 137–52; Cornish, *The Sable Arm*, 267–68; Redkey, ed., *A Grand Army of Black Men*, 31; Melvin Claxton and Mark Puls, *Uncommon Valor: A Story of Race, Patriotism, and Glory in the Final Battles of the Civil War* (Hoboken, N.J.: John Wiley & Sons, Inc., 2006), 99–100; Hallowell, *Papers of the Military Historical Society*

of Massachusetts, 308–9; Smith, ed., *Black Soldiers in Blue*, 138, 139–42; Yacovone, ed., *A Voice of Thunder*, 67, 295–96.

20. Adams, ed., *On the Altar of Freedom*, xxxi, 108–9, 114–15; Redkey, ed., *A Grand Army of Black Men*, 31; Emilio, *A Brave Black Regiment*, 162–73; Hallowell, *Papers of the Military Historical Society of Massachusetts*, 308–9; Smith, ed., *Black Soldiers in Blue*, 143–45. Historians have estimated that as many as fifty wounded blacks were killed after the fighting had ended. See Yacovone, ed., *A Voice of Thunder*, 67–69, 295–97; William A. Gladstone, *Men of Color* (Gettysburg, 1993), 36. For additional information on Andersonville, see William B. Hesseltine, ed., *Civil War Prisons* (Kent, Ohio: Kent State University Press, 1972, eight printing, 1995), 9–31. In death, Gooding left behind a wife, Ellen Louise Gooding, but no children. She applied for and was approved for a widow's pension, which commenced on February 20, 1864 and ended with her death in May 1903. She never remarried. See James H. Gooding Pension Files, 54th Massachusetts Infantry, Records of the Veterans Administration, Record Group 15. Toussaint L'Overture Delany was recruited at fifteen by his father, Martin Delany, to join the 54th. Martin worked for George L. Stearns as a recruiter for the 54th. Toussaint was enlisted at sixteen into Company D and served until the entire regiment was discharged in 1865; Toussaint L'Overture Delany Pension Files, 54th Massachusetts Infantry, Records of the Veterans Administration, Record Group 15.

21. Cornish, *The Sable Arm*, 268–69; Yacovone, ed., *A Voice of Thunder*, 69.

22. Redkey, ed., *A Grand Army of Black Men*, 31; Wilson, *Campfires of Freedom*, 52; Gladstone, *Men of Color*, 36; Yacovone, ed., *A Voice of Thunder*, 67.

23. Redkey, ed., *A Grand Army of Black Men*, 47–48.

24. Emilio, *A Brave Black Regiment*, 179.

25. Yacovone, ed., *The Voice of Thunder*, 292.

26. Ibid., 64, 70–71; Jenkins, *Climbing Up to Glory*, 34.

27. Wilson, *Campfires of Freedom*, 46; Yacovone, ed., *The Voice of Thunder*, 70–71, 309–10.

28. Hallowell served under Robert Gould Shaw and took over the regiment after Shaw's death at Fort Wagner, where Hallowell was also severely wounded. An abolitionist from Philadelphia with connections to Wendell Phillips, he fully supported the regiment's refusal to accept the decreased pay. But he was also committed to keeping order in his command. Glatthaar, *Forged in Battle*, 173; Yacovone, ed., *The Voice of Thunder*, 71–72; Yacovone, ed., *The Voice of Thunder*, 71–72; Berlin, et al., eds., *Freedom's Soldiers*, 30; Hallowell, *Papers of the Military Historical Society of Massachusetts*, 303; Redkey, ed., *A Grand Army of Black Men*, 229–31; Wilson, *Campfires of Freedom*, 47; William Walker Service Records, 21st USCT; Letter from Brigadier General T. Seymour to Head Quarters District of Florida, February 28, 1864, enclosed with William Walker Service Records. Walker's regiment, the 3rd South Carolina Colored Infantry (designated the 21st USCT on March 14, 1864), was in Florida at the time of the Battle at Olustee, but did not participate in the battle because it was held in reserve in Jacksonville away from the frontlines.

29. William Walker Service Records, 21st USCT; Letter from William Walker to Colonel Hall Provost Marshall, February 7, 1864, enclosed with William Walker Service Records.

30. Ibid.

31. Ibid. Walker was one of the few Union men who served in both the navy and army during the war. Wanting to serve the Union when the war began, similar to many African Americans, he probably joined the navy as a way to contribute to the war effort. Because of severe manpower shortages, the Union navy began enlisting blacks in September 1861, long before the army did. Black sailors made up 20 percent of the Union navy's total force. The Captain Worden who Walker was referring to was John Lorimer Worden. Worden commanded the USS Monitor in the famous naval battle against the Confederate vessel Virginia (originally named Merrimack) in first battle of ironclad ships on March 9, 1862. The battle changed naval warfare forever. See Reidy, "Black Men in Navy Blue."

32. Yacovone, ed., *The Voice of Thunder*, 72; Berlin, et al., eds., *Freedom's Soldiers*, 30; Hallowell, *Papers of the Military Historical Society of Massachusetts*, 303; Redkey, ed., *A Grand Army of Black Men*, 231.

33. Berlin et al., eds., *Freedom's Soldiers*, 30; Yacovone, ed., *The Voice of Thunder*, 72, 299.

34. Yacovone, ed., *The Voice of Thunder*, 73, 74–75, 317–18.

35. Jenkins, *Climbing Up to Glory*, 43; Yacovone, ed., *The Voice of Thunder*, 75, 317–18; Trudeau, *Like Men of War*, 257.

36. Wilson, *Campfires of Freedom*, 45, 47; Glatthaar, *Forged in Battle*, 172, 174; Nancy Weir to Abraham Lincoln, February 8, 1864, endorsement of E. N. Hallowell, March 3, 1864, W-264, 1864, Letters Received, series 360, Colored Troops Division, Record Group 94; Yacovone, ed., *The Voice of Thunder*, 75–78.

37. Claxton and Puls, *Uncommon Valor*, 114–17, 188; Cornish, *The Sable Arm*, 173, 175, 176, 177; McPherson, *The Negro's Civil War*, 220–26; Hargrove, *Black Union Soldiers*, 169–76; John Cimprich, "The Fort Pillow Massacre: Assessing the Evidence," *Black Soldiers in Blue*, 150–65; Forbes, *African American Women*, 46–47; Miller, Jr., *The Black Civil War Soldiers of Illinois*, 10, 39, 65; Blackett, ed., *Thomas Morris Chester*, 262, 267. For additional information on the Fort Pillow Massacre, see John Cimprich and Robert Mainfort, Jr., "The Fort Pillow Massacre: A Statistical Note," *The Journal of American History* 76 (December, 1989): 830–37; Richard L. Fuchs, *An Unerring Fire: The Massacre at Fort Pillow* (London: Associated University Presses, 1994; Andrew Ward, *River Run Red: The Fort Pillow Massacre in the American Civil War* (New York: Viking Press, 2005); Congress, Joint Committee on the Conduct of the War, *Fort Pillow Massacre and Returned Prisoners*, report prepared by B. F. Wade and D. W. Gooch, 38th Cong., 1st sess., 1864; Bruce Tap, *The Fort Pillow Massacre: North, South, and the Status of African Americans in the Civil War Era* (New York: Taylor & Francis, 2014); Tom Quinn, *American Massacre: Fort Pillow and the Day that Changed a War* (Self Published, 2014).

38. Cornish, *The Sable Arm*, 191–92; Chicago *Tribune*, January 28, 1864, May 1, 1864.

39. Redkey, ed., *A Grand Army of Black Men*, 237. Chelton Hills was the town just northwest of Philadelphia, where Camp William Penn was located.

40. Ibid.; Yacovone, ed., *The Voice of Thunder*, 73.

41. Berlin, et al., eds., *Freedom*, 714; Forbes, *African American Women*, 183; Glatthaar, *Forged in Battle*, 171; Hallowell, *Papers of the Military Historical Society of Massachusetts*, 303; Wilson, *Campfires of Freedom*, 47, 181.

42. McPherson, *The Negro's Civil War*, 207.

43. Yacovone, ed., *The Voice of Thunder*, 73; Emilio, *A Brave Black Regiment*, 179; Redkey, ed., *A Grand Army of Black Men*, 237.

44. Wilson, *Campfires of Freedom*, 177.

45. James S. Weir Service Records, 54th Massachusetts Infantry; Nancy M. Weir to Abraham Lincoln, February 8, 1864, endorsement of E. N. Hallowell, March 3, 1864, W-264, 1864, Letters Received, series 360, Colored Troops Division, Record Group 94; Emilio, *A Brave Black Regiment*, 191.

46. Nancy M. Weir to Abraham Lincoln, February 8, 1864, endorsement of E. N. Hallowell, March 3, 1864, W-264, 1864, Letters Received, series 360, Colored Troops Division, Record Group 94; Emilio, *A Brave Black Regiment*, 191.

47. Nancy M. Weir to Abraham Lincoln, January 9, 1865, C. W. Foster (Assistant Adjutant General) to Nancy M. Weir, January 30, 1865, W-72, 1865, Letters Received, series 360, Colored Troops Division, Record Group 94.

48. Ibid.

49. Grocery stores in the northern black community became the financial agencies for a community that had little or no access to credit or bank loans. They provided credit to people who were more likely to at times not have regular income. See Stephen Kendrick and Paul Kendrick, *Sarah's Long Walk: The Free Blacks of Boston and How Their Struggle for Equality Changed America* (Boston: Beacon Press, 2004), 30; Horton, *Black Bostonians*, 37. Nancy M. Weir to Abraham Lincoln, January 9, 1865, C. W. Foster to Nancy M. Weir, January 30, 1865, W-72, 1865, Letters Received, series 360, Colored Troops Division, Record Group 94. James survived the war and was mustered out with the 54th Massachusetts on August 20, 1865 in Charleston, South Carolina. He returned home and stayed there until 1867 when he move away. On September 11, 1872 in Detroit, Michigan, he married Victoria F. Dickenson, who was twenty-one years old. They had a child, Harriet Anna Weir, born on January 5, 1876, and they made it west to Chicago, Illinois, where James worked as a Pullman porter or conductor. He was later employed as a janitor and died at an early age, thirty-two, on June 20, 1879, after suffering for four years with kidney disease. He was buried in Detroit, Michigan. On July 21, 1890, Victoria, who moved to Minneapolis, Minnesota, and worked as a housekeeper at a school, filed a claim for a widow's pension. Her claim was finally approved on May 26, 1894, retroactive to the day after James's death; see James S. Weir Pension Files, 54th Massachusetts Infantry, Records of the Veterans Administration, Record Group 15.

50. John Bland to Edwin Stanton, March 28, 1864, C. W. Foster to John Bland Letter, April 28, 1864, B-33, 1864, Letters Received, series 360, Colored Troops Division, Record Group 94.

51. John Bland to Edwin Stanton, March 28, 1864, C. W. Foster to John Bland Letter, April 28, 1864, B-33, 1864, Letters Received, series 360, Colored Troops Division, Record Group 94; George Tolbert Service Records, 8th USCT; Israel Bourdney Service Records, 8th USCT; John D. Hart Service Records, 8th USCT; David Johnson Service Records, 8th USCT. Except for Johnson, the men survived the war and returned home. Johnson died of "disease" on September 16, 1865, at the post hospital in Brownsville, Texas.

52. Yacovone, ed., *The Voice of Thunder*, 77.

53. Ibid., 78–79; Glatthaar, *Forged in Battle*, 172, 174–75; Cornish, *The Sable Arm*, 192–94; Emilio, *A Brave Black Regiment*, 220–21; Hallowell, *Papers of the Military Historical Society of Massachusetts*, 304; Redkey, ed., *A Grand Army of Black Men*, 241–44.

54. Yacovone, ed., *The Voice of Thunder*, 78–79; Glatthaar, *Forged in Battle*, 172, 174–75; Cornish, *The Sable Arm*, 192–94; Emilio, *A Brave Black Regiment*, 220–21; Redkey, ed., *A Grand Army of Black Men*, 241–44.

55. Ira Berlin, *Families & Freedom*, 86–87; Yacovone, ed., *The Voice of Thunder*, 320.

56. Berlin et al., eds., *Families & Freedom*, 87

57. Yacovone, ed., *The Voice of Thunder*, 320.

58. Ibid.

59. Ibid., 325.

60. Rachel Ann Wicker to John A. Andrew, September 12, 1864, C. W. Foster to John A. Andrew, October 10, 1864, W-734, 1864, Letters Received, series 360, Colored Troops Division, Record Group 94.

61. Robert Wicker Service Records, 55th Massachusetts Infantry; Rachel Ann Wicker to John A. Andrew, September 12, 1864, C. W. Foster to John A Andrew, October 10, 1864, W-734, 1864, Letters Received, series 360, Colored Troops Division, Record Group 94. Robert survived the war and was discharged with his regiment on August 29, 1865; however, while living in Troy, Ohio, he accidently fell into the Miami & Erie Canal and drowned on December 12, 1881. Before his death, he applied for an invalid pension on March 23, 1880, based on an injury to his left ankle from enemy shellfire during the Battle at Olustee. His application was also based on injuries to both of his eyes from the accidental discharge of a cannon cartridge while he was loading the canon while in battle. By 1880, Robert alleged his injuries made him totally disabled and he could not work at his livelihood as a laborer. However, it appears his application was rejected for lack of evidence regarding his injuries. After Robert's death, his wife, Dorothy, applied for a widow's pension on May 1883, which was rejected on September 17, 1883. But she reapplied and was approved, effective July 9, 1890 for $8 a month, which she received until her death on February 8, 1894. They had no children. See Robert Wicker Pension Files, 55th Massachusetts Infantry, Records of the Veterans Administration, Record Group 15.

62. Hallowell, *Papers of the Military Historical Society of Massachusetts*, 303; Redkey, ed., *A Grand Army of Black Men*, 243.

63. Redkey, ed., *A Grand Army of Black Men*, 244–47.

64. Yacovone, ed., *The Voice of Thunder*, 79; Emilio, *A Brave Black Regiment*, 227–28; Redkey, ed., *A Grand Army of Black Men*, 247–48.

65. It is not clear how or where Emilio came up with his dollar figures but there is evidence some black troops squandered large amounts of money after being paid. See Emilio, *A Brave Black Regiment*, 228; Jenkins, *Climbing Up to Glory*, 35–36. Adams Express was the private nineteenth-century freight and cargo transport company (rail and stagecoach) by which most Union soldiers sent money home. For more information about Adams Express and its operation during the Civil War, see Harlow, *Old Waybills*, Chapter 16; *Harper's Weekly*, November 5, 1864, 709.

66. McRae, *Negroes in Michigan*, 67; Wiley, *The Life of Billy Yank*, 48–49; Berlin and Rowland, eds., *Families & Freedom*, 85. According to Article XLV-1338 of the Army

Regulations of 1861, "The troops will be paid in such manner that the arrears shall at no time exceed two months, unless the circumstances of the case render it unavoidable." However, more often than not, the circumstances made it impossible to keep that schedule. See *Revised United States Army Regulations of 1861, With an Appendix Containing the Changed and Laws Affecting Army Regulations and Articles of War to June 25, 1863* (Washington: Government Printing Office, 1863), 351.

67. Glatthaar, *Forged in Battle*, 65; Cornish, *The Sable Arm*, 188. For additional information on military bounties and their effect on recruiting, see McRae, *Negroes in Michigan*, 45–46.

68. Cornish, *The Sable Arm*, 188; Glatthaar, *Forged in Battle*, 171–72; Joseph G. Bilby, *Forgotten Warriors: New Jersey's African American Soldiers in the Civil War* (Hightstown, N.J.: 1993), 26; *Revised United States Army Regulations of 1861*, 351; Miller, Jr., *The Black Civil War Soldiers of Illinois*, 153; Harlow, *Old Waybills*, Chapter 16; Berlin et al., eds., *Families & Freedom*, 80, 85.

69. Judith Ann Giesberg, *Civil War Sisterhood: The U.S. Sanitary Commission and Women's Politics in Transition* (Boston: Northeastern University Press, 2000), 140; Berlin et al., eds., *Families & Freedom*, 85; Silber. *Daughters of the Union*, 17, 50, 61–63.

70. Giesberg, *Civil War Sisterhood*, 6–7; Silber, *Daughters of the Union*, 47. In one year, the national government's expenditure increased drastically from $67 million to $475 million, a 700 percent increase from 1861 to 1862. The Federal government had to find new ways of raising revenue in order to pay for the war. The traditional ways, income from customs duties and public land sales, were no longer adequate. Secretary of the Treasury Salmon Chase and Congress implemented revenue innovations in the form of new taxes on income, products, and services, as well as the issuance of paper money (or greenbacks) to quickly raise enough funds to pay and supply an army, and win a war. See Phillip S. Paludan, *A People's Contest: The Union and Civil War, 1861–1865* (New York: Harper & Row, 1988), Chapter 5.

71. Berlin et al., eds., *Families & Freedom*, 87–88; Giesberg, *Civil War Sisterhood*, 6–7; Paludan, *A People's Contest*, 113, 121, 182; Rachel Ann Wicker to John A. Andrew, September 12, 1864, C. W. Foster to John A. Andrew, October 10, 1864, W-734, 1864, Letters Received, series 360, Colored Troops Division, Record Group 94.

72. Berlin et al., eds., *Families & Freedom*, 85; Silber, *Daughters of the Union*, 49; Yacovone, ed., *The Voice of Thunder*, 63.

73. Berlin et al., eds., *Families & Freedom*, 85; Yacovone, ed., *The Voice of Thunder*, 63–64, 321n.1; J. Matthew Gallman, *Mastering Wartime: A Social History of Philadelphia During the Civil War* (Philadelphia: University of Pennsylvania Press, 1990), 46; Rachel Ann Wicker to John A. Andrew, September 12, 1864, C. W. Foster to John A. Andrew, October 10, 1864, W-734, 1864, Letters Received, series 360, Colored Troops Division, Record Group 94.

74. Hallowell, *Papers of the Military Historical Society of Massachusetts*, 294; Smith, ed., *Black Soldiers in Blue*, 29. Quite to the contrary, the 55th was not a typical regiment. Because it was only the second one formed in the North, it attracted many black recruits who were from states that had not yet created their own black regiments. Once other states began creating black regiments, the regiments consisted of more local recruits and fewer from outside the state.

75. February 12, 1863 diary memoranda, Records of the 54th Regiment (Captain Luis F. Emilio, of Salem), 1863–1915, Civil War Correspondence, Diaries, and Journals at the Massachusetts Historical Society, 1754–1926, reel 13.

76. The remaining 1,185 black soldiers were recruited by New Jersey agents who enlisted them in the USCT as newly freed men from the South. These troops contributed to New Jersey's recruitment quota. See Bilby, *Forgotten Warriors*, 10, 13, 18. New Jersey blacks were most heavily represented in the following USCT regiments: the 22nd (681), 25th (531), 32nd (319), 41st (254), 43rd (365) and 45th (230), all of which were organized at Camp William Penn.

77. Rosanna Henson to Abraham Lincoln, July 11, 1864, 993/D-732, 1864, Letters Received, series 7, Record Group 99.

78. Ibid.; Benjamin Henson Service Records, 22nd USCT; Benjamin Henson Pension Files, 22nd USCI, Records of the Veterans Administration, Record Group 15; James M. Johnson Service Records, 22nd USCT.

79. Julia Piner to Edwin Stanton, August 12, 1864, Lieutenant James Simon to Offices of U.S. Sanitary Commission and Ladies Relief Association, August 11, 1864, Julia Piner to Adjutant General's Office, no date, U.S. Sanitary Commission to Ladies Relief Association, August 8, 1864, Adjutant General's Office to Julia Piner, August 23, 1864, P-274, 1864, Letters Received, series 360, Colored Troops Division, Record Group 94.

80. Ibid. David served until honorably discharged on October 16, 1865. Though it does not appear Julia was ever able to obtain any relief funds while her two sons served their country, David was later able to get an invalid pension and upon his death on December 6, 1890, his wife Isabella was able to collect a widow's pension; see David T. Jones Pension Files, 22nd USCI, Records of the Veterans Administration, Record Group 15.

81. Glatthaar, *Forged in Battle*, 172; Attie, *Patriotic Toil*, 33–34; Giesberg, *Civil War Sisterhood*, 5; Silber; *Daughters of the Union*, 163, 177. The United States Sanitary Commission (USSC) was founded in June 1861 as a humanitarian organization focused on modernizing health care methods and practices in military camps and battlefields. See Melinda Lawson, *Patriot Fires: Forging a New American Nationalism in the Civil War North* (Lawrence: University Press of Kansas, 2002), Chapter 1.

82. Attie, *Patriotic Toil*, 33–34; Giesberg, *Civil War Sisterhood*, 5, 143–46; Silber; *Daughters of the Union*, 163–65, 185–86; Gallman, *Mastering Wartime*, 136–38, Chapter 6; Lawson, *Patriot Fires*, 14–18, 24–25.

83. Giesberg, *Civil War Sisterhood*, 140, 151; Cornish, *The Sable Arm*, 188; Attie, *Patriotic Toil*, 93.

84. Attie, *Patriotic Toil*, 93–94; Lisa Tendrich Frank, ed., *Women in the American Civil War*, Volume 1 (Santa Barbara, Calif.: ABC-CLIO, Inc., 2008), 286; Rhodes, *Mary Ann Shadd Cary*, 158; Forbes, *African American Women*, x, 93, 195–96; Painter, *Sojourner Truth*, 182, 213. Other ethnic groups, such as Germans and Jews, also created their own soldiers'-aid societies. See Gallman, *Mastering Wartime*, 124, 136.

85. Sojourner Truth, was a public activist, organizer, and speaker. Truth, a former slave in New York, became free in 1827 under the New York State Emancipation Act and became a prominent African-American abolitionist and women's rights activist. During the war, she volunteered her services to relief organizations to help black troops

and freedpeople, working tirelessly to collect food and supplies for both. See Painter, *Sojourner Truth*.

86. Forbes, *African American Women*, x, 93, 195–96; Rhodes, *Mary Ann Shadd Cary*, 158; Painter, *Sojourner Truth*, 182, 213. James Caldwell was taken prisoner in action on James Island, South Carolina, on July 16, 1863. He remained a prisoner-of-war in Florence, South Carolina, until March 4, 1865. He was discharged from the Union army, having never been paid, on May 12, 1865, in Boston, three months before the rest of his regiment. See James Caldwell Service Records, 54th Massachusetts Infantry. For more information about Lucy Stanton Day, see Ellen NicKenzie Lawson, *The Three Sarahs: Documents of Antebellum Black College Women* (New York: Edwin Mellen Press, 1984), Chapter 4.

87. Silber, *Daughters of the Union*, 166–67; Forbes, *African American Women*, 80, 94, 101–4; Giesberg, ed., *Emilie Davis's Civil War*, xx. Octavius V. Catto worked with George L. Stearns to recruit black men to enlist in the army and help fight for the Union cause. His efforts helped to fill the ranks of eleven of the black regiments formed in the Philadelphia area. After the war, he became a civil rights martyr when he was murdered on October 10, 1871, during an outbreak of violence aimed at preventing blacks from voting. Le Count was the one who identified his body. For additional information about his life, see Harry C. Silcox, "Nineteenth Century Philadelphia Black Militant: Octavius V. Catto (1839–1871)," *Pennsylvania History* 44, no. 1 (January 1977), 53–76; and Daniel R. Biddle and Murray Durbin, *Tasting Freedom: Octavius Catto and the Battle for Equality in Civil War America* (Philadelphia: Temple University Press, 2010). For additional information about Carolyn Le Count see Daniel R. Biddle and Murray Dubin, "One Woman's Drive for Equality," Philadelphia *Inquirer* (May 31, 2009).

88. Silber, *Daughters of the Union*, 166–67; Attie, *Patriotic Toil*, 93–94; Forbes, *African American Women*, 77, 79–80, 94, 101–4.

89. *Liberator*, May 20, 1864.

90. Forbes, *African American Women*, 77; Gallman, *Mastering Wartime*, 124; Silber, *Daughters of the Union*, 232–33, 235–36; Giesberg, ed., *Emilie Davis's Civil War*, xx, 166.

91. Gallman, *Mastering Wartime*, 124–26; Giesberg, *Civil War Sisterhood*, 140; Silber, *Daughters of the Union*, 232–33, 235–36. For additional information about the health and well being of African Americans during and after the war see, Jim Downs, *Sick from Freedom: African-American Illness and Suffering During the Civil War and Reconstruction* (Oxford: Oxford University Press, 2012).

92. In early March 1864, Congress finally approved a law that allowed for equal pay for all black troops from the point of their enlistment into service. See Glatthaar, *Forged in Battle*, 172, 174–75; Yacovone, ed., *The Voice of Thunder*, 78–79; Emilio, *A Brave Black Regiment*, 220–21; Redkey, ed., *A Grand Army of Black Men*, 241–44; Bilby, *Forgotten Warriors*, 26. Soldiers regularly did not see their pay for six to nine months, and often even longer. See Miller, Jr., *The Black Civil War Soldiers of Illinois*, 153; Berlin et al., eds., *Families & Freedom*, 85.

93. Ruby Cumback to Edwin Stanton, March 2, 1865, 2030/D-732, 1865, Letters Received, series 7, Record Group 99; Oliver Cumback Service Records, 20th USCT.

94. Ibid.

95. Glatthaar, *Forged in Battle*, 88–89; Oliver Cumback Service Records, 20th USCT.

96. William Chandler to Abraham Lincoln, November 21, 1864, 335/D-732, 1864, Letters Received, series 7, Record Group 99; Peter Peterson to Edwin Stanton, May 24, 1865, C. W. Foster to Peter Peterson, May 30, 1865, P-252, 1865, Letters Received, series 360, Colored Troops Division, Record Group 94; Samuel Peterson Service Records, 8th USCT. Peter Peterson mistakenly referred to the Battle of Olustee as the Battle of McAllister. Neither Samuel or his regiment were present at any of the battles that occurred at Fort McAllister, which was located near Savannah, Georgia.

97. William Chandler to Abraham Lincoln, November 21, 1864, 335/D-732, 1864, Letters Received, series 7, Record Group 99; Peter Peterson to Edwin Stanton, May 24, 1865, C. W. Foster to Peter Peterson, May 30, 1865, P-252, 1865, Letters Received, series 360, Colored Troops Division, Record Group 94; Samuel Peterson Service Records, 8th USCT.

98. Gibbs, *Black, Copper, & Bright*, iv.

99. William Sinclair to James A. Hardie (Assistant Adjutant General), March 8, 1865, James A. Hardie to William Sinclair, March 8, 1865, S-168, 1865, Letters Received, series 360, Colored Troops Division, Record Group 94.

100. Ibid.; William Sinclair to James A. Hardie (Assistant Adjutant General), March 8, 1865, James A. Hardie to William Sinclair, March 8, 1865, S-168, 1865, Letters Received, series 360, Colored Troops Division, Record Group 94.

101. Forbes, *African American Women*, 96, 165.

5. Violence on Two Fronts

1. Berlin and Rowland, eds., *Families & Freedom*, 80–81; Hallowell, *Papers of the Military Historical Society of Massachusetts*, 293; *Official Records*, series 2, vol. 5, 940–41; Burchard, *One Gallant Rush*, 144. In 1860, the black populations in South Carolina and Mississippi were substantially larger than the white populations. In Louisiana, the numbers were about equal. For additional population statistics, see *Population of the United States in 1860; Compiled From the Original Returns of the Eight Census* (Washington: Government Printing Office, 1864).

2. Hallowell, *Papers of the Military Historical Society of Massachusetts*, 293; *Official Records*, series 2, vol. 6, 163; Smith, ed., *Black Soldiers in Blue*, 46–49. For additional information about the treatment of black soldiers by the Confederacy, see Cornish, *The Sable Arm*, Chapter 9.

3. Hannah Johnson to Abraham Lincoln, July 31, 1863, J-17, 1863, Letters Received, series 360, Colored Troops Division, Record Group 94; Berlin and Rowland, eds., *Families & Freedom*, 80–81.

4. Paul David Escott, *Lincoln's Dilemma: Blair, Sumner, and the Republican Struggle Over Racism and Equality in the Civil War Era* (Charlottesville: University of Virginia Press, 2014), 166–69; Smith, ed., *Black Soldiers in Blue*, 45–46; Drew Gilpin Faust, *This Republic of Suffering: Death and the American Civil War* (New York: Alfred A. Knopf, 2008), 44–47.

5. Escott, *Lincoln's Dilemma*, 166–69. Race riots regularly occurred in the North before the war. These included a major anti-black riot in Cincinnati in 1829, five in Phila-

delphia between 1832 and 1849, and a one in New York in 1834. See William Loren, Katz, ed., *Anti-Negro Riots in the North* (New York: Arno Press, 1969), i–ii; Bernstein, *The New York City Draft Riots*, 5.

6. Wilma Wood Henrickson, ed., *Detroit Perspectives: Crossroads and Turning Points* (Detroit: Wayne Sate University Press, 1991), 157; Anonymous author, *A Thrilling Narrative From the Lips of the Sufferers of the Late Detroit Riot, March 6, 1863, with the Hair Breath escapes of Men, Women and Children, and Destruction of Colored Men's Property, Not Less Than $15,000* (Detroit: Published by author, 1863), 2. The author of *A Thrilling Narrative* is unknown. A compilation of several accounts, including from eyewitnesses, newspaper excerpts, and a poem at the end of the work, are used to tell the story of the victims of the riot. It appears the narrator was a white man who may or may not have been an eyewitness to the riots himself.

7. For additional information on the hostilities against Detroit blacks during the Civil War, see Katz, ed., *Anti-Negro Riots*, iii; McRae, *Negroes in Michigan*, 24, 33–34; Frank B. Woodford, *Father Abraham's Children: Michigan Episodes in the Civil War* (Detroit: Wayne State University, 1961, 1999 edition), 64; John C. Schneider, *Detroit and the Problem of Order, 1830–1880: A Geography of Crime, Riot and Policing* (Lincoln: University of Nebraska Press, 1980), 69–70; Escott, *Paying Freedom's Price*, 66.

8. Henrickson, ed., *Detroit Perspectives*, 157–60; Anonymous author, *A Thrilling Narrative*, 2; Schneider, *Detroit and the Problem of Order*, 70–72; McRae, *Negroes in Michigan*, 34; Woodford, *Father Abraham's Children*, 65–66. Detroit did not have a regular police department and the group of deputies and constables from the city's wards who were assembled to guard Faulkner was too small a force to protect him from the rowdy crowd. The military police, or provost guard, from an army barrack in Detroit were assigned to protect Faulkner while he was transported from the courthouse to the county jail.

9. Henrickson, ed., *Detroit Perspectives*, 159–62; Woodford, *Father Abraham's Children*, 66; McRae, *Negroes in Michigan*, 34–35; Anonymous author, *A Thrilling Narrative*, 2–3; Schneider, *Detroit and the Problem of Order*, 71–72.

10. Woodford, *Father Abraham's Children*, 68–69; Schneider, *Detroit and the Problem of Order*, 70–72; Henrickson, ed., *Detroit Perspectives*, 157; Patrick Rael, *Black Identity & Black Protest in the Antebellum North* (Chapel Hill: University of North Carolina Press, 2002), 120; Katz, ed., *Anti-Negro Riots*, iv. Many of the blacks who left Cincinnati migrated to Michigan, western Pennsylvania, New York, and Canada. Consequently, William Faulkner served seven years of his life sentence before being released from prison. He was proven innocent after Mary Brown confessed that the crime never occurred. The white girl, Brown, admitted the two girls lied about the rape to avoid being punished for coming home late. See McRae, *Negroes in Michigan*, 36. In the preface to *Anti Negro Riots*, James McPherson argues Faulkner was Spanish and Indian, not black, and one of the "orphan" girls was actually a prostitute who was "consorting" with Faulkner.

11. See Adrian Cook, *The Armies of the Streets: The New York City Draft Riots of 1863* (Lexington: University of Kentucky Press, 1974), 50–52; Bernstein, *The New York City Draft Riots*, 9–14; Escott, *Paying Freedom's Price*, 66–67. Peace Democrats or Copperheads were northern Democrats who opposed the Union war policy, and were in favor of a negotiated peace to immediately end the war and restore the Union. See Jennifer

Weber, *Copperheads: The Rise and Fall of Lincoln's Opponents in the North* (Oxford: Oxford University Press, 2006).

12. *New York Times*, July 14, 1863.

13. *New-York Tribune*, July 13, 1863; *New-York Tribune*, July 14, 1863; *New York Times*, July 14, 1863, July 18, 1863; Harris, *In the Shadow of Slavery*, 280; Cook, *The Armies of the Streets*, 55–58, 77; McPherson, *Battle Cry of Freedom*, 609–10.

14. Cook, *The Armies of the Streets*, 143–44; McPherson, *Battle Cry of Freedom*, 610. Blacks and whites competed with each other for jobs on the docks, and it did not help that racial tensions were already high since late spring 1863 when black labor was used by shipping companies to break a longshoreman's strike. See Bernstein, *The New York City Draft Riots*, 27. Katz, ed., *Anti-Negro Riots*, iv; Committee of Merchants for the Relief of Colored People Suffering From the Late Riots In the City of New York, *Report* (New York: George A. Whitehorne, Steam Printer, 1863), 21. Included in the *Report* are testimonies by victims of the riots as well as newspapers accounts.

15. *Report*, 14, 15–16, 17–18; Cook, *The Armies of the Streets*, 82–83, 140–41.

16. *Report*, 17–18; Cook, *The Armies of the Streets*, 135–36.

17. *Report*, 18–20; Burchard, *One Gallant Rush*, 130–31; Holice B. Young, "Our Firemen, The History of the NY Fire Departments," Chapter 32, Part III. *American History and Genealogy Project*, March 2001. http://www.newyorkroots.org/bookarchive/history ofnyfiredepartments/31-40/ch32pt3.html.

18. *New York Times*, vol. XII, July 15, 1863, 1; *Report*, 22–23; McPherson, *Battle Cry of Freedom*, 610–11.

19. *Report*, 23; *New York Times*, vol. XII, July 15, 1863, 8.

20. *New-York Tribune*, July 17, 1863, 4; *Report*, 24–25; Cook, *The Armies of the Streets*, 56, 158. City authorities did not anticipate resistance at the drawing of the names and were preparing instead for a show of force when conscripts were required to actually report to duty and "take their place in the ranks." See *New York Times*, vol. XII, July 14, 1863, 1.

21. *Report*, 22; Bernstein, *The New York City Draft Riots*, 66. And even days and weeks after the riots, blacks continued to wonder why they were made to suffer from such violence and degradation. They continued to be the victims of other random acts of violence at the hands of white groups. Some were severely injured after being kicked and beaten, but there were no other fatalities, and the appearance of police was enough to disperse the white hooligans.

22. Bernstein, *The New York City Draft Riots*, 66, 267; Cook, *The Armies of the Streets*, 174–75, 177–87.

23. *Report*, 4–5, 12; Bernstein, *The New York City Draft Riots*, 233; Cook, *The Armies of the Streets*, 174–75, 177–87.

24. Yacovone, ed., *The Voice of Thunder*, 48, 240, 250–51; Emilio, *A Brave Black Regiment*, 93; Burchard, *One Gallant Rush*, 130–31, 144; Robert John Simmons Service Records, 54th Massachusetts Regiment; Redkey, ed., *A Grand Army of Black Men*, 27–28; Robert John Simmons Pension Files, 54th Massachusetts Infantry, Records of the Veterans Administration, Record Group 15. As his mother and dependent, Mrs. Simmons applied for Robert's military pension on November 7, 1865. Her application was approved and she received payments until her death on October 9, 1881.

25. Yacovone, ed., *The Voice of Thunder*, 240; Cook, *The Armies of the Streets*, 80. Cook mistakenly refers to Powell, Sr. as William P. Powell. See Robert G. Slawson, *Prologue to Change: African Americans in Medicine in the Civil War Era* (Frederick, Maryland: The NMCWM Press, 2006), 25, 38–39. Also according to Slawson, William B. Powell, Jr., probably worked with the army as one of nine African-American "contract surgeons" and was not a soldier in the army. That explains why service records do not exist for him in the National Archives.

26. H. G. Mosee to Edwin Stanton, April 1, 1865, William Haig (Connecticut Headquarters) to H. G. Mosee, June 9, 1864, M-248, 1865, Letters Received, series 360, Colored Troops Division, Record Group 94.

27. Sterling, ed., *We Are Sisters*, 230–31. For additional information on the kidnapping of free blacks see Wilson, *Freedom At Risk*.

28. Horton, *Black Bostonians*, 99; Wilson, *Freedom At Risk*, 6–8, 17–39, 41–66.

29. Horton, *Black Bostonians*, 99; Harris, *In the Shadow of Slavery*, 215.

30. Horton, *Black Bostonians*, 97–98, 100–1; Harris, *In the Shadow of Slavery*, 210–15.

31. Proceedings and Debates of the House of Representatives of the United States at the Second Session of the Second Congress, Begun at the City of Philadelphia, November 5, 1792, "Annals of Congress, 2nd Congress, 2nd Session (November 5, 1792 to March 2, 1793)," 1414–15. Horton, *Black Bostonians*, 97–98; Wilson, *Freedom At Risk*, 40–42, 44, 54, 55.

32. Harris, *In the Shadow of Slavery*, 210–15.

33. Wilson, *Freedom at Risk*, 103–16. For additional information about Anthony Burns, see Albert J. Von Frank, *The Trials of Anthony Burns: Freedom and Slavery in Emerson's Boston* (Cambridge: Harvard University Press, 1998).

34. H. G. Mosee to Edwin Stanton, April 1, 1865, William Haig (Connecticut Headquarters) to H. G. Mosee, June 9, 1864, M-248, 1865, Letters Received, series 360, Colored Troops Division, Record Group 94.

35. Ibid. The "Contrabands" Mosee was referring to were probably white Confederate supporters in southern Indiana and Kentucky who had become refugees or displaced as a result of the economic hardships brought about by the war. Also, Mosee was referring to the Freedmen's Bureau (formally called the Bureau of Refugees, Freedmen, and Abandoned Lands), which had just been established by Congress on March 13, 1865. The Bureau's duties included dispensing rations—clothing, food, and fuel—to white and black refugees, or anyone in a distressed state and in need of rations. Over time, the Bureau assumed other responsibilities, such as helping freedmen secure employment through the use of labor contracts, the handling of disputes between freedmen and their former masters, and the establishment of schools for whites and blacks. For additional information about the Bureau, see Michael Perman, *Emancipation and Reconstruction, 1862–1879* (Arlington Heights, Ill.: Harlan Davidson, 1987), 22–23, and Eric Foner, *A Short History of Reconstruction, 1863–1877* (New York: Harper & Row, 1990), 31–32, 64–66.

36. Giesberg, ed., *Emilie Davis's Civil War*, 48–49; David G. Smith, "Race and Retaliation: The Capture of African-Americans during the Gettysburg Campaign," *In Virginia's Civil War*, edited by Peter Wallenstein and Bertram Wyatt-Brown (Charlottesville:

University of Virginia Press, 2005), 137; James Paradis, *African Americans and the Gettysburg Campaign* (Lanham, Md.: Scarecrow Press, 2005), xiii, 29–36.

37. Paradis, *African Americans and the Gettysburg Campaign*, 30. Smith, "Race and Retaliation," 138.

38. Giesberg, ed., *Emilie Davis's Civil War*, 48–49; Smith, "Race and Retaliation, 142; Paradis, *African Americans and the Gettysburg Campaign*, ix, xiii, 1–13, 29–36. Gettysburg's population was 8 percent black at the time of the Civil War. Many of the African Americans were involved in the abolitionist movement and the Underground Railroad to support runaway slaves.

39. Hargrove, *Black Union Soldiers*, 195–99; Faust, *This Republic of Suffering*, 44–47. For more information on the massacre at the Battle of Saltville, see Smith, ed., *Black Soldiers in Blue*, Chapter 7; and Thomas D. Mays, *The Saltville Massacre* (Civil War Campaigns and Commanders Series) (Abilene, Tex.: McWhiney Foundation Press, 1998). For additional information on the massacre of black troops by forces led by Nathan Bedford Forrest, see George S. Burkhardt, *Confederate Rage, Yankee Wrath: No Quarter in the Civil War* (Carbondale: Southern Illinois University Press, 2007), 1–4, 232–36; Tap, *The Fort Pillow Massacre*; Quinn, *American Massacre*.

40. Cornish, *The Sable Arm*, 176–80; Faust, *This Republic of Suffering*, 53–54. According to Joseph T. Glatthaar, there is little evidence Confederate threats to enslave or execute captured black troops deterred any blacks from military service. See Glatthaar, *Forged in Battle*, 202–3.

41. Wilson, *The Black Phalanx*, 348.

42. Gregory J. W. Urwin, ed., *Black Flag Over Dixie: Racial Atrocities and Reprisals in the Civil War* (Carbondale: Southern Illinois University Press, 2004), 9; Blackett, ed., *Thomas Morris Chester*, 113–14; Brayton Harris, *Blue & Gray in Black & White: Newspapers in the Civil War* (Washington: Brassey's, 2000), 308. "Johnnies" or "Johnny Reb" was applied as a slang term or nickname for Confederate soldiers by the Union soldiers in the Civil War. Its opposite by Confederate soldiers referring to Union soldiers was "Billy Yank."

43. McRae, *Negroes in Michigan*, 36–37.

44. Anonymous author, *A Thrilling Narrative*, 1.

45. McRae, *Negroes in Michigan*, 98; Marcus Dale Service Records, 102nd USCT.

46. Charles Jackson Service Records, 8th USCT; Alexander Newton Service Records, 29th Connecticut Volunteers.

47. For additional information about New York's black regiment, see William Seriale, *New York's Black Regiments During the Civil War* (New York: Routledge, 2001). McPherson *The Negro's Civil War*, 212–13; Bernstein, *The New York City Draft Riots*, 66–67.

48. Bernstein, *The New York City Draft Riots*, 234; Wilson, *Campfires of Freedom*, 73–74; Harris, *In the Shadow of Slavery*, 286–87; Yacovone, ed., *The Voice of Thunder*, 251.

6. Information Requests

1. Wilson, *Campfires of Freedom*, 179.

2. O. D. M. Baker (for family of John Pero) to Lorenzo Thomas, June 29, 1864, B-39, 1864, Letters Received, series 366, Colored Troops Division, Record Group 94; John Pero Service Records, 26th USCT; John Pero Pension Files, 26th USCI, Records of the

Veterans Administration, Record Group 15. It was very common for families to hire claim agents or attorneys to help them with the application process for securing soldiers' back pay and pensions. For additional information about the role of claims agents, see John William Oliver, *History of the Civil War Military Pensions, 1861–1865*, Bulletin of the University of Wisconsin, No. 844, Volume 4, Issue 1 (Madison: University of Wisconsin, 1917), 53–54.

3. Homer Augustus Nelson (for the mother of James Johnson) to Adjutant General, November 3, 1864, M-25, 1864, Letters Received, series 366, Colored Troops Division, Record Group 94.

4. Lucy Freeman to Abraham Lincoln, December 1, 1864, F-46, 1864, Letters Received, series 366, Colored Troops Division, Record Group 94; Charles Brown Service Records, 54th Massachusetts Infantry. There were two soldiers named Charles Brown in the 54th and both were in Company E. Their service records have them listed as Charles Brown (1st) and Charles Brown (2nd). Charles Brown (2nd) is cited here. What his family did not know was that since November 1864, during the time they lost contact with him, he was serving a sentence of one year and seven months for dereliction of duty. He was found sleeping at his post on November 27, 1864, while the regiment was assigned to Morris Island, South Carolina. His pay was also reduced by half. Though he would not serve the entire sentence, Charles was not mustered out of service until March 7, 1866, seven months after the 54th returned home from the war. His muster-out date was delayed probably so he could serve at least a portion of the sentence.

5. Elizabeth F. Gaines to Lorenzo Thomas, 1864, G-36, 1864, Letters Received, series 366, Colored Troops Division, Record Group 94; Noah Gaines Service Records, 54th Massachusetts Infantry.

6. Mrs. S. J. Bell to Mr. Samuel Peck, November 2, 1864, B-130, 1864, Letters Received, series 366, Colored Troops Division, Record Group 94.

7. Redkey, ed., *A Grand Army of Black Men*, 127–28; J. Cutler Adams, *The North Reports the Civil War* (Pittsburgh: University of Pittsburgh Press, 1955, 1983, paperback reprint 1985), 73–74; *New York Times*, August 13, 1862. For example, see the list of Union casualties at the assault on Fort Wagner on July 18, 1863, *New York Times*, July 28, 1863, and at the Battle of Olustee on February 18, 1864, *New York Times*, March 8, 1864.

8. James Givin (for Mrs. Samuel Waters) to Lorenzo Thomas, July, 27, 1864, G-18, 1864, Letters Received, series 366, Colored Troops Division, Record Group 94; Samuel Waters Service Records, 8th USCT; Gladstone, *Men of Color*, 36.

9. Sarah Lewis to Edwin Stanton, November 29, 1864, L-49, 1864, Letters Received, series 366, Colored Troops Division, Record Group 94; Alexander Lewis Service Records, 6th USCT. John J. Keefe wrote letters for illiterate families. He may have written the letters for a fee or he simply may have done it out of benevolence. Keefe may have been a grocer or landlord whom a number of family members owed money; therefore, it was in his best interest to transcribe the letters for the families. His handwriting is easily identifiable and the letters appear to be dictated to him because they show distinct differences related to a family's unique problem or need.

10. For information about the 6th USCT see Paradis, *Strike the Blow for Freedom*. For detailed information about the "Assault on Petersburg," see Trudeau, *Like Men of War*, 220–27; and Paradis, *Strike the Blow for Freedom*, 48–60.

11. Harriet Banks to Adjutant General's Office, October 26, 1864, B-121, 1864, Letters Received, series 366, Colored Troops Division, Record Group 94; James Banks Service Records, 6th USCT.

12. James Thomas Davis to Lorenzo Thomas, September 19, 1864, D-23, 1864, Letters Received, series 366, Colored Troops Division, Record Group 94; George Harris Service Records, 26th USCT.

13. James Thomas Davis to Lorenzo Thomas, December 5, 1864, D-47, 1864, Letters Received, series 366, Colored Troops Division, Record Group 94.

14. Jane Harris to Lorenzo Thomas, November 16, 1864, H-126, 1864, Letters Received, series 366, Colored Troops Division, Record Group 94; James T. Baker Service Records, 28th USCT.

15. Mrs. Banks to Lorenzo Thomas, November 16, 1864, B-147, 1864, Letters Received, series 366, Colored Troops Division, Record Group 94; John Brown Service Records, 22nd USCT.

16. Mary Ann Nickens to Lorenzo Thomas, October 25, 1864, W-23, 1864, Letters Received, series 366, Colored Troops Division, Record Group 94.

17. Robert Nickens Service Records, 27th USCT.

18. Jane Cable to Lorenzo Thomas, October 31, 1864, C-16, 1864, Letters Received, series 366, Colored Troops Division, Record Group 94.

19. William B. Cable Service Records, 20th USCT. State bounties were lower then federal bounties, which were usually $300.

20. Cornish, *The Sable Arm*, 188. Following the massacre of black troops on April 12, 1864 at Fort Pillow, Tennessee, by Confederate forces led by Nathan Bedford Forest, the Republican-controlled Congress decided to amend the pension laws to allow black wives access to pension funds. See Silber, *Daughters of the Union*, 85; Richard Reid, "USCT Veterans in Post-Civil War North Carolina," *Black Soldiers in Blue*, 409–10. For detailed information on the pension process involving African-American veterans, see Donald R. Shaffer, *After the Glory: The Struggles of Black Civil War Veterans* (Lawrence, University Press of Kansas, 2004); Elizabeth Regosin, *Freedom's Promise: Ex-Slave Families and Citizenship in the Age of Emancipation* (Charlottesville: University Press of Virginia, 2002), Chapter 1.

21. George Raimer to Lorenzo Thomas, November 28, 1864, R-83, 1864, Letters Received, series 366, Colored Troops Division, Record Group 94.

22. Newman Raimer Service Records, 54th Massachusetts Infantry; Newman Raimer Pension Files, 54th Massachusetts Infantry, Records of the Veterans Administration, Record Group 15. A copy of the army's reply to George Raimer's letter is not available in Newman Raimer's service records or pension files.

23. H. A. Nelson (for the wife of John Hart) to Lorenzo Thomas, November 5, 1864, N-26, 1864, Letters Received, series 366, Colored Troops Division, Record Group 94; John Hart Service Records, 20th USCT.

24. Elisha C. Clarke to Lorenzo Thomas, November 22, 1864, C-96, 1864, Letters Received, series 366, Colored Troops Division, Record Group 94.

25. Elisha C. Clarke to Adjutant General, November 22, 1864, Letters Received, Series 366, Colored Troops Division, Record Group 94; George Lippitt Service Rec-

ords, 14th Rhode Island Heavy Artillery; Henry Gardner Service Records, 14th Rhode Island Heavy Artillery; George Lippitt Pension Files, 14th Rhode Island Heavy Artillery, Records of the Veterans Administration, Record Group 15. George and Elizabeth never had children so an application for a minor's pension was never filed. Daniel Warmsley Service Records, 14th Rhode Island Heavy Artillery. Daniel Warmsley Pension Files, 14th Rhode Island Heavy Artillery, Records of the Veterans Administration, Record Group 15. Daniel and Rosilla were married August 10, 1863 and had no children together. Rosilla was nine years older than Daniel. On March 26, 1870, Rosilla remarried, taking Daniel's nephew as her new husband, an act that also ended her widow's pension because she was no longer a widow. Eventually, Susan M. Warmsley, Daniel's daughter from his first wife, Ann Eliza Perry, filed a dependent pension application on June 10, 1879, probably for the purpose of obtaining retroactive pay from her father's death until she turned sixteen years old. Susan was born on May 14, 1857 in South Kingston, Rhode Island.

26. Adams, *The North Reports the Civil War*, 73–74; *New York Times*, August 13, 1862. For example, see the list of Union casualties at the assault on Fort Wagner on July 18, 1863, *New York Times*, July 28, 1863, and at the Battle of Olustee on February 18, 1864, *New York Times*, March 8, 1864.

27. Mary Denby to Edwin Stanton, February 3, 1865, D-28, 1865, Letters Received, series 366, Colored Troops Division, Record Group 94. It is not clear if Peter Kelly, like John J. Keefe, wrote letters for a fee for illiterate families or if he simply did it out of benevolence. Also similar to Keefe, he may have been a grocer or landlord to whom a number of family members owed money. Kelly's handwriting is also easily identifiable and the letters appear to be dictated to him because they show distinct differences related to a family's unique problem or need.

28. Charlotte Harris to Edwin Stanton, February 28, 1865, H-75, 1865, Letters Received, series 366, Colored Troops Division, Record Group 94; David Harris Service Records, 55th Massachusetts Infantry. Charlotte Harris was referring to Folly Island, South Carolina, which is located outside of Charleston and was where Union forces gathered before executing their attempt to capture Charleston in June 1863. The July 18, 1863 attack on Fort Wagner was an outcome of that campaign; Trudeau, *Like Men of War*, 73–74.

29. According to David's pension file, he and Charlotte were married as slaves in Virginia. However, because most slave marriages were not recognized legally, it was Maria who had full access to the widow's pension because her later marriage to David (post slavery) was considered legal. Military records don't show if Charlotte or the children she had with David ever attempted to apply for a widow's or dependent's pension after the war; see David Harris Pension Files, 55th Massachusetts Regiment, Records of the Veterans Administration, Record Group 15.

30. Ellen Brunson to Lorenzo Thomas, April 15, 1865, B-197, 1865, Letters Received, series 366, Colored Troops Division, Record Group 94.

31. Matilda Dorsey to unknown, April 26, 1865, D-104, 1865, Letters Received, series 366, Colored Troops Division, Record Group 94; John Dorsey Service Records, 8th USCT. It is not clear whom the April 26, 1864 letter was sent to. The destination address is not in the letter and the salutation refers to "Dear Sir."

32. Matilda Dorsey to Edwin Stanton, May 3, 1865, D-117, 1865, Letters Received, series 366, Colored Troops Division, Record Group 94.

33. Matilda Dorsey to Edwin Stanton, July 19, 1865, D-197, 1865, Letters Received, series 366, Colored Troops Division, Record Group 94.

34. John Dorsey Service Records, 8th USCT; John Dorsey Pension Files, 8th USCI, Records of the Veterans Administration, Record Group 15.

35. John W. Hampton (for parents of Charles Williams) to General Samuel Breck, January 9, 1865, H-11, 1865, Letters Received, series 366, Colored Troops Division, Record Group 94; Charles Williams Service Records, 54th Massachusetts Infantry. Samuel Breck was an assistant in the adjutant-general's department at Washington, in charge of rolls, returns, and the preparation of the "Volunteer Army Register." He was breveted brigadier-general, for faithful services, on March 13, 1865. See http://famousamericans .net/samuelbreck1/.

36. Charles Williams Service Records, 54th Massachusetts Infantry. On May 1, 1869, sixty-two-year-old Sarah Williams filed an application for a mother's pension. Her husband, who appeared to be an alcoholic, suffered a stroke that led to paralysis in 1862. Also a bricklayer, he was never again able to work regularly to support his family before his death on March 26, 1869. Since her husband's paralysis, Sarah and her other three children had been dependent on her son for support, before and after he enlisted. Then, with both her husband and son dead, the family had very little means of support outside of her own labor—washing, house cleaning, and keeping boarders—until their home had to be sold to cover debts. That is when she put in her application for a mother's pension. George E. Stephens provided an affidavit for Sarah's application, which was approved for $8 a month on January 26, 1870, commencing January 31, 1865, the army's recorded date for her son's death in the prisoner-of-war camp. However, on February 27, 1877, the government suspended payments on the grounds Sarah gave inaccurate income statements on her 1869 application. The government investigated her pension case and it appears the payments were reinstated in August 1883. See Charles Williams Pension Files, 54th Massachusetts Infantry, Records of the Veterans Administration, Record Group 15.

37. Mary Brown (for her and Hester White) to Edwin Stanton, February 3, 1865, B-52, 1865, Letters Received, series 366, Colored Troops Division, Record Group 94.

38. James Brown Service Records, 25th USCT; Daniel White Service Records, 55th Massachusetts Infantry. Daniel probably went to Boston to join the 54th but ended up in the 55th after the 54th reached its allotment of 1,000 men. This explains his mother's confusion as to what regiment he was in and her lack of knowledge as to what company he belonged to. Of the 620,000 deaths in the war—360,00 Union and 260,000 Confederates—more than 414,000 were from disease while only 206,000 soldiers actually died in battle or from wounds directly obtained in battle. The reason for the high casualty rate by disease was the deficient state of medical science at the time. There existed a lack of understanding about bacteria and germs and their effects on the human body. However, another significant factor was the lack of adequate medical care, which was especially the case for black troops. See Margaret Humphreys, *Intensely Human: The Health of the Black Soldier in the American Civil War* (Baltimore: Johns Hopkins University Press, 2008).

39. Trudeau, *Like Men of War*, 314–31.

40. Patience Cain to Lorenzo Thomas, February 18, 1865, C-54, 1865, Letters Received, series 366, Colored Troops Division, Record Group 94; George Bazel Service Records (the army spelled his name Bazel not Bazil), 55th Massachusetts Infantry.

41. George Bazil Service Records, 55th Massachusetts Infantry.

42. John Brunson to Lorenzo Thomas, March 29, 1865, B-151, 1865, Letters Received, series 366, Colored Troops Division, Record Group 94; David Brunson Service Records, 54th Massachusetts Infantry. John and his son, David, may have been related to Ellen and her husband, Charles, given that they shared the same last name and were from the same small town, Blairsville, Pennsylvania.

43. David Brunson Service Records, 54th Massachusetts Infantry.

44. Peter Kelly referred to Julia as Julia Henry, but that was probably a transcription error because he clearly stated Charles was her husband and she his wife. Julia Henry to Edwin Stanton, March 11, 1865, H-101, 1865, Letters Received, series 366, Colored Troops Division, Record Group 94. Charles's service records list his occupation as "Dealer," but they do not provide an explanation or any other information as to what that specifically meant. It probably referred to some type of commodity or product Charles sold to make a living. See Charles Henry Green Service Records, 32nd USCT. Trudeau, *Like Men of War*, 330–31.

45. Mary Lloyd to Edwin Stanton, March 18, 1865, L-50, 1865, Letters Received, series 366, Colored Troops Division, Record Group 94.

46. Forbes, *African American Women*, 196.

47. Faust, *This Republic of Suffering*, xv–xvi, 48, 51–52, 55. Faust argued African Americans' understanding of death was not just about dying for the Union cause but also killing for the cause. Violence and killing were active ways of managing and conceptualizing the reality of death and the war and more important than dying.

48. Mary Fisher to Edwin Stanton, March 4, 1865, F-27, 1865, Letters Received, series 366, Colored Troops Division, Record Group 94.

49. Joshua Fisher Service Records, 25th USCT; Joshua Fisher Pension Files, 25th USCI, Records of the Veterans Administration, Record Group 15.

50. Noah Davis Service Records, 8th USCT; John Demby Service Records, 24th USCT; John Demby Pension Files, 31st USCI, Records of the Veterans Administration, Record Group 15.

51. Jane Mares to Edwin Stanton, April 12, 1865, M-141, 1865, Letters Received, series 366, Colored Troops Division, Record Group 94; John Mares Service Records, 25th USCT. John's wife, Mary Ellen Maris, applied for a widow's pension and it was approved on October 26, 1866. It commenced April 26, 1865 for $8 a month. They had been married since December 7, 1856 and had no children. She received the pension until her death "of old age and being an invalid" on March 2, 1909. See John Mares Pension Files, 25th USCI, Records of the Veterans Administration, Record Group 15.

52. Elizabeth Adams to Edwin Stanton, April 6, 1865, A-92, Letters Received, series 366, Colored Troops Division, Record Group 94; John Quincy Adams Service Records, 45th USCT; Charles W. Roy Service Records, 45th USCT; George S. Rico Service Records, 45th USCT.

53. Humphreys, *Intensely Human*, 6–7, 10–11. Of the more than 37,000 black soldiers who died in Union uniforms, only 4,000 died directly from battle wounds. The rest died

from disease. The most common diseases for all Civil War soldiers were diarrhea, cholera, pneumonia, dysentery, typhoid fever, measles, small-pox, tuberculosis, and malaria.

54. Sarah Brown to Edwin Stanton, April 8, 1865, B-67, 1865, Letters Received, series 366, Colored Troops Division, Record Group 94; Samuel Brown Service Records, 25th USCT; Asa Miller Service Records, 25th USCT; George H. Washington Service Records, 25th USCT.

55. Samuel Brown Service Records, 25th USCT; George H. Washington Service Records, 25th USCT; Asa Miller Service Records, 25th USCT.

56. Victoria Covington to Lorenzo Thomas, April 7, 1865, C-157, 1865, Letters Received, series 366, Colored Troops Division, Record Group 94; Evans Covington Service Records, 54th Massachusetts Infantry.

57. Victoria Covington to Lorenzo Thomas, April 7, 1865, C-157, 1865, Letters Received, series 366, Colored Troops Division, Record Group 94; Evans Covington Service Records, 54th Massachusetts Infantry. Evans was admitted into the asylum because he was affected by chronic epilepsy dementia, which led to death. In question was whether his illness was war related or a condition he already suffered from before he enlisted. After repeated application attempts after the war ended, Victoria was unsuccessful in securing a widow's pension. See Evans Covington Pension Files, 54th Massachusetts Infantry, Records of the Veterans Administration, Record Group 15.

58. Gideon Granger (for Annis E. Holland) to Edward D. Townsend (Assistant Adjutant General), February 24, 1863, G-35, 1865, Letters Received, series 366, Colored Troops Division, Record Group 94; Adam Holland Service Records, 31st USCT.

59. Adam Holland Service Records, 31st USCT; Gideon Granger (for Annis E. Holland) to Edward D. Townsend (Assistant Adjutant General), February 24, 1863, G-35, 1865, Letters Received, series 366, Colored Troops Division, Record Group 94; Adam Holland Service Records, 31st USCT; Adam Holland Pension Files, 31st USCI, Records of the Veterans Administration, Record Group 15.

60. E. Chandlee (for Ann Elizer Palmer (alias Pammer) to Lorenzo Thomas, March 13, 1865, C-88, Letters Received, series 366, Colored Troops Division, Record Group 94; Jacob Palmer (alias Pammer) Service Records, 22nd USCT.

61. E. Chandlee (for Ann Elizer Palmer (alias Pammer) to Lorenzo Thomas, March 13, 1865, C-88, Letters Received, series 366, Colored Troops Division, Record Group 94.

62. Ibid.; Jacob Palmer (Alias Pammer) Service Records, 22nd USCT; Jacob Palmer (Alias Pammer) Pension Files, 22nd USCI, Records of the Veterans Administration, Record Group 15. According to the pension records, there was confusion with Jacob's correct date of death. Even after September 30, 1864 he remained on the regiment's muster rolls as absent until October 16, 1865, when he was reported killed. Eventually, the army verified he actually died in September 1864, though his death was not correctly recorded. It was probably Ann's efforts to get the correct dates in order to obtain Jacob's pension that caused the army to correct its records.

7. Discharge Requests

1. Jane Welcome to Abraham Lincoln, November 21, 1864, C. W. Foster to Jane Welcome, December 2, 1864, W-934, 1864, Letters Received, series 360, Colored Troops Division, Record Group 94.

2. Ibid.; Martin Welcome Service Records, 6th USCT.

3. Julia Rouser to Abraham Lincoln, September 24, 1864, endorsement of Mrs. L. W. Boyd, et al., no date, endorsement of Louis W. Richie, M.D., September 24, 1864, R. H. Tyson to Edwin Stanton, 1864, Adjutant General's Office Memorandum, October 13, 1864, Adjutant General's Office to Julia Rouser, October 18, 1864, R-389, 1864, Letters Received, series 360, Colored Troops Division, Record Group 94.

4. Ibid.

5. Ibid.; Army policy required a recruit be substituted prior to being assigned to a regiment. Once William had been assigned to the 10th USCT, it was too late for him to be allowed to use a substitute. William Rouser Service Records, 10th USCT.

6. Glatthaar, *Forged in Battle*, 65–66, 76; McRae, *Negroes in Michigan*, 46; Jim Murphy, *The Boys' War: Confederate and Union Soldiers Talk About the Civil War* (New York: Clarion Books, 1990), 2–3, 8–11; Dennis M. Keesee, *Too Young to Die: Boy Soldiers of the Union Army, 1861–1865* (Huntington, W. Va.: Blue Acorn Press, 2001), 4–5, 12, 190; G. Clifton Wisler, *When Johnny Went Marching: Young Americans Fight the Civil War* (New York: HarperCollins, 2001), viii.

7. William C. Davis, *Rebels and Yankees: Fighting Men of the Civil War* (New York: Smithmark Publishers, 1991), 17; Cate Lineberry, "The Boys of War," *New York Times* (October 2011), http://opinionator.blogs.nytimes.com/2011/10/04/the-boys-of-war/; Rebecca Beatrice Brooks, "Child Soldiers in the Civil War," *Civil War Saga* (December 16, 2011), http://civilwarsaga.com/child-soldiers-in-the-civil-war/; Tabitha Thompson to Lorenzo Thomas, October 10, 1864, Adjutant General's Office to Tabitha Thompson, October 13, 1864, T-318, 1864, Letters Received, series 360, Colored Troops Division, Record Group 94; John Alexander Thompson Service Records, 26th USCT.

8. Ibid.; John Alexander Thompson Pension Files, 26th USCI, Records of the Veterans Administration, Record Group 15. John Thompson's younger sister, Margaret (Thompson) Lee, revealed her brother's untruth when she completed an affidavit supporting John's second wife's application for a widow's pension in 1918. John died December 23, 1910. The pension files also reveal John was actually fourteen when he joined the Union army, not twelve, as his mother stated in her letter to the Adjutant General. For additional information on boy soldiers in the Civil War, see Murphy, *The Boys' War*; Davis, *Rebels and Yankees*; Lineberry, "The Boys of War"; Brooks, "Child Soldiers in the Civil War"; Keesee, *Too Young to Die*. For information specific to African-American boys in the Civil War, see Keesee, *Too Young to Die*, 190–91, and Wisler, *When Johnny Went Marching*, 70–76.

9. Alicia Bass to Abraham Lincoln, December 7, 1864, B-186, 1864, Letters Received, series 366, Colored Troops Division, Record Group 94.

10. Armon Bass Service Records, 27th USCT. Armon Bass Pension Files, 27th USCI, Records of the Veterans Administration, Record Group 15; a deposition was provided

by George Beesley (May 1909) regarding a pension application for Bass's second wife, Lida R. Bass.

11. William Chandler to Abraham Lincoln, November 21, 1864, 335/D-732, 1864, Letters Received, series 7, Record Group 99. In spite of having lost his arm, William was probably listed as still being on a furlough because he was not officially discharged from the army. For some reason, his discharge was delayed until December 26, 1865. William Chandler Service Records, 8th USCT.

12. William Chandler to Abraham Lincoln, November 21, 1864, 335/D-732, 1864, Letters Received, series 7, Record Group 99. William Chandler Service Records, 8th USCT. William Chandler Pension Files, 8th USCI, Records of the Veterans Administration, Record Group 15.

13. Rebecca Smith to Edwin Stanton, April 1865, endorsements of Phillip Nolan and Archibald Lewis, April 18, 1865, note from Pension Division, November 26, 1889, note from Auditor's Office, November 21, 1889, S-257, 1865, Letters Received, series 360, Colored Troops Division, Record Group 94; Moses Smith Service Records, 43rd USCT; Silber, *Daughters of the Union*, 50. In spite of serving a short time in the army, Moses applied for an invalid pension on October 13, 1890. He was suffering from rheumatism and eczema, which he felt was due to his service during the war. However, his application was denied on June 23, 1891 because he did not serve the minimum of 190 days required for eligibility for a soldier's pension under the Congressional Act of June 27, 1890; for additional information, see Moses Smith Pension Files, 43rd USCI, Records of the Veterans Administration, Record Group 15.

14. Julia Rouser to Abraham Lincoln, September 24, 1864, endorsement of Mrs. L. W. Boyd, et al., no date, endorsement of Louis W. Richie, M.D., September 24, 1864, R. H. Tyson to Edwin Stanton, 1864, Adjutant General's Office Memorandum, October 13, 1864, Adjutant General's Office to Julia Rouser, October 18, 1864, R-389, 1864, Letters Received, series 360, Colored Troops Division, Record Group 94. The army's policy was to require a recruit be substituted prior to getting assigned to a regiment. Once William was assigned to the 10th USCT, it was too late for him to use a substitute. By 1865, the army clearly had changed its policy. William Rouser Service Records, 10th USCT.

15. John W. Hoag, et al. (for family of Daniel Johnson) to Edwin Stanton, July 10, 1865, C. W. Foster to John W. Hoag, July 19, 1865, P-363, 1865, Letters Received, series 360, Colored Troops Division, Record Group 94; Daniel Johnson Service Records, 14th USCT. The letter writer was referring to Union policy that allowed draftees to be exempted from military duty if they could show "that they were the sole means of support for a widow, an orphan sibling, a motherless child, or an indigent parent," as described in McPherson, *Battle Cry of Freedom*, 601. The average black household in 1850 and 1860 contained four people, usually a married couple and two children. This is based on the censuses for those years. See Horton, *Black Bostonians*, 15.

16. John W. Hoag, et al. (for the family of Daniel Johnson) to Edwin Stanton, July 10, 1865, C. W. Foster to John W. Hoag, July 19, 1865, P-363, 1865, Letters Received, series 360, Colored Troops Division, Record Group 94; Daniel Johnson Service Records, 14th USCT.

17. Lyddia Ann Bartley to Lorenzo Thomas, April 6, 1865, B-218, 1865, Letters Received, series 360, Colored Troops Division, Record Group 94; Joseph S. Bartley Service Records, 38th USCT.

18. C. W. Foster to Lyddia Ann Bartley, April 28, 1865, B-256, Letters Sent, series 352, Colored Troops Division, Record Group 94. In this response the army explained the content of its first letter (sent April 11, 1865) to Lyddia Ann Bartley.

19. Lyddia Ann Bartley to Lorenzo Thomas, April 26, 1865, endorsements of George Brewer, no date, notarized statement of Lyddia Ann Bartley, et al, no date, note from Captain & Provost Marshall (Second District, Penna), March 23, 1865, B-256, 1865, Letters Received, series 360, Colored Troops Division, Record Group 94; C. W. Foster to Lyddia Ann Bartley, April 28, 1865, B-256, Letters Sent, series 352, Colored Troops Division, Record Group 94; Joseph S. Bartley Service Records, 38th USCT.

20. Hilton Sand to Edwin Stanton, March 9, 1865, endorsements of Joseph Sheldon, March 18, 1865, statement from Provost Marshall's Office, March 31, 1865, consent form of Caroline Sands, February 17, 1863, Description of Recruit form of William Hamlin, February 18, 1863, miscellaneous notes, no date, S-180, 1865, Letters Received, series 360, Colored Troops Division, Record Group 94; John Sands Service Records, 11th USCHA; Wallace Sands Service Records, 29th Connecticut Regiment. Wallace was discharged early from the army due to a disability and was probably already receiving a disability pension when he provided a notarized affidavit for John's pension case.

21. Hilton Sand to Edwin Stanton, March 9, 1865, endorsements of Joseph Sheldon, March 18, 1865, statement from Provost Marshall's Office, March 31, 1865, consent form of Caroline Sands, February 17, 1863, Description of Recruit form of William Hamlin, February 18, 1863, miscellaneous notes, no date, S-180, 1865, Letters Received, series 360, Colored Troops Division, Record Group 94; John Sands Service Records, 11th USCHA. John Sands Pension Files, 11th USCHA, Records of the Veterans Administration, Record Group 15.

8. The Conclusion of the War

1. For additional information on the Confederate army's will to fight, especially near the war's end, see Gary W. Gallagher, *The Confederate War: How Popular Will, Nationalism, and Military Strategy Could Not Stave Off Defeat* (Cambridge: Harvard University Press, 1997); see also, Gabor S. Boritt, ed., *Why the Confederacy Lost* (New York: Oxford University Press, 1992); Richard E. Beringer, Herman Hattaway, Archer Jones, and William N. Still, Jr., *Why the South Lost the Civil War* (Athens: University of Georgia Press, 1986); Michael Perman and Amy Murrell Taylor, eds., *Major Problems in the Civil War and Reconstruction, Documents and Essays, Third Edition* (Boston: Wadsworth, Cengage Learning, 2011), 256–75; and Andrew F. Smith, *Starving The South: How the North Won the Civil War* (New York: St. Martin's Press, 2011).

2. Glatthaar, *Forged in Battle*, 147–48.

3. See McPherson, *Battle Cry of Freedom*, 844; Claxton, *Uncommon Valor*, 120–21; Wilson, *The Black Phalanx*, 378; Blackett, ed., *Thomas Morris Chester*, 268, 270–71; Trudeau, *Like Men of War*, 375. For more details about Grant's 1864 campaigns in the

east, see McPherson, *Battle Cry of Freedom*, 721–43. For specific information about the role of black soldiers in Grant's campaigns in 1864, see Quarles, *The Negro in the Civil War*, 296–97.

4. Hargrove, *Black Union Soldiers*, 199; Miller, Jr., *The Black Civil War Soldiers of Illinois*, 140; Berlin, et al., eds., *Freedom*, 26.

5. Redkey, ed., *A Grand Army of Black Men*, 88–89; Blackett, ed., *Thomas Morris Chester*, 41, 203–19; Gibbs, *Black, Copper & Bright*, 95–97, 134–35, 152; Dobak, *Freedom by the Sword*, 403–5, 406–7; McPherson, *Battle Cry of Freedom*, 819–20, 821; Trudeau, *Like Men of War*, 358–64; Kelly D. Mezurek, *For Their Own Cause: The 27th United States Colored Troops* (Kent, Ohio: Kent State University Press, 2016). This was the Union's second attempt to take the fort. The first one, which occurred on December 24, 1864, had failed and led to General Grant relieving General Butler of command and replacing him with Terry.

6. Smith, ed., *Black Soldiers in Blue*, xviii, 6; Trudeau, *Like Men of War*, 353–58; Emilio, *A Brave Black Regiment*, 281, 284. To leave very little to Yankee forces, Confederates torched anything that could be of military value to them. See Quarles, *The Negro in the Civil War*, 325–26.

7. Smith, ed., *Black Soldiers in Blue*, xviii, 6; Trudeau, *Like Men of War*, 353–58; Emilio, *A Brave Black Regiment*, 281, 284; Redkey, ed., *A Grand Army of Black Men*, 78–79.

8. Yacovone, ed., *A Voice of Thunder*, 80–81, 265.

9. McPherson, *Battle Cry of Freedom*, 844–46, 847–49; Hargrove, *Black Union Soldiers*, 200; Burkhardt, *Confederate Rage, Yankee Wrath*, 239; Blackett, ed., *Thomas Morris Chester*, 253, 279–80. Trudeau, *Like Men of War*, 424–32, 455. Participating in the final campaign against Lee's army and leading to the surrender were the 7th, 8th, 29th, 31st, 41st, 45th, 109th, 116th, and 127th USCTs. Black soldiers (the 4th, 6th, 27th, 30th, and 107th USCTs) were also present when General Joseph E. Johnston surrendered his army to Sherman; see Gladstone, *Men of Color*, 175. For additional information on an analysis of the effects of letters from southern women to their soldiers, see Perman and Taylor, eds., *Major Problems in the Civil War and Reconstruction*, 256–75.

10. Clayton Johnson Service Records, 54th Massachusetts Infantry. Living in Brooklyn and employed as a truck driver after the war, Johnson applied for an invalid pension, which was approved due to his permanent hand injury that "destroys the grip of his right hand." Payments began November 20, 1865. After his death on May 28, 1906, his second wife, Josephine A. Johnson (his first wife, Amanda, died after two or three years of marriage), petitioned for and was approved for an $8 a month pension; Clayton had one child with his first wife (a daughter who died as a baby) and two kids with Josephine (a son and then a son who died at seven months old); Josephine received a widow's pension until her death on January 29, 1917; see Clayton Johnson Pension Files, 54th Massachusetts Infantry, Records of the Veterans Administration, Record Group 15. Minié balls are rifle bullets with conical heads used in muzzle-loading firearms, the primary weapon by both sides in the Civil War. Emilio, *A Brave Black Regiment*, 304; Yacovone, ed., *A Voice of Thunder*, 81–82; Trudeau, *Like Men of War*, 390–95.

11. Redkey, ed., *A Grand Army of Black Men*, 82.

12. Claxton, *Uncommon Valor*, 212. In *The Sable Arm*, 264–67, Cornish analyzed the

Civil War statistics on the participation of black soldiers in major campaigns, battles, and skirmishes as provided by the *Official Army Register* and Dyer's *Compendium*.

9. After the War: A Different Kind of Battle

1. Anna Wright to Edwin Stanton, April 10, 1865, W-145, 1865, Letters Received, series 366, Colored Troops Division, Record Group 94.

2. Archibald Wright Service Records, 54th Massachusetts Infantry. The New Markets Heights battle took place on September 29, 1864, when black Union soldiers attacked a heavily fortified position near Richmond, Virginia. In a very hard fought victory with many casualties on both sides, fourteen of the black soldiers were later awarded the Congressional Medal of Honor for their exceptional bravery during the battle. See James S. Price and O. James. Lighthizer, *The Battle of New Market Heights: Freedom Will Be Theirs by the Sword* (Charleston, S.C.: The History Press, 2011); Paradis, *Strike the Blow for Freedom*, 69–79.

3. Rebecca Beverly to unknown, May 3, 1865, B-207, 1865, Letters Received, series 366, Colored Troops Division, Record Group 94.

4. Hull Fauton (for father of William Lewis) to Lorenzo Thomas, May, 4 1865, F-67, 1865, Letters Received, series 366, Colored Troops Division, Record Group 94.

5. Richard Beverly Service Records, 32nd USCT.

6. William Lewis Service Records, 8th USCT.

7. May Bullett to unknown, May 10, 1865, B-237, 1865, Letters Received, series 366, Colored Troops Division, Record Group 94. Though the letter referred to a May Bullett, the pension records make it clear the letter writer, John J. Keefe, was referring to Althea Bullett.

8. Mary Graham to Edwin Stanton, May 29, 1865, G-99, 1865, Letters Received, series 366, Colored Troops Division, Record Group 94.

9. Henry Bullett Service Records, 25th USCT. On July 8, 1865, just weeks after receiving confirmation Henry was dead, Althea filed for a widow's pension, which was not approved until December 2, 1870. The payments commenced September 8, 1864, the day after her husband died. She received $8 a month for herself and another $2 each for her and Henry's daughter, Martha Selena Bullet, and son, William Bullet. The children were two and one years old when she applied. On May 7, 1866, Henry's mother, Martha Bullett, applied for a mother's pension, feeling she was more entitled than Henry's wife. Then, on November 5, 1990, Althea's payments were canceled after the government determined Althea had lied about once being married to Henry and becoming his widow. An investigation revealed she was Henry's mistress for many years, not his wife, and Althea may have been married twice after Henry's death. Martha Bullet's claim for a mother's pension, which had originally been denied, was reopened on March 6, 1891 but the records don't show if her pension claim was ever approved. See Henry Bullett Pension Files, 25th USCI, Records of the Veterans Administration, Record Group 15.

10. James Graham Service Records, 22nd USCT.

11. Either during or shortly after the war, Mary Graham died. It is not clear. Ten years later, on May 10, 1876, he married Annie Wright; see James Graham Pension Files, 22nd USCI, Records of the Veterans Administration, Record Group 15.

12. Rebecca Berry to Adjutant General's Office, June 8, 1865, B-295, 1865, Letters Received, series 366, Colored Troops Division, Record Group 94; Charles H. Blake Service Records, 22nd USCT; Jeremiah Cummings Service Records, 32nd USCT; Charles H. Blake Pension Files, 22nd USCI, Records of the Veterans Administration, Record Group 15. The problem with verifying Charles's death began because no one in the regiment was present to complete the proper paperwork. The regiment left the area while he remained in the hospital. With the officers and regimental surgeons gone, he was probably forgotten about, especially given that the war ended soon afterwards and most of the regiment's officers were discharged and returned home. By May 1865, the rest of the regiment was headed to Texas.

13. Charles H. Blake Pension Files, 22nd USCI, Records of the Veterans Administration, Record Group 15.

14. Glatthaar, *Forged in Battle*, 209–10; Redkey, ed., A *Grand Army of Black Men*, 455–56; Smith, ed., *Black Soldiers in Blue*, 379.

15. Berlin, et al., eds., *Freedom*, 733–34; Smith, ed., *Black Soldiers in Blue*, 361.

16. Lawson, *Patriot Fires*, 180; Smith, ed., *Black Soldiers in Blue*, xviii, 6; Trudeau, *Like Men of War*, 455–56. These figures are based on the number of black soldiers still in the service as of July 15, 1865. See Cornish, *The Sable Arm*, 288; Berlin et al., eds., *Freedom—*, 733–34. Some historians have argued black troops were not purposely excluded from the parade. Instead, they were not there because they remained in the South to complete their three-year terms of enlistment and they were needed to perform occupation duties. See Gary W. Gallagher, *The Union War* (Cambridge: Harvard University Press, 2011), 19–21.

17. Glatthaar, *Forged in Battle*, 164–65, 316n46; Redkey, ed., A *Grand Army of Black Men*, 178–80.

18. Redkey, ed., A *Grand Army of Black Men*, 161–82, 178–80; Trudeau, *Like Men of War*, 456; Berlin et al., eds., *Freedom*, 734.

19. Redkey, ed., A *Grand Army of Black Men*, 178–80.

20. Ibid., 190–91.

21. This timeline was determined by reviewing service records of soldiers, which list when a soldier was last paid, when he mustered out of the service, or when he died.

22. Mrs. John W. Wilson to Edwin Stanton, May 27, 1865, W-416, 1865, Letters Received, series 360, Colored Troops Division, Record Group 94.

23. Ibid.

24. John Wesley Wilson Service Records, 102nd USCT.

25. Gibbs, *Black, Copper & Bright*, 182.

26. Redkey, ed., A *Grand Army of Black Men*, 170–72; Glatthaar, *Forged in Battle*, 210–11; Perman, *Emancipation and Reconstruction*, 22–23; McPherson, *Battle Cry of Freedom*, 842; Foner, *A Short History of Reconstruction*, 31–32, 64–66; Berlin, et al., eds., *Freedom's Soldiers*, 158.

27. Berlin et al., eds., *Freedom's Soldiers*, 49; Glatthaar, *Forged in Battle*, 214–15, 217–18; Trudeau, *Like Men of War*, 464; Berlin et al., eds., *Freedom*, 33–34, 735–36; Redkey, ed., A *Grand Army of Black Men*, 161, 192; Trudeau, *Like Men of War*, 457; Rosen, *Terror in the Heart of Freedom*, 47–49, 54.

28. Glatthaar, *Forged in Battle*, 218; Yacovone, ed., *A Voice of Thunder*, 87–88.

29. Redkey, ed., *A Grand Army of Black Men*, 180.

30. Ibid., 195.

31. Martha Douglass to the War Department, July, 6, 1865, AGO note, no date, D-222, 1865, Letters Received, series 360, Colored Troops Division, Record Group 94.

32. Lewis Douglass Service Records, 43rd USCT.

33. Adjutant General's Office to Martha Douglass, D-222, 1865, Letters Received, series 354, Colored Troops Division, Record Group 94.

34. David M. Burke Service Records, 38th USCT.

35. Isleanor Burke to Edwin Stanton, June 17, 1865, note from C. W. Foster, June 19, 1865, H-281, 1865, Letters Received, series 360, Colored Troops Division, Record Group 94.

36. Ibid.; Scrophula is a type skin of disease. It is a tuberculous infection of the skin on the neck, usually affecting the lymph nodes.

37. Isleanor Burke to Edwin Stanton, June 17, 1865, note from C. W. Foster, June 19, 1865, H-281, 1865, Letters Received, series 360, Colored Troops Division, Record Group 94.

38. David M. Burke Service Records, 38th USCT.

39. Rachel Batties to Edwin Stanton, September 13, 1865, C. W. Foster to Mrs. Rachel Batties, September 20, 1865, B-698, 1865, Letters Received, series 360, Colored Troops Division, Record Group 94.

40. Charles Batties Service Records, 24th USCT; John Batties Service Records, 24th USCT; Edward Batties Service Records, 24th USCT. John and Edward were probably twins.

41. Rachel Batties to Edwin Stanton, September 13, 1865, C. W. Foster to Mrs. Rachel Batties, September 20, 1865, B-698, 1865, Letters Received, series 360, Colored Troops Division, Record Group 94.

42. John Batties lived a very long life and was ninety-five when he died. He outlived his brothers and his wife, Eliza Jackson Batties. He married Eliza on November 26, 1866 and they had three children together (two daughters and one son). She died on January 24, 1911. He applied for and was approved for invalid pension on October 3, 1902, which he received until his death on April 16, 1941 in Philadelphia. Before he died, he was one of the few black Civil War veterans still alive. His family received $100 from Veteran's Administration to cover a portion of the cost for his funeral and burial. See John Batties Pension Files, 24th USCI, Records of the Veterans Administration, Record Group 15.

43. Martin Clayburn Service Records, 32nd USCT.

44. R. W. Downey (for family of Martin Clayburn) to Edwin Stanton, July 11, 1865, C. W. Foster to R. W. Downey, July 19, 1865, AGO note, no date, D-225, 1885, Letters Received, series 360, Colored Troops Division, Record Group 94.

45. Ibid.

46. Robert Anderson Service Records, 6th USCT.

47. Mrs. A. Hartman, et al., (for Mary Anderson) to Edwin Stanton, July 18, 1865, War Department note, July 14, 1865, AGO note, no date, endorsements of Mrs. F. M. Hartwell (Freedmen's Aid Society, Washington, D.C.) to C. W. Foster, July 14, 1865, J. H. Hilton to

General Hardy, July 14, 1865, H-401, 1865, Letters Received, series 360, Colored Troops Division, Record Group 94.

48. Ibid.

49. Ibid.

50. Ibid.

51. Ruben Mann Service Records, 8th USCT.

52. A. J. Fox, et al., (for Ruben Mann) to Edwin Stanton, 1865, AGO note, no date, Lyman Balcom to Edwin Stanton, no date, C. W. Foster to R. B. Vanvelkenburg, June 9, 1865, V-120, 1865, Letters Received, series 360, Colored Troops Division, Record Group 94.

53. Ibid.

54. John M. Johnson to Lidy Johnson, Jun 22, 1865, Lidy A. Johnson to Samuel Brock, June 26, 1865, C. W. Foster to Sydia A. Johnson, July 1, 1865, J-89, 1865, Letters Received, series 360, Colored Troops Division, Record Group 94; John Johnson Service Records, 6th USCT.

55. John M. Johnson to Lidy Johnson, Jun 22, 1865, Lidy A. Johnson to Samuel Brock (Assistant Adjutant General), June 26, 1865, C. W. Foster to Sydia A. Johnson, July 1, 1865, J-89, 1865, Letters Received, series 360, Colored Troops Division, Record Group 94.

56. John Johnson Service Records, 6th USCT.

57. John S. Driver Service Records, 32nd USCT; Noel (Noah) B. Jacobs Service Records, 32nd USCT, including Deed of Manumission and Release of service form and accompanying documents.

58. Angeline Jacobs to Edwin Stanton, June 3, 1865, J-71, 1865, Letters Received, series 366, Colored Troops Division, Record Group 94.

59. Sally Davis to Edwin Stanton, May 5, 1865, D-176, 1865, Letters Received, series 366, Colored Troops Division, Record Group 94.

60. William E. Davis Service Records, 43rd USCT.

61. Adam Willet Service Records, 45th USCT.

62. Mary Fitzgerald to Edwin Stanton, July 18, 1865, F131, 1865, Letters Received, series 366, Colored Troops Division, Record Group 94.

63. Joseph Fitzgerald Service Records, 32nd USCT. John J. Keefe wrote her letter and also served as a witness for the documentation provided with her pension application.

64. Edmund H. Anderson to Edwin Stanton, July, 25, 1865, A-193, 1865, Letters Received, series 366, Colored Troops Division, Record Group 94.

65. Edmund H. Anderson Service Records, 3rd USCT.

66. D. B. Booth Letter (for the family of John M. Coley) to unknown, July 15, 1865, B-452, 1865, Letters Received, series 366, Colored Troops Division, Record Group 94.

67. John M. Coley Service Records, 29th Connecticut Infantry.

68. John Lewis Service Records, 41st USCT.

69. Margaret Lewis to Edwin Stanton, August 16, 1865, L-153, 1865, Letters Received, series 366, Colored Troops Division, Record Group 94.

70. Clayton Johnson Service Records, 6th USCT.

71. Mary Ann Johnson to Edmund [Edwin] M. Stanton, July 15, 1865, J-95, 1865, Letters Received, series 366, Colored Troops Division, Record Group 94.

72. Ibid.

73. Clayton Johnson Service Records, 6th USCT.

74. Henry Fletcher (for Lavinia Cromwell) to Edwin Stanton, July 8, 1865, F-117, 1865, Henry Fletcher (for Lavinia Cromwell) to Mr. Taggard (probably referring to Assistant Adjutant General Samuel L. Taggart), July 8, 1865, J-152, 1865, Letters Received, series 366, Colored Troops Division, Record Group 94; Obediah Cromwell Service Records, 6th USCT.

75. Henry Fletcher (for Lavinia Cromwell) to Edwin Stanton, July 8, 1865, F-117, 1865, Henry Fletcher (for Lavinia Cromwell) to Mr. Taggard (probably referring to Assistant Adjutant General Samuel Taggart), August 21, 1865, J-152, 1865, Letters Received, series 366, Colored Troops Division, Record Group 94.

76. Lavinia C. Cromwell to unknown, August 24, 1865, C-340, 1865, Lavinia C. Cromwell to unknown, December 2, 1865, C-487, 1865, Letters Received, series 366, Colored Troops Division, Record Group 94.

77. Obediah Cromwell Pension Files, 6th USCI, Records of the Veterans Administration, Record Group 15. Lavinia received $8 a month until she remarried on March 30, 1870. She also received an extra $2 a month for each of her two dependent children until they reached sixteen years of age.

78. Eliza Lukens to Edwin Stanton, August 9, 1865, L-149, 1865, Letters Received, series 366, Colored Troops Division, Record Group 94.

79. Benjamin Augustus Service Records, 127th USCT. After Augustus's death, the prisoners were "placed under fire" by order of General B. F. Butler.

80. Charles Lukens Service Records, 45th USCT; George Lukens to Edwin Stanton, December 6, 1865, S-241, 1865, Letters Received, series 366, Colored Troops Division, Record Group 94; Rebecca Berry to Adjutant General's Office, June 8, 1865, B-295, 1865, Letters Received, series 366, Colored Troops Division, Record Group 94; Charles H. Blake Service Records, 22nd USCT; Charles H. Blake Service Records, 22nd USCT. Charles Lukens's service records don't shed light on if and when he may have died and a pension file does not exist under his name.

81. Gibbs, *Black, Copper & Bright*, 182.

82. Lieutenant Colonel W. B. Lane to Adjutant General's Office, December 18, 1865, L-391 and S-258, 1865, Letters Received, series 366, Colored Troops Division, Record Group 94.

10. Even Farther Away from Home: Occupation Duty Continues

1. Miller, Jr., *The Black Civil War Soldiers of Illinois*, 152–53; Humphreys, *Intensely Human*, 119–20, 121–22. The Monroe Doctrine was a United States policy introduced by President James Monroe in an annual message to Congress on December 2, 1823. He declared the American continents were no longer to be subject to new colonization by European governments. To do so, he claimed, would be considered by the United States to be a threat to the United States's peace and safety. The Doctrine became the foundation of future U.S. foreign policy in Central and South America.

2. Berlin et al., eds., *Freedom*, 734, 736; Humphreys, *Intensely Human*, 122; Miller, Jr., *The Black Civil War Soldiers of Illinois*, 152–53; Trudeau, *Like Men of War*, 458–61; Redkey, ed., *A Grand Army of Black Men*, 163; Glatthaar, *Forged in Battle*, 219–20.

3. Miller, Jr., *The Black Civil War Soldiers of Illinois*, 153–55; Glatthaar, *Forged in Battle*, 219; Frankel, *Freedom's Women*, 15–27, 28–55.

4. Miller, Jr., *The Black Civil War Soldiers of Illinois*, 155–56; Glatthaar, *Forged in Battle*, 219; Cornish, *The Sable Arm*, 288; Alexander H. Newton, *Out Of The Briars: An Autobiography And Sketch Of The Twenty-Ninth Regiment, Connecticut Volunteers* (1910) (Philadelphia: The A.M.E. Book Concerns, 1910), 69–70.

5. Miller, Jr., *The Black Civil War Soldiers of Illinois*, 156–57; Glatthaar, *Forged in Battle*, 219; Humphreys, *Intensely Human*, 119, 122.

6. Glatthaar, *Forged in Battle*, 219–20; Humphreys, *Intensely Human*, 119–20, 122–24; Redkey, ed., *A Grand Army of Black Men*, 198–99; Trudeau, *Like Men of War*, 459–60.

7. William J. Kauffman (for the family of William B. Peterson) to Lorenzo Thomas, November 16, 1865, R-97, 1865, Letters Received, series 366, Colored Troops Division, Record Group 94.

8. William B. Peterson Service Records, 127th USCT; William B. Peterson Pension Files, 127th USCI, Records of the Veterans Administration, Record Group 15. For a reason not explained in the military records, Peterson's children did not apply for their father's pension until October 1891, when they were no longer minors. By the time they applied, three of the five children were deceased. The remaining two were William, who was thirty-two years old, and Charles, who was twenty-eight, both living in Philadelphia. Because they had long since reached the age of sixteen, pension officials rejected their applications. Hence, the Peterson family received very little monitory compensation for William's ultimate sacrifice while serving.

9. No disease affected the men more than the outbreak of scurvy. The situation became so critical during the summer of 1865 that about sixty percent of the troops succumbed to scurvy, with two percent, or 2,500 men, dying from the disease; however, these numbers may be at the conservative end because of underreporting of both cases and deaths. Glatthaar, *Forged in Battle*, 220–21; Miller, Jr., *The Black Civil War Soldiers of Illinois*, 158–60, 160; Humphreys, *Intensely Human*, 120, 125–27, 132–34; Trudeau, *Like Men of War*, 460; Redkey, ed., *A Grand Army of Black Men*, 200–2.

10. Redkey, ed., *A Grand Army of Black Men*, 199–200. George Broden, to Edwin Stanton, August 14, 1865, B-671, 1865, Letters Received, series 360, Colored Troops Division, Record Group 94. It is unclear whether Broden's request was approved or denied because his service record is not available.

11. Redkey, ed., *A Grand Army of Black Men*, 199–200; Mrs. S. E. Draper (written for Mrs. Maria Herbert) to Oliver Howard, August 22, 1865, Samuel L. Taggart (Assistant Adjutant General) to Department of Refugees, August 23, 1865, A-9865, 1865, Unregistered Letters Received, series 457, D.C. Assistant Commissioner, Record Group 105.

12. Ibid.

13. Ibid.

14. Glatthaar, *Forged in Battle*, 221–22; Trudeau, *Like Men of War*, 460.

15. Redkey, ed., *A Grand Army of Black Men*, 182; Glatthaar, *Forged in Battle*, 222–23, 224; Berlin et al., eds., *Freedom*, 424–25. Described in *The Civil War Dictionary*, buck and gag (or bucking) was a form of corporal punishment. The offending soldier "was gagged and seated with his hands and feet tied. His knees were drawn up, the arms

passed around them, and a rod was inserted, horizontal to the ground, between the arms and the backs of the knees." The soldier was left in this immobile and in a highly uncomfortable position for a period of time comparable to the magnitude of the soldier's transgression. See Mark M. Boatner, ed., *The Civil War Dictionary*, 95. For information about general discipline in the Union army, see Steven J. Ramold, *Baring the Iron Hand: Discipline in the Union Army* (DeKalb: Northern Illinois University Press, 2010).

16. Glatthaar, *Forged in Battle*, 222–23, 224.

17. Ibid., 226; Berlin et al., eds., *Freedom*, 611; Wilson, *The Black Phalanx*, 503–7; Wilson, *Campfires of Freedom*, 83–84, 94–95, 98. Historian Christopher Hager argued that the act of writing displayed a sense of independence and freedom not experienced before by African Americans, and explains why they valued literacy for themselves and their children; see Hager, *Word by Word*. For additional information about the strong desire by black troops to become literate see Heather Andrea Williams, *Self-Taught: African American Education in Slavery and Freedom* (Chapel Hill: University of North Carolina Press, 2007).

18. Berlin et al., eds., *Freedom*, 611–12, 617–18; Wilson, *Campfires of Freedom*, 84–87, 94–95. Samuel Armstrong kept his regiment's school open for many hours so the troops could take advantage of the opportunity to learn. He would remain committed to this cause even after the war when in 1868 he founded Hampton Institute, in Hampton, Virginia, a manual arts college for black students. Its most famous graduate was Booker T. Washington. Today, Hampton Institute is known as Hampton University.

19. Berlin et al., eds., *Freedom*, 612; Glatthaar, *Forged in Battle*, 226–27.

20. Wilson, *Campfires of Freedom*, 84, 88–89; Berlin et al., eds., *Freedom*, 612; Gibbs, *Black, Copper & Bright*, 130–34; Glatthaar, *Forged in Battle*, 226–27.

21. Robert Stevenson, "America's First Black Music Historian," *Journal of the American Musicological Society* 26 (Autumn 1973): 383–404; Wilson, *The Black Phalanx*, 505–7.

22. Wilson, *The Black Phalanx*, 84, 99; Berlin et al., eds., *Freedom*, 612; Gibbs, *Black, Copper & Bright*, 31; Glatthaar, *Forged in Battle*, 226–27.

23. Berlin et al., eds., *Freedom—*, 611; Wilson, *Campfires of Freedom*, 84–85, 101; Yacovone, ed., *A Voice of Thunder*, 5. It is not exactly known where Stephens attended school.

24. Stevenson, "America's First Black Music Historian," 383–404; Wilson, *The Black Phalanx*, 505–7; Joseph T. Wilson, "James Monroe Trotter (1842–1892)," *African-American Experience in Ohio 1850–1920*. The Ohio Historical Society, http://dbs.ohio history.org/africanam/det.cfm?ID'10044; "James M. Trotter," Ohio History Central, November 11, 2008, http://www.ohiohistorycentral.org/w/James_M._Trotter Records, 55th Massachusetts Infantry.

25. James M. Trotter Service Records, 55th Massachusetts Infantry. The first African American promoted to the rank of second lieutenant was Stephen Atkin Swails of the 54th Massachusetts Infantry. On March 11, 1864, Colonel Edward N. Hallowell recommended Swails for a commission as a second lieutenant and Governor John Andrew accepted the request. However, because of prejudice, the Union army did not recognize his appointment. Nevertheless, he served as an officer for ten months until January 1865, when the army officially awarded his commission, but not until Andrew sent months of pleas and protests to Washington. See Yacovone, ed., *A Voice of Thunder*, 89–90.

26. Wilson, *Campfires of Freedom*, 89; Forbes, *African American Women*, 113; Sterling, ed., *We Are Your Sisters*, 261; Glatthaar, *Forged in Battle*, 226–27.

27. Wilson, *Campfires of Freedom*, 89; Forbes, *African American Women*, 125; Glatthaar, *Forged in Battle*, 226–27. According to the Freedmen's Bureau, almost one-third of all teachers working in the South by 1867 were commissioned by the AMA. The AMA played a pivotal role in the education of freedmen throughout the South by providing dedicated and talented teachers, and by helping to establish elementary schools, high schools, and colleges and universities. The AMA chartered eight historically black institutions of higher education and had much to do with the founding of many others. See Clara Merritt DeBoer, *His Truth Is Marching On: African Americans Who Taught the Freedmen for the American Missionary Association, 1861–1877* (New York: Garland, 1995), 4–7; Sterling, ed., *We Are Your Sisters*, 261n.

28. DeBoer, *His Truth Is Marching On*, xiii, 46–49; Sterling, ed., *We Are Your Sisters*, 263; Henry Barnard, ed., *American Journal of Education*, Volume III (Hartford: Office of American Journal of Education, 1870), 224; Forbes, *African American Women*, 114.

29. Sterling, ed., *We Are Your Sisters*, 279–86. Charlotte Forten's father was the son of the family's patriarch, James Forten. Robert Forten Service Records, 43rd USCT. Burchard, *One Gallant Rush*, 146; Stevenson, ed., *Charlotte Forten Grimke*, 14–15, 37–49, 490, 494–98.

30. Charles Highgate was a member of Company B, 185th New York Infantry, which was organized in Syracuse, New York, and mustered in on September 19, 1864. Why he joined a white regiment is unclear, especially since black regiments had been organizing since March 1863. He must have used his very light complexion to pass as white, an act members of his family had a history of doing when they felt it would work to their advantage. DeBoer, *His Truth is Marching On*, 50–54, 95, 121; Sterling, ed., *We Are Your Sisters*, 294–305. Edmonia's mother, Mrs. H. F. Highgate, and two sisters, Winella and Carrie, would also follow her and teach in the South. See Forbes, *African American Women*, 129, 131, 143, 195–96.

31. Forbes, *African American Women*, 114–24, 126–29; DeBoer, *His Truth Is Marching On*, xiii, Chapter 14; Sterling, ed., *We Are Your Sisters*, 265n.

32. Glatthaar, *Forged in Battle*, 226; Berlin et al., eds., *Freedom*, 613; Wilson, *Campfires of Freedom*, 91–92, 102.

33. Wilson, *Campfires of Freedom*, 92–93, 104; Berlin et al., eds., *Freedom*, 613; Gibbs, *Black, Copper & Bright*, 184; Glatthaar, *Forged in Battle*, 226–27.

34. Stevenson, "America's First Black Music Historian," 383–404; Wilson, *The Black Phalanx*, 507.

35. Berlin et al., eds., *Freedom*, 736; Glatthaar, *Forged in Battle*, 209–10; Redkey, ed., *A Grand Army of Black Men*, 161–62; Foner, *A Short History of Reconstruction*, 89; Dobak, *Freedom by the Sword*, 473.

36. Elizabeth Conrad to Edwin Stanton, November 18, 1865, AGO note, no date, C. W. Foster to Elizabeth Conrad, November 28, 1865, C-766, 1865, Letters Received, series 360, Colored Troops Division, Record Group 94. Service Records, 5th USCHA.

37. Ibid.

38. Ibid.

39. Elizabeth Conrad to Edwin Stanton, November 18, 1865, AGO note, no date, C. W. Foster to Elizabeth Conrad, November 28, 1865, C-766, 1865, Letters Received, series 360, Colored Troops Division, Record Group 94. Thomas Conrad Pension Files, 5th USCHA, Records of the Veterans Administration, Record Group 15.

40. Thomas A. Conrad Service Records, 5th USCHA.

41. Sarah Odrich to Edwin Stanton, October 11, 1865, C. W. Foster to Sarah Odrich, January 10, 1866, O-109, 1865, Letters Received, series 360, Colored Troops Division, Record Group 94.

42. Ibid.

43. Charles Lukens Service Records, 10th USCHA.

44. George B. Clark (for the family of William F. Miner) to Edwin Stanton, October 23, 1865, C. W. Foster to George B. Clark, November 1, 1865, Treasury Department Auditor's Report, April 24, 1888, Auditor's Final Statement, April 28, 1888, AGO note, no date, C-728, 1865, Letters Received, series 360, Colored Troops Division, Record Group 94.

45. Ibid.

46. Ibid.

47. William F. Miner Service Records, 38th USCT; William F. Miner Pension Files, 38th USCI, Records of the Veterans Administration, Record Group 15.

48. Robert T. Seagrave (on the behalf of John Adams) to Miss D. L. Dix, October 16, 1865, D-370, 1865, Letters Received, series 360, Colored Troops Division, Record Group 94.

49. John Adams Service Records, 8th USCT.

50. Adams's service records show he was a patient at the Fort Monroe hospital, but it is not clear when he left there and returned to Philadelphia. See John Adams Service Records, 8th USCT. It is because Adams remarried that we know so much about him since there was very little information in his service records. His second wife, Josephine, wrote letters and provided affidavits from individuals who knew John, in her attempt after he died to obtain his pension funds as his widow. She had a difficult time proving they were legally married. See John Adams Pension Files, 8th USCI, Records of the Veterans Administration, Record Group 15.

51. Miller, Jr., *The Black Civil War Soldiers of Illinois*, 170.

52. B. M. Albany (for Willis Clark) to Edwin Stanton, September 16, 1865, A-237, 1865, Letters Received, series 366, Colored Troops Division, Record Group 94.

53. Ibid.

54. William Elbridge Clark Service Records, 23rd USCT. A pension file does not exist under William Elbridge Clark, which might have explained if he died in the hospital, was discharged from the army, or returned home to his family.

55. A. B. Hutchinson (for Rachel Whitten) to Lorenzo Thomas, October 31, 1865, H-457, 1865, Letters Received, series 366, Colored Troops Division, Record Group 94. Point of Rocks, Virginia, was only eleven miles from the general hospital near Petersburg, Virginia, and Joseph was probably transferred there as the 8th USCT moved into position to support the Union siege around Petersburg.

56. Joseph W. Witten Service Records, 8th USCT.

57. Joseph W. Witten Pension Files, 8th USCI, Records of the Veterans Administration, Record Group 15. In December 1862, Jefferson Davis threatened to send black soldiers into slavery or have them executed if captured by Confederate forces. On May 1, 1863, the Confederate Congress followed their president by passing a joint resolution that authorized Jefferson Davis to follow through with his threat. In practice, if captured black troops lived and were not murdered after being captured during a battle, Confederate forces tended to treat captured free black troops as prisoners of war. It is unclear how often former slaves were returned to slavery or free blacks sold into slavery, as Joseph stated happened to him. For additional information about the fair treatment of black soldiers by the Confederacy, see Cornish, *The Sable Arm*, Chapter 9.

58. Redkey, ed., *A Grand Army of Black Men*, 162, 202–3; Berlin et al., eds., *Freedom*, 736; Foner, *A Short History of Reconstruction*, 89; Trudeau, *Like Men of War*, 461; Thomas Boswell Service Records, 116th USCT.

59. Trudeau, *Like Men of War*, 461, 466; Dobak, *Freedom by the Sword*, 475; Berlin et al., eds., *Freedom*, 12, 14.

60. Gibbs, *Black, Copper & Bright*, 184.

61. Redkey, ed., *A Grand Army of Black Men*, 199–200.

62. Ibid., 201.

63. Glatthaar, *Forged in Battle*, 227.

64. Kantrowitz, *More Than Freedom*, 312–20.

11. Home Again

1. Redkey, ed., *A Grand Army of Black Men*, 285; Miller, Jr., *The Black Civil War Soldiers of Illinois*, 167.

2. Redkey, ed., *A Grand Army of Black Men*, 283; Berlin, et al., eds., *Freedom*, 767; Trudeau, *Like Men of War*, 461.

3. Yacovone, ed., *A Voice of Thunder*, 90; Emilio, *A Brave Black Regiment*, 318–19; Redkey, ed., *A Grand Army of Black Men*, 283.

4. Yacovone, ed., *A Voice of Thunder*, 90; Redkey, ed., *A Grand Army of Black Men*, 283; Emilio, *A Brave Black Regiment*, 317–18, 319–20. While on Gallop's Island in Boston Harbor, the 54th received its final payment from the paymaster on September 1, 1865 and was officially discharged afterwards. The regiment crossed the harbor the next day for the welcome-home festivities planned in the city.

5. Gibbs, *Black, Copper & Bright*, 166–70; *Daily National Republican*, October 10, 1865.

6. Miller, Jr., *The Black Civil War Soldiers of Illinois*, 169.

7. Newton, *Out Of The Briars*, 89.

8. Cornish, *The Sable Arm*, 290.

9. Escott, *Paying Freedom's Price*, Chapter 5.

10. Stevenson, "America's First Black Music Historian," 383–404; Joseph T. Wilson, "James Monroe Trotter (1842–1892)," *African-American Experience in Ohio 1850–1920*. The Ohio Historical Society, http://dbs.ohiohistory.org/africanam/det.cfm?ID'10044; "James M. Trotter," Ohio History Central, November 11, 2008, http://www.ohiohistory

central.org/entry.php?rec'3356. Trotter's son, William Monroe Trotter, graduated from Harvard University. A very close associate of W. E. B. Du Bois, William was a charter member of the Niagara Movement in 1905 and helped to found the National Association for the Advancement of Colored People in 1909.

11. Charles R. Douglass Service Records, 54th Massachusetts Regiment. On February 20, 1889, Charles applied for an invalid pension, which was approved for $20 monthly, effective April 14, 1890. By 1889, he had lost all hearing in his right ear and partial hearing in his left. The damage resulted from the discharge of cannon fire near him on June 16, 1864, as his company was supporting a heavy artillery regiment. After Charles's death, his wife, Laura, applied for a widow's pension. Though she provided extensive documentation, it's not clear if her petition was ever approved; see Charles R. Douglass Pension Files, 54th Massachusetts Regiment, Records of the Veterans Administration, Record Group 15.

12. Yacovone, ed., *A Voice of Thunder*, 99–109. George's wife, Catherine, received a widow's pension, commencing June 17, 1891 at $8 a month, until her death on March 3, 1921. Their son received a dependent child's benefit of $2 a month until he turned sixteen in May 1892. See George E. Stephens Pension Files, 54th Massachusetts Infantry, Records of the Veterans Administration, Record Group 15.

13. Yacovone, ed., *A Voice of Thunder*, 257n16.

14. Marcus Dale Pension Files, 102nd USCI, Records of the Veterans Administration, Record Group 15.

15. Charles Jackson Service Records, 8th USCT; Charles Jackson Pension Files, 8th USCI, Records of the Veterans Administration, Record Group 15. Along with the multiple aliases, other signs pointing to the possibility that Charles was a runaway from the South include the fact that no one seemed to know exactly where he was born. Several acquaintances stated New York, Rhode Island, and Pennsylvania. In addition, Eliza stated she never met any of his family members, which was probably because he left them behind when he escaped to the North. Lastly, William F. Pennington, who appeared to be his best friend in the army, stated in an affidavit after the war that Charles was originally from the South. All these instances surely did not help Eliza's application but helped explain why her application was never approved.

16. See Painter, *Sojourner Truth*. Rhodes, *Mary Ann Shadd Cary*, 186–91, 209; Forbes, *African American Women*, 89n46. The first black woman lawyer was Charlotte E. Ray, who graduated from the Howard University School of Law in 1872.

17. For additional information on Charlotte Forten Grimke, see Stevenson, ed., *Charlotte Forten Grimke*; see also Winch, *A Gentleman of Color*.

18. DeBoer, *His Truth Is Marching On*, 121; Stanley, *From Bondage to Contract*, 53; Sterling, ed., *We Are Your Sisters*, 297–305. This probably was First Lieutenant John H. Vosburg, who was a member of Company F and E, 66th Pennsylvania Infantry, see John H. Vosburg Service Records, 66th Pennsylvania Infantry.

19. The role of newly freed women in the South was vastly different than the role of their sisters in the North. For example, after the war nearly 50 percent of the workforce suddenly disappeared from the rural workforce. With most former slaves choosing sharecropping over wage labor contracts, married men worked the fields while they

chose to keep their wives home to raise children and run households, usually to the consternation of their former masters. For additional information see Stanley, *From Bondage to Contract*, Chapter 4; and Frankel, *Freedom's Women*, 56–78.

20. All women, North and South, white and black, rich and poor, were transformed by the war and reached a sense of independence and functioning in the public sphere that many of them had not experienced before; see Faust, *Mothers of Invention*, 234–54; Etcheson, *A Generation at War*, 17.

21. For additional information about the struggle for northern blacks for equal rights in the Reconstruction North, see Hugh Davis, *We Will Be Satisfied with Nothing Less: The African American Struggle for Equal Rights in the North During Reconstruction* (Ithaca: Cornell University Press, 2011).

Cited Literature

Primary Sources

Manuscript Sources at the National Archives, Washington, D.C.

"General Index to Pension Files, 1861–1934" (Microfilm No. T288) [Individual Soldier Records].

"Index to Compiled Service Records of Volunteer Union Soldiers Who Served with the United States Colored Troops" (Microfilm No. M589) [Individual Soldier Records].

Record Group 15, Records of the Veterans Administration [Individual Soldier Records].

Record Group 94, Records of the Adjutant General's Office, 1780s–1917.

Letters Sent (December 1863–March 1888), series 352, Colored Troops Division.

Letters Received (1863–1888), series 360, Colored Troops Division.

Letters Received Relating to Recruiting (1863–1888), series 366, Colored Troops Division.

Other Manuscript Collections

Emilio, Luis F. February 12, 1863, diary. *Records of the 54th Regiment.* Civil War correspondence, diaries, and journals at the Massachusetts Historical Society, 1754–1926, microfilm edition, 29 reels (Boston: Massachusetts Historical Society, 1954–1959).

Published Sources

Adams, Virginia Matzke, ed. *On the Altar of Freedom: A Black Soldier's Civil War Letters from the Front.* Amherst: University of Massachusetts, 1991.

Andrews, Charles C. *The History of the New York African Free-Schools: From Their Establishment in 1787, to the Present Time (1830).* New York: Negro Universities Press, 1969 (reprint of the 1830 edition).

Anonymous author. *A Thrilling Narrative From the Lips of the Sufferers of the Late Detroit Riot, March 6, 1863, with the Hair Breath escapes of Men, Women and Children, and Destruction of Colored Men's Property, Not Less Than $15,000.* Detroit: Published by author, 1863.

Berlin, Ira, Joseph P. Reidy, and Leslie S. Rowland, eds. *Freedom: A Documentary History of Emancipation, 1861–1867,* Series 2, *The Black Military Experience.* New York: Cambridge University Press, 1982.

———, eds. *Freedom's Soldiers: The Black Military Experience in the Civil War.* Cambridge: Cambridge University Press, 1998.

Berlin, Ira, and Leslie Rowland, eds. *Families & Freedom: A Documentary History of African-American Kinship in the Civil War Era.* New York: The New Press, 1997.

Blackett, R. J. M., ed. *Thomas Morris Chester, Black Civil War Correspondent: His Dispatches from the Virginia Front.* New York: Da Capo Press, 1989.

Brown, William Wells. *The Negro in the American Rebellion: His Heroism and His Fidelity*. Athens: Ohio University Press, 2003. First published 1867.

Committee of Merchants for the Relief of Colored People Suffering From the Late Riots In the City of New York. *Report*. New York: George A. Whitehorne, Steam Printer, 1863.

Duncan, Russell, ed. *Blue-Eyed child of Fortune: The Civil War Letters of Colonel Robert Gould Shaw*. Athens: University of Georgia Press, 1992.

Emilio, Luis. *A Brave Black Regiment*. New York: Bantam Books, 1992. First published 1894.

Foner, Philip S. ed. *The Life and Writings of Frederick Douglass*. Vol. 2. New York: International Publishers, 1952.

———, ed. *The Life and Writings of Frederick Douglass*. Vol. 3, *The Civil War, 1861–1865*. New York: International Publishers, 1952.

Giesberg, Judith, ed. *Emilie Davis's Civil War: The Diaries of a Free Black Woman in Philadelphia, 1863–1865*. University Park: Pennsylvania State University Press, 2014.

Keckley, Elizabeth. *Behind the Scenes in the Lincoln White House: Memoirs of an African-American Seamstress*. Mineola, N.Y.: Dove Publications, 2012. First published 1868.

Hallowell, Norwood. "The Negro as a Soldier in the War of the Rebellion," *Civil and Mexican Wars, 1861, 1846: Papers of the Military Historical Society of Massachusetts*. Vol. 13. Boston: The Military Historical Society of Massachusetts, 1913.

Higginson, Thomas Wentworth. *Army Life in a Black Regiment and Other Writings*. New York: Penguin Books, 1997. First published 1870.

Mottelay, Paul F., T. Campbell-Copeland, eds. *The Soldier in Our Civil War: A Pictorial History of the Conflict, 1861–1865*, Vol. 1. New York: G. W. Carleton, 1885.

———, eds. *The Soldier in Our Civil War: A Pictorial History of the Conflict, 1861–1865*, Vol. 2. New York: G. W. Carleton, 1885.

Newton, Alexander H. *Out Of The Briars: An Autobiography and Sketch of the Twenty-Ninth Regiment, Connecticut Volunteers*. Philadelphia: The A.M.E. Book Concern, 1910.

Redkey, Edwin S., ed. *A Grand Army of Black Men: Letters of African-American Soldiers in the Union Army, 1861–1865*. New York: Cambridge University Press, 1992.

Stauffer, John, ed. *The Works of James McCune Smith: Black Intellectual and Abolitionist*. Oxford: Oxford University Press, 2006.

Stevenson, Brenda, ed. *The Journals of Charlotte Forten Grimke*. New York: Oxford University Press, 1988.

Wilson, Joseph T. *The Black Phalanx: African American Soldiers in the War of 1812 & the Civil War*. Cambridge: Da Capo Press, 1994.

Yacovone, Donald, ed. *A Voice of Thunder: The Civil War Letters of George E. Stephens*. Urbana: University of Illinois Press, 1997.

Government Publications and Documents

Dobek, William A. *Freedom by the Sword: The U.S. Colored Troops, 1862–1867*. Washington: U.S. Government Printing Office, 2011.

Gibson, Campbell, and Kay Jung. *Historical Census Statistics on Population Totals By Race, 1790 to 1990, and By Hispanic Origin, 1970 to 1990, For the United States, Regions, Divisions, and States*. Population Division, U. S. Census Bureau, Working Paper Series No. 56. Washington, D.C., 2002. http://www.census.gov/population/www/documentation/twps0076/twps0076.html.

Population of the United States in 1860; Compiled From the Original Returns of the Eighth Census. Washington: Government Printing Office, 1864.

Proceedings and Debates of the House of Representatives of the United States at the Second Session of the Second Congress, Begun at the City of Philadelphia, November 5, 1792. *Annals of Congress*, 2nd Congress, 2nd Session.

Revised United States Army Regulations of 1861, With an Appendix Containing the Changed and Laws Affecting Army Regulations and Articles of War to June 25, 1863. Washington: Government Printing Office, 1863.

The Seventh Census of the United States: 1850. Washington: Robert Armstrong, Public Printing, 1853.

U.S. Congress. Joint Committee on the Conduct of the War. *Fort Pillow Massacre and Returned Prisoners. Report prepared by B. F. Wade and D. W. Gooch*. 38th Cong., 1st sess., 1864.

The War of the Rebellion: Official Records of the Union and Confederate Armies, 128 vols. Washington, 1880–1902.

The War of the Rebellion: A Compilation of the Official Records of the Union and Confederate Navies, 30 vols. Washington, 1874–1922.

Secondary Sources

Books

Adams, J. Cutler. *The North Reports the Civil War*. Pittsburgh: University of Pittsburgh Press, paperback reprint 1985. First published 1955.

Anbinder, Tyler. *Nativism and Slavery: The Northern Know Nothings and the Politics of the 1850s*. New York: Oxford University Press, 1992.

Ash, Stephen V. *A Massacre in Memphis: The Race Riot That Shook the Nation One Year After the Civil War*. New York: Hill & Wang Books, 2013.

Attie, Jeanie. *Patriotic Toil: Northern Women and the American Civil War*. Ithaca: Cornell University Press, 1998.

Bacon, Margaret Hope. *But One Race: The Life of Robert Purvis*. Albany: SUNY Press, 2007.

Bercaw, Nancy. *Gendered Freedoms: Race, Rights, and the Politics of Household in the Delta, 1861–1875*. Gainesville: University Press of Florida, 2003.

Berlin, Ira. *Slaves Without Masters: The Free Negro in the Antebellum South*. New York: The New Press, 2007. First published 1974.

Berlin, Ira, and Leslie Harris, eds. *Slavery in New York*. New York: New Press, 2005.

Beringer, Richard E., Herman Hattaway, Archer Jones, and Still, Jr., William N. *Why the South Lost the Civil War*. Athens: University of Georgia Press, 1986.

Bernstein, Iver. *The New York City Draft Riots: Their Significance for American Society and Politics in the Age of the Civil War*. New York: Oxford University Press, 1990.

Biddle, Daniel R., and Durbin, Murray. *Tasting Freedom: Octavius Catto and the Battle for Equality in Civil War America*. Philadelphia: Temple University Press, 2010.

Bilby, Joseph G. *Forgotten Warriors: New Jersey's African American Soldiers in the Civil War*. Highstown, N.J. Longstreet House, 1993.

Blassingame, John W. *The Slave Community: Plantation Life in the Antebellum South*. Oxford: Oxford University Press, 1979.

Blight, David W. *Frederick Douglass' Civil War: Keeping Faith in Jubilee*. Baton Rouge: Louisiana State University Press, 1989.

Boatner, Mark M., ed. *The Civil War Dictionary*. New York: Vintage Books, 1991.

Boritt, Gabor S., ed. *Why the Confederacy Lost*. New York: Oxford University Press, 1992.

Burchard, Peter. *One Gallant Rush: Robert Gould Shaw and His Brave Black Regiment*. New York: St. Martin's Press, 1965.

Burkhardt, George S. *Confederate Rage, Yankee Wrath: No Quarter in the Civil War*. Carbondale: Southern Illinois University Press, 2007.

Castel, Albert. *Civil War in Kansas: Reaping the Whirlwind*. Lawrence: University of Kansas Press, 1997.

Cecelski, David S. *The Fire of Freedom: Abraham Galloway and the Slaves' Civil War*. Chapel Hill: University of North Carolina Press, 2012.

Clark, Peter. *The Black Brigade of Cincinnati*. New York: Arno Press, 1969.

Claxton, Melvin, and Mark Puls. *Uncommon Valor: A Story of Race, Patriotism, and Glory in the Final Battles of the Civil War*. Hoboken, N.J.: John Wiley & Sons, 2006.

Clinton, Catherine. *Harriet Tubman: The Road to Freedom*. New York: Little, Brown and Company, 2004.

Cook, Adrian. *The Armies of the Streets: The New York City Draft Riots of 1863*. Lexington: University of Kentucky Press, 1974.

Cornish, Dudley Taylor. *The Sable Arm: Black Troops in the Union Army, 1861–1865*. Lawrence: University of Kansas Press, 1987. First published1956.

Current, Richard N., ed. *Encyclopedia of the Confederacy*. New York: Simon & Schuster, 1993.

Davis, Hugh. *We Will Be Satisfied with Nothing Less: The African American Struggle for Equal Rights in the North During Reconstruction*. Ithaca: Cornell University Press, 2011.

Davis, William C. *Rebels and Yankees: Fighting Men of the Civil War*. New York; Smithmark Publishers, 1991.

DeBoer, Clara Merritt. *His Truth Is Marching On: African Americans Who Taught the Freedmen for the American Missionary Association, 1861–1877*. New York: Garland, 1995.

Downs, Jim. *Sick from Freedom: African-American Illness and Suffering During the Civil War and Reconstruction*. Oxford: Oxford University Press, 2012.

Dray, Philip. *Capitol Men: The Epic Story of Reconstruction Through the Lives of the First Black Congressmen*. Boston: Houghton Mifflin Company, 2008.

Dru Stanley, Amy. *From Bondage to Contract: Wage Labor, Marriage, and the Market in the Age of Slave Emancipation*. Cambridge: Cambridge University Press, 1998.

Dunaway, Wilma A. *The African-American Family in Slavery and Emancipation.* Cambridge: Cambridge University Press, 2003.

Dunbar, Erica Armstrong. *A Fragile Freedom: African American Women and Emancipation in the Antebellum City.* New Haven: Yale University Press, 2008.

Dyer, Frederick H. *A Compendium of the War of the Rebellion. Compiled and Arranged from Official Records of the Federal and Confederate Armies Reports of the Adjutant Generals of the Several States, the Army Registers and Other Reliable Documents and Sources.* Des Moines, Iowa: The Dyer Pub. Co., 1908.

Escott, Paul David. *Lincoln's Dilemma: Blair, Sumner, and the Republican Struggle Over Racism and Equality in the Civil War Era.* Charlottesville: University of Virginia Press, 2014.

———. *Paying Freedom's Price: A History of African Americans in the Civil War.* Lanham, Md.: Rowman & Littlefield Publishing Group, 2016.

———. *"What Shall We Do with the Negro?": Lincoln, White Racism, and Civil War America.* Charlottesville: University of Virginia Press, 2019.

Etcheson, Nicole. *A Generation at War: The Civil War in a Northern Community.* Lawrence: University Press of Kansas, 2011.

Farrow, Edward Samuel. *A Dictionary of Military Terms.* New York: Thomas Y. Crowell Company Publishers, 1918.

Faust, Drew Gilpin. *Mothers of Invention: Women of the Slaveholding South in the American Civil War.* Chapel Hill: University of North Carolina Press, 1996.

———. *This Republic of Suffering: Death and the American Civil War.* New York: Alfred A. Knopf, 2008.

Fleischner, Jennifer. *Mrs. Lincoln and Mrs. Keckley: The Remarkable Story of the Friendship Between a First Lady and a Former Slave.* New York: Broadway Books, 2003.

Foner, Eric. *Free Soil, Free Labor, Free Men: The Ideology of the Republican Party Before the Civil War.* New York: Oxford University Press, 1995. First published 1970.

———. *A Short History of Reconstruction, 1863–1877.* New York: Harper & Row Publishers, 1990.

Forbes, Ella. *African American Women During the Civil War.* New York: Garland Publishing, 1998.

Fox, William F. *Regimental Losses In The American Civil War, 1861–1865, A Treatise On The Extent And Nature Of The Mortuary Losses In The Union Regiments, With Full And Exhaustive Statistics Compiled From The Official Records On File In The State Military Bureaus And At Washington.* Albany, New York: Albany Pub. Co., 1889.

Frank, Lisa Tendrich, ed. *Women in the American Civil War,* Vol. 1. Santa Barbara, Calif.: ABC-CLIO, 2008.

Frankel, Noralee. *Freedom's Women: Black Women and Families in Civil War Era Mississippi.* Bloomington: Indiana University Press, 1999.

Fuchs, Richard L. *An Unerring Fire: The Massacre at Fort Pillow.* London: Associated University Presses, 1994.

Gallagher, Gary W. *The Confederate War: How Popular Will, Nationalism, and Military Strategy Could Not Stave Off Defeat.* Cambridge: Harvard University Press, 1997.

———. *The Union War.* Cambridge: Harvard University Press, 2011.

Gallman, J. Matthew. *Mastering Wartime: A Social History of Philadelphia During the Civil War*. Philadelphia: University of Pennsylvania Press, 1990.

———. *The North Fights the Civil War: The Home Front*. Chicago: Ivan R. Dee, 2013.

Genovese, Eugene D. *Roll, Jordan, Roll: The World the Slaves Made*. New York: Vintage Books, 1976.

Gibbs, C. R. *Black, Copper & Bright: The District of Columbia's Black Civil War Regiment*. Silver Spring, Md.: Three Divisional Publishing, 2002.

Giesberg, Judith. *Army at Home: Women and the Civil War on the Northern Home Front*. Chapel Hill: University of North Carolina Press, 2009.

Giesberg, Judith Ann. *Civil War Sisterhood: The U.S. Sanitary Commission and Women's Politics in Transition*. Boston: Northeastern University Press, 2000.

Gladstone, William A. *Men of Color*. Gettysburg, Thomas Publications, 1993.

Glatthaar, Joseph T. *Forged in Battle: The Civil War Alliance of Black Soldiers and White Officers*. New York: Free Press, 1990.

Gutman, Herbert G. *The Black Family in Slavery and Freedom, 1750–1925*. New York: Vintage Books, 1977.

Hager, Christopher. *Word by Word: Emancipation and the Act of Writing*. Cambridge: Harvard University Press, 2013.

Hargrove, Hondon B. *Black Union Soldiers in the Civil War*. Jefferson, N.C.: McFarland & Company, 1988.

Harlow, Alvin F. *Old Waybills: The Romance of the Express Companies*. New York: Arno Press, 1976.

Harris, Brayton. *Blue & Gray in Black & White: Newspapers in the Civil War*. Washington: Brassey's, 2000.

Harris, Leslie M. *In the Shadow of Slavery: African Americans in New York City, 1626–1863*. Chicago: University of Chicago Press, 2003.

Henrickson, Wilma Wood, ed. *Detroit Perspectives: Crossroads and Turning Points*. Detroit: Wayne Sate University Press, 1991.

Hesseltine, William B., ed. *Civil War Prisons*. Kent, Ohio: Kent State University Press, 1995. First published 1972.

Hollandsworth, James G., Jr. *The Louisiana Native Guards: The Black Military Experience During the Civil War*. Baton Rouge: Louisiana State University Press, 1995.

Horton, James Oliver, and Lois E. Horton. *Black Bostonians: Family Life and Community Struggle in the Antebellum North*. New York: Holmes & Meier Publishers, 1979.

Humphreys, Margaret. *Intensely Human: The Health of the Black Soldier in the American Civil War*. Baltimore: Johns Hopkins University Press, 2008.

———. *Marrow of Tragedy: The Health Crisis of the American Civil War*. Baltimore: Johns Hopkins University Press, 2013.

Jenkins, Wilbert L. *Climbing Up to Glory: A Short History of African Americans During the Civil War and Reconstruction*. Wilmington: Scholarly Resources Inc., 2002.

Johnson, Charles Beneulyn. *Muskets and Medicine: Or, Army Life in the Sixties*. Philadelphia: F. A. Davis, 1917.

Johnson, James Elton. *A History of Camp William Penn and Its Black Troops in the Civil War, 1863–1865*. PhD diss., University of Pennsylvania, 1999.

Jones, Martha S. *All Bound Up Together: The Woman Question in African American Public Culture, 1830–1900*. Chapel Hill: University of North Carolina Press, 2007.

Kantrowitz, Stephen. *More Than Freedom: Fighting for Black Citizenship in a White Republic, 1829–1889*. New York: Penguin Press, 2012.

Katz, William Loren, ed. *Anti-Negro Riots in the North*. New York: Arno Press, 1969.

Keesee, Dennis M. *Too Young to Die: Boy Soldiers of the Union Army, 1861–1865*. Huntington, W.Va.: Blue Acorn Press, 2001.

Kendrick, Stephen, and Paul Kendrick. *Sarah's Long Walk: The Free Blacks of Boston and How Their Struggle for Equality Changed America*. Boston: Beacon Press, 2004.

Lanning, Michael Lee. *African Americans in the Revolutionary War*. New York: Kensington Publishing, 2000.

Lardas, Mark. *African American Soldier in the Civil War: USCT 1862–66*. Oxford: Osprey Publishing, 2006.

Lawson, Ellen NicKenzie. *The Three Sarahs: Documents of Antebellum Black College Women*. New York: Edwin Mellen Press, 1984.

Lawson, Melinda. *Patriot Fires: Forging a New American Nationalism in the Civil War North*. Lawrence: University Press of Kansas, 2002.

Lerner, Gerda. *The Grimké Sisters from South Carolina: Pioneers for Woman's Rights and Abolitionism*. Oxford: Oxford University Press, 1998.

Long, Alecia P., Lee Ann Whites, eds. *Occupied Women: Gender, Military Occupation, and the American Civil War*. Baton Rouge: Louisiana State University Press, 2009.

Lowry, Beverly. *Harriet Tubman: Imagining a Life*. New York: Anchor Books edition, 2008.

Luke, Bob, and John David Smith. *Soldiering for Freedom: How the Union Army Recruited, Trained, and Deployed the U.S. Colored Troops*. Baltimore: Johns Hopkins University Press, 2014.

Mays, Thomas D. *The Saltville Massacre* (Civil War Campaigns and Commanders Series). Abilene, Texas: McWhiney Foundation Press, 1998.

McCaul, Robert L. *The Black Struggle for Public Schooling in Nineteenth-Century Illinois*. Carbondale: Southern Illinois University Press, 1987.

McPherson, James. *Battle Cry of Freedom: The Civil War Era*. Oxford: Oxford University Press, 1988.

———. *The Negro's Civil War: How American Blacks Felt and Acted During the War for the Union*. New York: Ballantine Books, 1991. First published 1965.

———. *Antietam: The Battle That Changed the Course of the War*. Oxford: Oxford University Press, 2002.

McRae, Norman. *Negroes in Michigan During the Civil War*. Lansing: Michigan Civil War Centennial Observance Commission, 1966.

Mezurek, Kelly D. *For Their Own Cause: The 27th United States Colored Troops*. Kent, Ohio: Kent State University Press, 2016.

Miller, Edward A., Jr. *The Black Civil War Soldiers of Illinois: The Story of the Twenty-ninth U.S. Colored Infantry*. Columbia: University of South Carolina Press, 1998.

Murphy, Jim. *The Boys' War: Confederate and Union Soldiers Talk About the Civil War*. New York: Clarion Books, 1990.

Oliver, John William. *History of the Civil War Military Pensions, 1861–1865*. Bulletin of the University of Wisconsin, no. 844, Vol. 4, no. 1. Madison: University of Wisconsin, 1917.

Painter, Nell Irvin. *Sojourner Truth: A Life, A Symbol*. New York: Norton, 1996.

Paludan, Phillip S. *A People's Contest: The Union and Civil War, 1861–1865*. New York: Harper & Row, 1988.

Paradis, James M. *Strike the Blow for Freedom: The 6th United States Colored Infantry in the Civil War*. Shippensburg, Pa.: White Mane Books, 1998.

———. *African Americans and the Gettysburg Campaign*. Lanham, Md.: Scarecrow Press, 2005.

Perman, Michael. *Reunion Without Compromise: The South and Reconstruction, 1865–1868*. Cambridge: Cambridge University Press, 1973.

———. *Emancipation and Reconstruction*. Arlington Heights, Ill.: Harlan Davidson, 1987.

Perman, Michael, and Amy Murrell Taylor, eds. *Major Problems in the Civil War and Reconstruction, Documents and Essays*. Boston: Wadsworth, Cengage Learning, 2011.

Perry, Mark. *Lift Up Thy Voice: The Grimke Family's Journey from Slaveholders to Civil Rights Leaders*. New York: Viking Press, 2001.

Price, James S., and O. James Lighthizer. *The Battle of New Market Heights: Freedom Will Be Theirs by the Sword*. Charleston, S.C.: History Press, 2011.

Quarles, Benjamin. *The Negro in the Civil War*. New York: Da Capo Press, 1989. First published 1953.

Quarles, Benjamin. *The Negro in the American Revolution*. Chapel Hill: University of North Carolina Press, 1996. First published 1964.

Quinn, Tom. *American Massacre: Fort Pillow and the Day That Changed a War*. Self Published, 2014.

Rael, Patrick. *Black Identity & Black Protest in the Antebellum North*. Chapel Hill: University of North Carolina Press, 2002.

———. *African-American Activism before the Civil War: The Freedom Struggle in the Antebellum North*. New York: Routledge, 2008.

Ramold, Steven J. *Slaves, Sailors, Citizens: African Americans in the Union Navy*. DeKalb: Northern Illinois University Press, 2002.

———. *Baring the Iron Hand: Discipline in the Union Army*. DeKalb: Northern Illinois University Press, 2010.

Regosin, Elizabeth. *Freedom's Promise: Ex-Slave Families and Citizenship in the Age of Emancipation*. Charlottesville: University Press of Virginia, 2002.

Reid, Richard. *Freedom for Themselves: North Carolina's Black Soldiers in the Civil War*. Chapel Hill: University of North Carolina Press, 2008.

Rhodes, Jane. *Mary Ann Shadd Cary: The Black Press and Protest in the Nineteenth Century*. Bloomington: Indiana University Press, 1998.

Rodriguez, Junius P., ed. *Encyclopedia of Slave Resistance and Rebellion: Greenwood Milestones in African American History*. Vol. 1. Westport, Conn.: Greenwood Press, 2007.

Rosen, Hanna. *Terror in the Heart of Freedom: Citizenship, Sexual Violence, and the Meaning of Race in the Postemancipation South*. Chapel Hill: University of North Carolina Press, 2009.

Samito, Christian G. *Becoming American Under Fire: Irish Americans, African Americans, and the Politics of Citizenship During the Civil War Era.* Ithaca, N.Y.: Cornell University Press, 2009.

Schneider, John C. *Detroit and the Problem of Order, 1830–1880: A Geography of Crime, Riot and Policing.* Lincoln: University of Nebraska Press, 1980.

Schultz, Jane E. *Women at the Front: Hospital Workers in Civil War America.* Chapel Hill: University of North Carolina Press, 2007.

Scott, David Sr. *Camp William Penn: 1863–1865.* Atglen, Pa., Schiffer Publishing, 2012.

Seriale, William. *New York's Black Regiments During the Civil War.* New York: Routledge, 2001.

Sernett, Milton C. *North Star Country: Upstate New York and the Crusade for African American Freedom.* Syracuse: Syracuse University Press, 2002.

Shaffer, Donald R. *After the Glory: The Struggles of Black Civil War Veterans.* Lawrence: University Press of Kansas, 2004.

Silber, Nina. *Daughters of the Union: Northern Women Fight the Civil War.* Cambridge: Harvard University Press, 2005.

Slawson, Robert G. *Prologue to Change: African Americans in Medicine in the Civil War Era.* Frederick, Md.: The NMCWM Press, 2006.

Smith, Andrew F. *Starving the South: How the North Won the Civil War.* New York: St. Martin's Press, 2011.

Smith, David G. "Race and Retaliation: The Capture of African-Americans during the Gettysburg Campaign." In *Virginia's Civil War,* edited by Peter Wallenstein and Bertram Wyatt-Brown. Charlottesville: University of Virginia Press, 2005.

Smith, John David, ed. *Black Soldiers in Blue: African American Troops in the Civil War.* Chapel Hill: University of North Carolina Press, 2002.

———, ed. *Race and Recruitment: Civil War History Readers, Volume 2.* Kent, Ohio: Kent State University Press, 2013.

Spurgeon, Ian Michael. *Soldiers in the Army of Freedom: The 1st Kansas Colored, the Civil War's First African American Combat Unit.* Norman: University of Oklahoma Press, 2014.

Sterling, Dorothy, ed. *We Are Sisters: Black Women in the Nineteenth Century.* New York: Norton, 1997. First published 1984.

Tap, Bruce. *The Fort Pillow Massacre: North, South, and the Status of African Americans in the Civil War Era.* New York: Taylor & Francis, 2014.

Trudeau, Noah Andrea. *Like Men of War: Black Troops in the Civil War.* Boston: Little Brown, 1998.

Urwin, Gregory J. W., ed. *Black Flag Over Dixie: Racial Atrocities and Reprisals in the Civil War.* Carbondale: Southern Illinois University Press, 2004.

Von Frank, Albert J. *The Trials of Anthony Burns: Freedom and Slavery in Emerson's Boston.* Cambridge: Harvard University Press, 1998.

Ward, Andrew. *River Run Red: The Fort Pillow Massacre in the American Civil War.* New York: Viking Press, 2005.

Weber, Jennifer. *Copperheads: The Rise and Fall of Lincoln's Opponents in the North.* Oxford: Oxford University Press, 2006.

Wiley, Bell I. *The Life of Billy Yank: The Common Soldier of the Union*. Indianapolis: Bobbs-Merrill Co., 1952.

Wilhelm, Thomas. *A Military Dictionary and Gazetteer: Comprising Ancient and Modern Military*. Philadelphia: L. R. Hamersly, 1881.

Williams, David. *I Freed Myself: African American Self-Emancipation in the Civil War Era*. New York: Cambridge University Press, 2014.

Williams, Heather Andrea. *Self-Taught: African American Education in Slavery and Freedom*. Chapel Hill: University of North Carolina Press, 2007.

Wilson, Carol. *Freedom At Risk: The Kidnapping of Free Blacks in America, 1780–1865*. Lexington: University Press of Kentucky, 1994.

Wilson, Keith P. *Campfires of Freedom: The Camp Life of Black Soldiers during the Civil War*. Kent, Ohio: Kent Sate University Press, 2002.

Winch, Julie. *Philadelphia's Black Elite: Activism, Accommodation, and the Struggle for Autonomy, 1787–1848*. Philadelphia: Temple University Press, 1988.

———. *A Gentleman of Color: The Life of James Forten*. Oxford: Oxford University Press, 2002.

———. *Between Slavery and Freedom: Free People of Color in America From Settlement to the Civil War*. Laham, Md.: Rowman & Littlefield, 2014.

Wisler, G. Clifton. *When Johnny Went Marching: Young Americans Fight the Civil War*. New York: HarperCollins, 2001.

Woodford, Frank B. *Father Abraham's Children: Michigan Episodes in the Civil War*. Detroit: Wayne State University, 1999. First published 1961.

Articles

Biddle, Daniel R. and Dubin, Murray. "One Woman's Drive for Equality." *Philadelphia Inquirer* (May 31, 2009).

Blackburn, George, and Sherman L. Ricards. "The Mother-Headed Family Among Free Negroes in Charleston, South Carolina, 1850–1860." *Phylon* 42, no. 1 (1981): 15.

Levy, Leonard W. "The 'Abolition Riot': Boston's First Slave Rescue." *The New England Quarterly* 25, no. 1 (March, 1952): 85–92.

Martin, Tony. "The Banneker Literary Institute of Philadelphia: African American Intellectual Activism before the War of the Slaveholders' Rebellion." *The Journal of African American History* 87 (Summer 2002): 303–22.

May, Robert E. "Invisible Men: Blacks and the U.S. Army in the Mexican War." *Historian* 49, issue 4 (August 1987): 463–77.

Silcox, Harry C. "Nineteenth Century Philadelphia Black Militant: Octavius V. Catto (1839–1871)." *Pennsylvania History* 44, no. 1 (January 1977): 53–76.

Stevenson, Robert. "America's First Black Music Historian." *Journal of the American Musicological Society* 26 (Autumn 1973): 383–404.

Taylor, Brian. "A Politics of Service: Black Northerners' Debates over Enlistment in the American Civil War." *Civil War History* 58, no. 4 (December 2012): 451–80.

Tremel, Andrew T. "The Union League, Black Leaders, and the Recruitment of Philadelphia's African American Civil War Regiments." *Pennsylvania History* 80, no. 1 (Winter 2013): 13–36.

Wert, Jeffry D. "Camp William Penn and the Black Soldier." *Pennsylvania History* 46, no. 4 (October 1979): 335–46.

Wilson, Joseph T. "James Monroe Trotter (1842–1892)," *African-American Experience in Ohio 1850–1920.* The Ohio Historical Society. http://dbs.ohiohistory.org/africanam/ det.cfm?ID'10044.

Websites

Brooks, Rebecca Beatrice. "Child Soldiers in the Civil War." *Civil War Saga* (December 16, 2011). http://civilwarsaga.com/child-soldiers-in-the-civil-war/.

Lineberry, Cate. "The Boys of War." *New York Times* (October 2011). http://opinionator .blogs.nytimes.com/2011/10/04/the-boys-of-war/.

National Park Service. The Civil War Soldiers and Sailors System. http://www.nps.gov/ civilwar/soldiers-and-sailors-database.htm.

Ohio History Central. *James M. Trotter.* http://www.ohiohistorycentral.org/w/James_M. _Trotter.

Online Encyclopedia. *Purvis, Charles Burleigh (1842–1929), Surgeon, Physician, Educator, Chronology, Attends College and Joins the Military.* http://encyclopedia.jrank.org/ articles/pages/4428/Purvis-Charles-Burleigh-1842-1929.html#ixzz0KbIdPNa7&C.

Reidy, Joseph P. "Black Men in Navy Blue." *Prologue Magazine* 33, no. 3 (2001). https:// www.archives.gov/publications/prologue/2001/fall/black-sailors-1.html.

Virtualology.com. *Samuel Breck.* http://famousamericans.net/samuelbreck1/.

Young, Holice B. American History and Genealogy Project. *Our Firemen, The History of the NY Fire Departments.* Chapter 32, Part III, March 2001. http://www.newyorkroots .org/bookarchive/historyofnyfiredepartments/31-40/ch32pt3.html.

Index

THE NORTH'S CIVIL WAR
Andrew L. Slap, series editor

Anita Palladino, ed., *Diary of a Yankee Engineer: The Civil War Story of John H. Westervelt, Engineer, 1st New York Volunteer Engineer Corps.*

Herman Belz, *Abraham Lincoln, Constitutionalism, and Equal Rights in the Civil War Era.*

Earl J. Hess, *Liberty, Virtue, and Progress: Northerners and Their War for the Union.* Second revised edition, with a new introduction by the author.

William L. Burton, *Melting Pot Soldiers: The Union's Ethnic Regiments.*

Hans L. Trefousse, *Carl Schurz: A Biography.*

Stephen W. Sears, ed., *Mr. Dunn Browne's Experiences in the Army: The Civil War Letters of Samuel W. Fiske.*

Jean H. Baker, *Affairs of Party: The Political Culture of Northern Democrats in the Mid–Nineteenth Century.*

Frank L. Klement, *The Limits of Dissent: Clement L. Vallandigham and the Civil War.* With a new introduction by Steven K. Rogstad.

Lawrence N. Powell, *New Masters: Northern Planters during the Civil War and Reconstruction.*

John A. Carpenter, *Sword and Olive Branch: Oliver Otis Howard.*

Thomas F. Schwartz, ed., *"For a Vast Future Also": Essays from the* Journal of the Abraham Lincoln Association.

Mark De Wolfe Howe, ed., *Touched with Fire: Civil War Letters and Diary of Oliver Wendell Holmes, Jr.* With a new introduction by David Burton.

Harold Adams Small, ed., *The Road to Richmond: The Civil War Letters of Major Abner R. Small of the 16th Maine Volunteers*. With a new introduction by Earl J. Hess.

Eric A. Campbell, ed., *"A Grand Terrible Dramma": From Gettysburg to Petersburg: The Civil War Letters of Charles Wellington Reed*. Illustrated by Reed's Civil War sketches.

Herbert Mitgang, ed., *Abraham Lincoln: A Press Portrait*.

Harold Holzer, ed., *Prang's Civil War Pictures: The Complete Battle Chromos of Louis Prang*.

Harold Holzer, ed., *State of the Union: New York and the Civil War*.

Paul A. Cimbala and Randall M. Miller, eds., *Union Soldiers and the Northern Home Front: Wartime Experiences, Postwar Adjustments*.

Mark A. Snell, *From First to Last: The Life of Major General William B. Franklin*.

Paul A. Cimbala and Randall M. Miller, eds., *An Uncommon Time: The Civil War and the Northern Home Front*.

John Y. Simon and Harold Holzer, eds., *The Lincoln Forum: Rediscovering Abraham Lincoln*.

Thomas F. Curran, *Soldiers of Peace: Civil War Pacifism and the Postwar Radical Peace Movement*.

Kyle S. Sinisi, *Sacred Debts: State Civil War Claims and American Federalism, 1861–1880*.

Russell L. Johnson, *Warriors into Workers: The Civil War and the Formation of Urban-Industrial Society in a Northern City*.

Peter J. Parish, *The North and the Nation in the Era of the Civil War*. Edited by Adam L. P. Smith and Susan-Mary Grant.

Patricia Richard, *Busy Hands: Images of the Family in the Northern Civil War Effort*.

Michael S. Green, *Freedom, Union, and Power: The Mind of the Republican Party During the Civil War*.

Christian G. Samito, ed., *Fear Was Not In Him: The Civil War Letters of Major General Francis S. Barlow, U.S.A.*

John S. Collier and Bonnie B. Collier, eds., *Yours for the Union: The Civil War Letters of John W. Chase, First Massachusetts Light Artillery*.

Grace Palladino, *Another Civil War: Labor, Capital, and the State in the Anthracite Regions of Pennsylvania, 1840–1868*.

Christian B. Keller, *Chancellorsville and the Germans: Nativism, Ethnicity, and Civil War Memory*.

Sidney George Fisher, *A Philadelphia Perspective: The Civil War Diary of Sidney George Fisher*. Edited and with a new Introduction by Jonathan W. White.

Robert M. Sandow, *Deserter Country: Civil War Opposition in the Pennsylvania Appalachians*.

Craig L. Symonds, ed., *Union Combined Operations in the Civil War*.

Harold Holzer, Craig L. Symonds, and Frank L. Williams, eds., *The Lincoln Assassination: Crime and Punishment, Myth and Memory*. A Lincoln Forum Book.

Earl F. Mulderink III, *New Bedford's Civil War*.

David G. Smith, *On the Edge of Freedom: The Fugitive Slave Issue in South Central Pennsylvania, 1820–1870*.

George Washington Williams, *A History of the Negro Troops in the War of the Rebellion, 1861–1865*. Introduction by John David Smith.

Randall M. Miller, ed., *Lincoln and Leadership: Military, Political, and Religious Decision Making*.

Andrew L. Slap and Michael Thomas Smith, eds., *This Distracted and Anarchical People: New Answers for Old Questions about the Civil War-Era North*.

Paul D. Moreno and Johnathan O'Neill, eds., *Constitutionalism in the Approach and Aftermath of the Civil War.*

Steve Longenecker, *Gettysburg Religion: Refinement, Diversity, and Race in the Antebellum and Civil War Border North.*

Harold Holzer, Craig L. Symonds, and Frank L. Williams, eds., *Exploring Lincoln: Great Historians Reappraise Our Greatest President.* A Lincoln Forum Book.

Lorien Foote and Kanisorn Wongsrichanalai, eds., *So Conceived and So Dedicated: Intellectual Life in the Civil War–Era North.*

William B. Kurtz, *Excommunicated from the Union: How the Civil War Created a Separate Catholic America.*

Kanisorn Wongsrichanalai, *Northern Character: College-Educated New Englanders, Honor, Nationalism, and Leadership in the Civil War Era.*

Ryan W. Keating, *Shades of Green: Irish Regiments, American Soldiers, and Local Communities in the Civil War Era.*

Robert M. Sandow, ed., *Contested Loyalty: Debates over Patriotism in the Civil War North.*

Grant R. Brodrecht, *Our Country: Northern Evangelicals and the Union During the Civil War Era.*

James G. Mendez, *A Great Sacrifice: Northern Black Soldiers, Their Families, and the Experience of Civil War.*

CPSIA information can be obtained
at www.ICGtesting.com
Printed in the USA
LVHW030849030119
602600LV00001B/2

MAY 02 2019